# Earth Jurisprudence

This book argues that the institution of private property is anthropocentric and needs to be reconceived. Drawing on international case law, indigenous views of property and the land use practices of agrarian communities, Peter Burdon considers how private property can be reformulated in a way that fosters duties towards nature.

The dominant rights-based interpretation of private property entrenches the idea of human dominion over nature. Accordingly, nature is not attributed any inherent value and becomes merely the matter of a human property relationship. *Earth Jurisprudence: Private Property and the Environment* explores how an alternative conception of property might be instead grounded in the ecocentric concept of an Earth community. Recognising that human beings are deeply interconnected with and dependent on nature, this concept is proposed as a standard and measure for human law. Using the theory of earth jurisprudence as a guide, this book outlines an alternative ecocentric description of private property, as a relationship between and among members of the Earth community.

This book will appeal to those researching in law, justice and ecology, as well as anyone pursuing an interest more particularly in earth jurisprudence.

**Peter D. Burdon** is a Senior Lecturer at the Adelaide Law School. His professional life seeks to blend theory and praxis. To this end, he has been an active campaigner with Friends of the Earth and also sits on the Ethics Specialist Group of the International Union for the Conservation of Nature.

# Earth Jurisprudence

## Private Property and the Environment

Peter D. Burdon

Routledge
Taylor & Francis Group
a GlassHouse Book

First published 2015
by Routledge
2 Park Square, Milton Park, Abingdon, Oxon OX14 4RN

and by Routledge
711 Third Avenue, New York, NY 10017

a GlassHouse Book

Routledge is an imprint of the Taylor & Francis Group, an informa
business

British Library Cataloguing in Publication Data
A catalogue record for this book is available from the British Library

*Library of Congress Cataloging-in-Publication Data*

A catalog record has been requested for this book

ISBN: 978-0-415-63317-8 (hbk)
ISBN: 978-0-203-79701-3 (ebk)

Typeset in Garamond
by Apex CoVantage, LLC

MIX
Paper from
responsible sources
FSC
www.fsc.org   FSC® C013604

Printed and bound by CPI Group (UK) Ltd, Croydon, CR0 4YY

Dedicated to the life and work
of William 'Thomas' Berry (1914–2009)
and
to my friend and mentor, Ron Engel

# Contents

# Acknowledgements

I would like to express gratitude to my wife Shani, my daughter Freya and son Arlo. Many times over the last few years, this book has has kept me away from parties, concerts, trips to the beach and even breakfast. You have all always given me support, understanding and love. For all of this I am more grateful than I can put into words.

Thank you to my parents, Jenny and Terry Burdon, for never telling me who to be or what to do, but providing the space and support for me to grow into my own person. Thank you also for teaching me respect, compassion and empathy.

To my colleagues, Paul Babie, Alex Reilly and Klauss Bosselmann. Thank you all for your friendship and the *many* hours you have spent reading, critiquing and supporting this book. Thank you also to Samuel Alexander and Claire Nettle for generously reading the complete draft of this book. Thank you also to Mary Heath for reading and providing critical comments on an earlier draft of Chapter 4. And thank you to Ngaire Naffine for providing critical advice and help during the development of this manuscript into a book.

I would like to acknowledge with gratitude the support I received from the JA Joyner Scholarship in law, which provided financial support for my family over my three-year dissertation. Thank you also to the Adelaide Law School for providing a stimulating work environment and the resources to suport my research.

My thanks must also go to the staff at Routledge, in particular Melanie Fortmann-Brown, Rebekah Jenkins and Colin Perrin for their engagement with the project. Finally, I would like to thank Anna Grear for her comments, humour, encouragement and support in pushing this project to completion. Without her clear vision and intellect, the book would not have reached its current state of scholarship.

# Series editor's introduction

Taking Earth jurisprudence – an ecocentric theory of law based on the work of Thomas Berry – as its foundation, this book engages in a lively analysis of modes of normative human coordination with and within an all-embracing Earth community made up of a multitude of ecosystems and other-than-merely-human subjectivities and subjects. The book offers a wide-ranging and eclectic engagement with central problems related to humanistic formulations of law and normative relations, subjecting anthropocentrism and – in particular – 'the anthropocentric notion of private property' to scrutiny within a broadly natural law conception of Earth jurisprudence.

Appealing to Earth jurisprudence and to a 'theory of social change' drawing on vernacular law and the contemporary inadequacies of law as a response to eco-violation, Burdon argues for modes of resistive political subjectivity and a juridical re-invention responsive to a wider, deeper vision of a common good embracing the entire living order. Human law – all human law – argues Burdon, should be situated 'within the physical context of the Earth's system' and 'directed toward the common good of the entire Earth community and not just human or corporate interests'. In other words, Burdon seeks to argue that ecocentric ethics should be understood to be inherent to law. The implications of this for the centrally important institution of private property – an analysis of which forms a core concern of this book – are not, Burdon argues, that private property is inherently inconsistent with ecocentric ethics or that private property should be discarded as a social institution. What his analysis indicates, he suggests, is that a 'more nuanced understanding of private property is required' – one responsive to 'nature as a subject rather than an object'. While some might wish to take issue with Burdon concerning his characterisation of the liberal tradition – and while others may resist his conclusions – Burdon issues an important and timely challenge to revisit cherished assumptions in the search for a more radical, a more eco-humane, juridical order.

The questions and debates that Burdon invites in this work offer one more strand in the now multiply threaded, critical and insistent conversation taking place the world over in the search for renewing dynamics between law, justice and ecology.

Anna Grear

# Foreword

This book pushes the boundaries of jurisprudence, i.e. the school of legal reasoning and investigation into the nature of law. Since Aristotle's *Nicomachean Ethics*, jurisprudential thinking has centered on the idea of justice, but only in the context of human relationships. The modern ecological crisis, however, has challenged this way of thinking. Why should justice be confined to inter-human relationships when humans collectively discriminate against all other species? Must the non-human part of nature stay outside the realm of law as the leading modern theorist of justice, John Rawls, insisted? Or have we reached a stage of maturity that makes it feasible, perhaps necessary to include nature into the realm of law? This is the central idea of Earth jurisprudence.

Peter Burdon is an environmental lawyer and, like all scholars of this field, concerned with protecting the environment from human overuse. However, unlike most of his colleagues Burdon defines the overuse problem not in anthropocentric, but ecocentric terms. He agrees with the common notion of private property as a bundle of rights, but organises this bundle in a different way. Some user rights may stay as they are, while those affecting the environment – land, water, air, animals and plants – need to respect additional boundaries. Translated into law, environmental boundaries mark the new limitations to private property. Hence, overuse does not occur when other people are affected in their entitlement to the environment, but a lot earlier: the environment itself, the integrity and functioning of ecosystems, describes the threshold for overuse.

The practical implications of this idea are easy to grasp. As humans become mindful of their ecological dependencies, they will organise their laws accordingly. In the future, private property holders – from car drivers to land owners right through to multinational corporate organisations – will have to pay for their use of the environment and will be prevented from environmental overuse. Considering the magnitude of our current crisis, this seems a very good idea. And yet, we are not likely to see such radical legal reform anytime soon. Too much is at stake. After all, in capitalism private property is sacred and any tempering with the motors of wealth and prosperity are readily dismissed as ideologically driven.

Ideologies (or paradigms) are belief systems that are relatively immune against new ideas, no matter how ethical, realistic and convincing they may be. So is the Earth jurisprudence movement driven by an ideological agenda, as its critics might suggest? I suggest that the position is the very reverse – for nothing could be more ideological than the belief that money generates wealth, that private property is sacred and economic growth indispensable. This is not the same as saying that money, property and growth may be useful within a given purpose. The issue is one of context and right balance. Our world is falling apart precisely because of gross imbalances in the prevailing economic system. The rich get richer at the expense of the poor and altogether we ruin the planet, our common home. The systemic nature of the process of bringing ourselves to the brink of extinction is almost beyond belief. Yet, our political leaders seem not to care: the 'tino' ('there is no alternative') ideology sits too deeply in their hearts and heads.

This book presses against the closures of contemporary ideology. The book conceives of private property as a relationship between and among members of the Earth community. In the age of the Anthropocene, surely this is a realistic and convincing proposition – at least to those who find the notion of an Earth community appealing. This in turn will depend on narrowness or broadness of the mind: our thinking will either be narrowly contrived to protect the status quo or it may be broader, literally open minded, depending on our horizons of time and space.

So far *homo sapiens* has been remarkably narrow minded. *Homo sapiens* sees 'himself' as the centre and crown of the universe. The Earth may appear huge to such a two-legged dwarf, but is merely a speck of dust in the universe and not even in the middle of it, as we should know since Copernicus. The centre of our planetary system, the sun, is only one of further 300 billion other stars in our Milky Way, which itself is just one of an estimated 100 billion galaxies with some 70 sexillion stars (a number with 21 zeros). How special does that make *homo sapiens*?

Ours is a tiny place and the time span we occupy is not that impressive either. If we condense the history of the universe to two calendar years beginning with the Big Bang on 1 January, we can say that *homo sapiens* appeared on 31 December a few minutes before midnight. During the last fraction of a second he does everything to destroy his fellow species and their common habitat, Earth. And how many seconds will we have in the New Year? One? Ten? If we make it to one minute after midnight (26,065 years) *homo sapiens* will have proved to be surprisingly successful, but reaching the end of the first hour of the New Year (1.5 million years) will take a miracle. From all we currently know, primates will not be around come 2 January (37.5 million years). The sun will have lost its life-supporting power around 14 January, and by early March, Earth will look like Mars today, while at the end of July,

Earth is likely to crash into the sun. On this time scale *homo sapiens* is, at best, a dayfly.

This brief story of space and time should teach us humility. How dare we think of ourselves as special – as if evolution has reached its final goal? What could possibly be right with an anthropocentric mindset? The only realistic perspective is to see ourselves as a small part in an evolutionary process of life. Thomas Berry has described this reality as a miracle that humans – and possibly only humans – are able consciously to witness and marvel at. It is this perspective of humility and awe – not the ignorance of *homo* (not so) *sapiens* – that will broaden our mind. And only this will allow us to begin the 'Great Work'.

Seen from this angle, the notion of Earth community is highly attractive as it locates humanity in space and time realistically. As Albert Schweitzer put it: we humans are life that wants to live, in the midst of life that wants to live. And what could be more important for contemporary jurisprudence than helping to organise legal principles and instruments around this awareness?

This book makes a timely contribution to Earth jurisprudence, but even more so to bringing property rights in line with ecological realities. Will the author succeed? The good news is that transformation always starts with the thoughts and actions of individuals. What may seem as unthinkable will over time become the norm. When Christopher Stone, the early pioneer of the eco-law movement, wrote his famous essay, he pointed out just how changeable legal morality is. Slavery was once seen as perfectly justified. For some time now, any form of gender, racial or religious discrimination has become unlawful and increasingly discrimination against animals is being outlawed.

Today, it is no longer unthinkable to outlaw any form of discrimination against nature. Sooner or later ecological realities will sink in and teach us an entirely new morality. This book shows the implications of the new morality for a central concept of law. Scholars and students will greatly benefit from it.

Klaus Bosselmann
Professor of Law
University of Auckland

# Chapter 1

# Introduction

The present legal system is supporting exploitation rather than protecting
the natural world from destruction by the relentless industrial economy.
(Berry 2006: 107)

## 1.1 The inquiry

Thomas Berry was a theologian and cultural historian. His observation that
law is central to the present environmental crisis is the motivation behind
a growing movement in law called Earth jurisprudence. In this chapter, I
introduce the inquiry and outline the fundamental themes on which the
book is built. I begin by introducing the environmental crisis and describe
the relationship between law, culture and environmental harm. I also introduce the concepts of paradigm and paradigm shift, which are used in this
book to analyse how law and legal concepts such as private property can shift
from an anthropocentric (human-centred) to an ecocentric (Earth-centred)
foundation.

### 1.1.1 The environmental crisis

Our biosphere is sick and is behaving like an infected organism. As carbon has
been collecting in our atmosphere, it has also been accumulating in the ocean
and as time has passed, deforestation, soil erosion, vanishing wetlands and a
whole host of other problems have continued unabated. We face a conver-
gence of crises, all of which present a significant moral and survival challenge
for the human species. In 2001 the United Nations Millennium Assessment
undertook a four-year study, involving over 2000 scientists from 95 countries,
on the health of the planet. Released in March 2005, the report found that
60 percent of global ecosystem services 'are being degraded or used unsustain-
ably' resulting in 'substantial and largely irreversible loss in the biodiversity of
life on Earth.' It further estimated that humans are responsible for the extinction of between 50–55 thousand species each year (Millennium Ecosystem
Assessment 2005: 81), a rate unequalled since the last great extinction some

65 million years ago (Berry 2006: 107). These systems and species provide the basis for all life and their devastation undermines the health and future flourishing of all components of the environment.

The scale of the present crisis is so great that in 2000, atmospheric chemist Paul Crutzen argued that the period from the industrial revolution to the present constituted a new geological era. Crutzen (Crutzen and Stoermer 2000: 17) labelled this period the 'anthropocene' to describe the significant impact of human activity on the Earth.[1] The term 'anthropocene' follows the geological tradition that divides the Phanerozoic eon into Paleozoic, Mesozoic and Cenozoic eras. Commenting on this characterisation, David Suzuki (2010: 17) argues that human beings have 'become a force of nature'. Indeed, it was not so long ago that hurricanes, tornadoes, floods and droughts were accepted as natural disasters. 'But now', Suzuki argues (2010: 17), 'we have joined God, powerful enough to influence these events.'

Chapter 2 of this book will demonstrate how the institution of private property has facilitated the emergence of the anthropocene and the current environmental crisis. For now, it is sufficient to note that the crisis is very real and largely anthropogenic. These two points were forcibly advocated before the international community in 1992 when 1700 senior scientists (including 104 Nobel Prize winners, comprising more than half of all laureates alive at the time) signed a document called 'World Scientists Warning to Humanity' (1992). The opening words read:

> Human beings and the natural world are on a collision course. Human activities inflict harsh and often irreversible damage on the environment and on critical resources. If not checked, many of our current practices put at risk the future that we wish for human society . . . and may so alter the living world that it will be unable to sustain life in the manner that we know. Fundamental changes are urgent if we are to avoid the collision our present course will bring about.

The authors went on to list the areas of collision from the atmosphere to water resources, oceans, soil, forests, species and population. The document also warns:

> No more than one or a few decades remain before the chance to avert the threats we now confront will be lost and the prospects for humanity immeasurably diminished. We the undersigned, senior members of the world's scientific community, hereby warn all humanity of what lies

1. In adopting the term 'anthropocene' I agree with the comments made by Dispesh Chakrabarty that the term should not denote reference to a single subject 'mankind'. As Chakrabarty (2009: 216) argues, talk of mankind can 'simply serve to hide the reality of capitalist production and the logic of imperial domination that it fosters'.

ahead. A great change in our stewardship of the Earth and life on it, is required, if human misery is to be avoided and our global home on this planet is not to be irretrievably mutilated.

The failure of the international community to respond adequately to this and other similar warnings is already devastating communities around the world and has the potential to put the future of most components of the Earth community in great jeopardy.'

### 1.1.2 Environmental crisis and ethics

At the dawn of the twenty-first century there is no greater challenge confronting human beings than the fate of the environment and the community of life it supports. There are many different ways to understand and interpret this crisis. Some of the most visible explanations in environmental-political discourse include industrial capitalism (Foster 2010), consumerism (Alexander 2009), overpopulation (Ehrlich & Ehrlich 1972), patriarchy (Merchant 1980) and anthropocentrism (Ehrenfeld 1978). These approaches are not mutually exclusive and interact in a complex cultural, social, political and economic web. Commenting on this mixture, some theorists have begun to characterise the present environmental crisis as a crisis of culture. Environmental psychologist Ralph Metzner (1999: 99) supports this characterisation: '[t]here is a growing chorus of agreement that the deepest roots of the ecological crisis must lie in the attitudes, values, perceptions and basic worldview that we humans of the global industrial society have come to hold.'

Philosopher John Livingston (1981: 24) expands this analysis, noting that disasters are commonly portrayed as a series of separate issues. He writes: 'Oil spills, endangered species, ozone depletion and so forth are presented as separate incidents and the overwhelming nature of these events means that we seldom look deeper.' 'However' Livingston argues that such 'issues are analogous to the tip of an iceberg, they are simply the visible portion of a much larger entity, most of which lies beneath the surface, beyond our daily inspection.'

In my view, the most sophisticated explanation of the root causes of the environmental crisis was developed by social ecologist, Murray Bookchin. According to Bookchin (1982: 4; Price 2012: 133–160), the domination of nature by human beings stems from and takes the same form as myriad ways in which human beings exploit one another. The key to this analysis is 'hierarchy' – a term that encompasses 'cultural, traditional and psychological systems of obedience and command' (Bookchin 1982: 4–5). Hierarchy includes the domination of the young by the old, of women by men, of one ethnic group by another, of the wealthy over the poor and of human beings over the environment.

Bookchin (1982: 62–88) argues that hierarchy has its ultimate founda-tion in the 'raw materials' of early civilisation. However, he also recognises that its emergence and elaboration has a dual effect that is both material and subjective. On a material level, Bookchin (1982: 89) argues that hierarchy attained sophisticated form in 'the emergence of the city, the state, authoritar-ian technics, and a highly organized market economy'. On a subjective level, hierarchy found expression 'in the emergence of a repressive sensibility and body of values – in various ways of mentalizing the entire realm of experience along the lines of command and obedience'. Bookchin (1982: 89) labelled these subjective elements 'epistemologies of rule' to denote the emergence of a body of knowledge that normalises the characteristics of a bifurcated hierarchical society.

What attracts me to Bookchin's statement on hierarchy is that it allows one to theorise myriad ways in which negative hierarchical relationships contribute to environmental harm in an open and dialectical way. It rec-ognises both structural and biopolitical analysis and invites conversation about anthropocentrism, gender, racism and economics. It also provides a foundation for thinking through how these root causes interact with one another. For example, how environmental harm often works in conjunc-tion with racism and class (Bullard 2000), or how poor women are dis-proportionately affected by environmental catastrophes such as flooding, draught and forced migration (Sontheimer 1991). Thus, while my investi-gation focuses primarily on anthropocentrism as the 'deepest cause of the present devastation' (Berry 1999: 4) I will also move beyond this instance of hierarchy to consider other (mental and material) explanations for the environmental crisis. Specifically, I consider how anthropocentric hierar-chy is supplemented and works in conjunction with economic and gender hierarchy.

### 1.1.3 The relationship between law, culture and power

> The law and legal disciplines are not created in a vacuum. Though they appear 'natural' and almost self-evident, the law and legal disciplines always tend, to a greater or narrower extent, to mirror the reality in which they are born and in which they grow. (Zamboni 2008: 63)

Legal systems and philosophies emerge from a social context and tend to be animated by the worldview and moral horizon of the political class of a given society (Pashukanis 1989). The political class has historically been closed on the basis of race and gender (Wallerstein 2011a: 77) and continues to be rep-resented predominately by the wealthy (Burdon 2013a). Law is one of the key mechanisms through which this class analyses itself and projects their image to the world. It also represents the dominant operative theory of society and environment within that society.

The instant we begin to approach law from this perspective, the questions we ask about law and the ideas we have regarding its development shift. This point is explicitly recognised by Kermit Hall (Hall and Karsten 2009: 1) in his description of law as a 'magic mirror'. Hall borrows this phrase from Justice Oliver Wendell Holmes Jr (1981: 17) who noted: 'This abstraction called Law is a magic mirror, [wherein] we see reflected, not only our own lives, but the lives of all men that have been!' For Hall, the description of law as a 'magic mirror' has two aspects. First, law is understood as a 'cultural artefact' and legal historians are encouraged to explore the social choices and moral imperatives that underpin a legal system and its normative concepts (Hall and Karsten 2009: 1). Further, Hall contends that a proper understanding of the relationship between law and society allows one to consider and perhaps even influence the future direction of law.

From this perspective, law mirrors the values, perceptions and goals of the dominant class in society. Further, the future of our legal system depends intimately on how these values perceptions and goals change or adapt to future need – not to mention whose needs they recognise. Reflecting a vast heritage of anthropocentric philosophy and theology, the next section argues that the dominant concept of law in analytic jurisprudence is fundamentally human centred. Following this, I introduce my argument about how our legal system can adapt to reflect ecological goals as reflected in the concept of Earth community.

### 1.1.4 Law and anthropocentrism

Our law is deeply anthropocentric and directed toward maintaining hierarchical structures for the protection of property and economic growth. To illustrate this point I turn first to legal theory, which as Karl Llewellyn (1962: 372) notes 'is as big as law – and bigger'. Legal theory deeply informs our concept of law and plays a critical role in shaping the contours and provisions of positive law, i.e. legislation and case law.

Despite great variation, legal theory is predominately anthropocentric. This is specifically true for both natural law and legal positivism, which are concerned ultimately with human beings and human good. More specifically, legal theory is concerned with 'relations between individuals, between communities, between states and between elementary groupings themselves' (Graham 2011: 15). Only in rare circumstances does legal theory consider the environment as relevant to human law (Blomley 2001). Indeed, 'the separation and hierarchical ordering of the human and non-human worlds' represents a fundamental presupposition on which the cannon of Western law has been constructed (Graham 2011: 15).

In orthodox legal theory, legal positivism is the dominant school of thought. Positivism describes law as a science and holds that no external element (i.e. morality, the environment or religion) enters into the definition of law. Legal provisions are identified by empirically observable criteria, such as legislation, common law and custom. Positivism focuses on the identification and definition of law with reference to 'abstract legal categories' and regards those doctrines as 'authoritative rules' applicable to each question and dispute requiring legal adjudication (Graham: 2011: 15). This method explicitly considers the influence of the environment, non-human animals, and place irrelevant. As a result, legal categories and prescriptions can be exported across the globe without reference to the unique landscape or populace on which they will operate.

The human-centred nature of legal positivism is expressed further by the passivity of courts to receive cultural evidence (Brown 1999) and their refusal to allow advocates to seek for protection for the environment in its own right (Taylor 2010: 203). As Graham (2011: 15) argues: 'By imagining and juxtaposing objective and subjective thought, abstract rules and particular contexts and then by privileging objectivity and abstraction, legal positivism epitomises anthropocentric logic.'

In Chapter 2, I describe how private property has been shaped to reflect anthropocentric thinking and the way it not only maintains but also perpetuates a dichotomy between human beings and the environment. Considered through the lens of private property, the environment possesses no inherent value and receives only instrumental value and protection through human property rights. Law and economics scholars are particularly unapologetic on this point. Richard Posner (1986: 32) typifies the instrumentalist view of the environment in his advocacy for privatisation: 'If every valuable (meaning scarce as well as desired) resource were owned by someone (universality), ownership connotes the unqualified power to exclude everybody else from using the resource (exclusivity) as well as to use it oneself, and ownership rights were freely transferable or as lawyers say alienable (transferable), value would be maximized.'

Neoliberal commentators have used Posner's justification in their advocacy for the further privatisation of the environment and the enclosure of all common space. And yet, I contend, if human beings are going to survive the ecological crisis (let alone thrive) then we need to shift our law from its current focus on the exclusive rights of private individuals to the needs and interests of the comprehensive Earth community.

### 1.1.5 Paradigm shift and the concept of earth community

> Revolutions are inaugurated by a growing sense . . . that existing institutions have ceased adequately to meet the problems posed by an environment that they have in part created. (Kuhn 1996: 92)

Physicist and philosopher Thomas Kuhn first articulated the concepts of paradigm and paradigm shift. Writing specifically with regard to science, Kuhn (1996: 43) defined a paradigm as: 'A constellation of achievements – concepts, values, techniques, etc. – shared by a scientific community and used by that community to define legitimate problems and solutions.' Cultural and legal theorists have also adopted the term 'paradigm' to explain how laws adapt and evolve. Consistent with this literature, for the purpose of this book I define a paradigm as a *constellation of concepts, values, perceptions and practices shared by a community, which forms a particular vision of reality that is the basis of the way the community organises itself and creates law* (Capra 1985: 11).

Commenting on the notion of paradigm shift, Kuhn (1996: 66–69) argued that social factors or developments in knowledge could lead to a paradigm crisis. This occurs when the dominant paradigm becomes dysfunctional, impacts negatively or loses its meaning for a given society. When this occurs, a society may go through a brief period of dissonance, which is followed by a shift toward a new paradigm. Importantly, Kuhn notes that a society may be completely ignorant or even deny that a paradigm crisis is on them. Broad acknowledgment is not a prerequisite to paradigm shift. However, when a crisis occurs it is not a question of if, but when, a culture adapts to meet the new paradigm. Kuhn (1996: 77) contends: 'The decision to reject one paradigm is always simultaneously the decision to accept another, and the judgment leading to that decision involves the comparison of both paradigms with nature and with each other.'

The concepts of paradigm and paradigm shift can also be considered alongside analyses of social and cultural epochs captured by writers such as Pitirim Sorokin (1970), Lewis Mumford (1956), Thomas Berry and Brian Swimme (1992). The analysis conducted by Berry and Swimme is explored in Chapter 3 of this book. In contrast to Crutzen's geological description 'anthropocene', Berry and Swimme envision that mental ideas of the world and ethics can catalyse a transition from the terminal Cenozoic era to the emerging Ecozoic era. As the name suggests, this latter period is characterised by ecocentric ethics and seeks to facilitate 'mutually enhancing human–Earth relations' (1992: 280). Commenting on this transition, Berry (1988: 42) writes:

> Presently, we are entering another historical period, one that might be described as the ecological age. I use the term *ecological* in its primary meaning as the relation of an organism to its environment, but also as an indication of the interdependence of all the living and nonliving systems of the earth. [Entering this age] is not simply adaptation to a reduced supply of fuels or to some modification in our systems of social or economic controls. Nor is it some slight change in our educational system. What is happening is something of a far greater magnitude. It is a radical change in our mode of consciousness.

The term 'ecocentric' is an alternative paradigm to anthropocentrism and denotes an Earth-centred (as opposed to human-centred) system of values.

Commenting on the distinction between the two paradigms, Klaus Bossel-mann (2008b: 92) argues that the 'relationship between anthropocentrism and ecocentrism is not one of gradual difference, but one of paradigmatic dichotomy.' In this book, I promote the ecocentric paradigm most visibly in the concept of Earth community.

Berry (1992: 243) captures the essence of Earth community in his contention that 'the universe is communion of subjects and not a collection of objects.' Berry's use of the term 'communion' is metaphorical and intends to communicate something richer than an impersonal description of human–Earth relations. Indeed, he suggests that existence is 'derived from and sustained' by an 'intimacy of each being with every other being of the universe' (1992: 243). In making this claim, Berry also seeks to dissolve the anthropocentric dichotomy between human beings and the environment. The community consists of ecological subjects who interact through horizontal relationships across time and place.

At the ecosystemic level, Berry's term 'Earth community' provides four fundamental insights. First, ecosystems are comprised of and influenced by natural and social systems (1999: 4). Second, ecosystems involve the individual behaviours of organisms. These organisms are understood as members (not isolated parts) of ecosystems (1999: 4). Third, members of ecosystems have various degrees of interiority or subjectivity (1999: 162–163). Finally, members of ecosystems interact within and across species to create horizons of shared meaning and understanding (1999: 4). These broad points share some similarity with the discipline of integral ecology (Wilber 1995). In particular, both make the radical claim that nature is more than a complex network of exterior strands of energy flows and holistic input/outputs. Rather, nature is also a space of intimacy and communion between ecological subjects. From this perspective, organisms are not just parts of an ecosystem – they are partners within an Earth community and intersubjective space. All organisms are subjects – they have interiors and lifeworlds.[2] Berry (1990: 15x) is very clear on this point:

> Nothing on earth [is] a mere 'thing'. Every thing [has] its own divine, numinous subjectivity, its self, its center, its unique identity. Every being [is] a presence to every other being.[3]

---

2. Perhaps the most illustrative example is Uexküll (1957: 11).

3. Berry (1988: 133) argues further: 'If the demand for objectivity and the quantitative aspect of the real has led scientists to neglect subjectivity and the qualitative aspect of the real, this has been until now a condition for fulfilling their historic task. The most notable single development within science in recent years, however, has been a growing awareness of the integral physical-psychic dimension of reality.' See also Bennett (2010). Bennett aims to develop a theory of 'vital materialism' – vital in the sense that matter has the capacity 'not only to impede or block the will and designs of humans but also to act as quasi agents or forces with trajectories, propensities, or tendencies of their own' (Bennett 2010: viii). See also Latour (2004).

From this quotation, it is clear that Berry's description of the Earth community is not limited by the strict Cartesian dichotomy between 'alive' and 'dead' matter.[4] Indeed, Berry often talks about the numinous, psychic aspects of species and matter in the context of the Earth as a sacred community. In making this description, Berry draws heavily from the French Jesuit, Pierre Teilhard de Chardin. In the *Phenomenon of Man*, Teilhard maintained that there was an intimate unity between human beings and the rest of the universe. He claimed that this unity was not merely physical or genetic. Rather, Chardin (1959: 56) held that matter had an inner and an outer reality – 'coextensive with their Without, there is a Within to things.' Besides the physical that one senses, there was a mental aspect to the whole universe;[5] this was the aspect that came to self-reflective consciousness in the human species (1959: 54–56). Thus, because there is consciousness in human beings and because we have evolved from the Earth, then from the beginning some form of consciousness or interiority has been present in the process of evolution. Consciousness is an intrinsic part of reality and is the thread that links all members of the Earth community (1959: 56).

Reflecting on these comments, Berry observes (1990: 15x) that 'while Darwin saw the human appearing only out of the physical Earth, Teilhard de Chardin saw the human emerging out of both the physical and the psychic dimensions of the earth.' Matter is not simply dead or inert but a numinous reality.[6] In his early writing, Berry was clear that the psychic dimension of the universe identified by Teilhard was a key element that needed to be further developed. This concern is consistent with a fundamental tenant of integral ecology – with exterior ecosystems come interior ecocommunities (Esjörn-Hargens 2011: 101). Berry (1990: 15x) outlines this argument as follows:

> That there is an organizing force within the Earth process with both physical and psychic dimensions needs to be acknowledged in language and in imagery. It needs to be named and spoken of in its integral form. It has a unified functioning similar to the more particular organisms with which we are acquainted. When we speak of Earth we are speaking of a numinous maternal principle in and through which the total complex of Earth phenomena takes its shape.

4. In support of this interpretation, see Berry (1990: 15x): 'The universe is not a vast smudge of matter, some jelly-like substance extended indefinitely in space. Nor is the universe a collection of unrelated particles. The universe is, rather, a vast multiplicity of individual realities with both qualitative and quantitative differences all in spiritual-physical communion with each other.'

5. This mental aspect was shaped with reference to the concept 'nöosphere' developed by Russian mineralogist and geochemist Vernadsky (1992).

6. Berry uses the term 'numinous' variously in his writing to indicate the powerful experience of a place where one is compelled to contemplate the mysteries and meanings of the universe. The best example of this is (1999: 12–20).

For both Teilhard and Berry, the perspective of evolution provides the most comprehensive context for understanding human beings in relation to other members of the Earth community. In this regard, Berry (Swimme & Berry 1992: 66–78) frequently noted that since the publication of the *Origin of Species* we have become aware that the universe exists not as part of a static cosmos, but an unfolding cosmogenesis. The theory of evolution provides a distinctive realisation of development in the universe that resituates human beings in a huge sweep of geological time. This implies that human beings are but one species among others.

As suggested by Klaus Bosselmann (1995: 7), the ecocentric paradigm 'points towards the necessity of putting ecological correlations and networks of which humankind is only "one" aspect, into the centre of our thoughts and not humanity'. In this respect, the concept of Earth community advocates a 'shift of the centre of human thought about humans to the network of interrelations between humans and the environment' (Bosselmann 1995: 7). As I detail further in Chapter 5, this reasoning does not deny the moral status of human beings or claim that all forms of non-human animals have moral equivalence with humanity (Low & Gleeson 1998: 97; Ott 2008: 48). Instead, it seeks to shift our focus away from hierarchies and asserts that all components of the Earth community have value as Earth subjects.

## 1.2 Outline of the argument

Every text stands on the shoulders of past authors, ideas and debates. An interesting text is one that aims to move beyond those texts and make a novel or interesting intervention into the scholarship. In this book, I am concerned primarily with the intellectual insights offered in environmental philosophy, legal theory, political economy and critical theory. In exploring my thesis, I am also influenced by the thoughts offered by a young Karl Marx in his article 'For a Ruthless Criticism of Everything that Exists'. In this piece, Marx describes the critical method as a process of taking what others have said and working on it to transform thought – and the world it describes – into something new. For Marx (1978: 14), new knowledge arises out of taking radically different conceptual blocks and rubbing them together to create revolutionary fire.

This is effectively what I hope to achieve in this book – bringing together divergent intellectual traditions to create a new framework for knowledge and praxis. Beyond this introduction, the book consists of five substantive chapters and a conclusion. The following chapter overviews sketch an outline of the central arguments.

### 1.2.1 Chapter 2: Anthropocentrism and private property

In Chapter 2, I argue that the concept of private property reflects anthropocentric ideas and promotes environmental harm. To support this argument,

I examine four important periods in the development of private property from antiquity, the scientific revolution, the Industrial Revolution and the influence of modern liberal and neoliberal political philosophy.

Beginning in antiquity, I argue that the fundamental starting point for Western theories of property is human dominion over nature. The cultural roots of this perception can be traced back to Greek Stoic philosophy and the writing of Plato and Aristotle. Aristotle, for example, argued that all of the Earth was organised in a hierarchy with the physical environmental and non-human animals representing instruments for human use and happiness. This argument was influential for Roman Stoic jurists who constructed the first sophisticated legal definition of property in the concept dominion. This concept was subsequently developed by Christian jurists who blended Roman law with their own mythology concerning human dominium over 'creation'. I argue that despite enormous progression, Western theories of property have never shifted away from this basic starting point and continue to define nature as the object of human property relationships.

Following antiquity, the scientific revolution had a significant impact on Western theories of property. Increasingly during this period the environment came to be seen in mechanistic terms or as a lifeless machine. This worldview directly influenced philosophical writings on property and promoted the removal of longstanding community and environmental protections during the Industrial Revolution. Alongside this historical narrative, I capture these changes through an examination of the writing of John Locke, Jeremy Bentham and Wesley Newcomb Hohfeld. Each of these theorists conceptualised private property as a person–person relationship. According to this conception, property is divorced from the physical and the notion of inherent limits on property was discarded in favour of whatever regulation (if any) was prescribed by state law.

Finally, I consider how private property developed in the context of liberal and neoliberal political philosophy. Liberalism promotes individual freedom or choice without necessarily placing any duties on owners to have regard to human society or the environment. I argue that this conception is the ultimate product of anthropocentric philosophy and invites owners to live as isolated individuals who are concerned only with their own self-interest. I contend that this image of private property is misleading and promotes environmental harm. Indeed, property choices take place in a vast interconnected network of human and ecological relations. Our choices do not occur in a vacuum and instead have very real and immediate consequence for other human beings and the broader environment.

### 1.2.2 Chapter 3: Earth community: narrative and action

In Chapter 3, I advance an alternative foundation for law based on the eco-centric concept of Earth community. To support this concept, I bring together and critically examine scientific theories contained within quantum physics, ecology and Gaia theory. I also analyse the critique of holism advanced by Timothy Morton and describe his ecological concept of 'the mesh'. While there is not uniform agreement among these theories, I contend that each provides sophisticated support for the description of Earth community articulated earlier.

Following this analysis, I suggest that it is not sufficient to put forward an alternative worldview and assume that it will influence law. Instead, an explanation must also be provided that explains how this worldview can become assimilated and infused in law. I discuss this process first with reference to the 'new story' proposed by Thomas Berry. The 'new story' describes contemporary ecological insights in narrative form and offers an alternative cosmology for Western culture. Its intention is to address the psychological and cultural aspects of legal development by providing the foundation for an ecocentric worldview.

Following this, I contend that while an examination of 'mental ideas' about the world is arguably necessary, it is not sufficient to enact broad social and legal change. As a result, I seek to move beyond idealist philosophy and strengthen my analysis with respect a theory of social change advanced by Karl Marx. While Marx is often depicted as a determinist social thinker who positions the proletariat at the centre of historical development, his sociological writings are actually far more complex. He argues that social change occurs through a dialectical transformation across six spheres: technology, relation to nature, the process of production, the production and reproduction of daily life, social relations and mental conceptions of the world.

While I do not have the space to analyse each of these spheres, I supplement my analysis of Berry's 'new story' with a discussion of the role of social relations and social justice movements in legal development. In particular, I position the current movement for Earth jurisprudence as a social movement that is engaged in a grassroots collaborative struggle aimed at shifting laws toward an ecological foundation. I consider one key example of this in the worldwide advocacy for the rights of nature. However, I also conclude that the movement will need to politicise, build networks of solidarity and engage in further robust struggle to realise Berry's vision of an ecocentric era. Indeed, without such coordinated development, there is no reason why the environmental consequences of the anthropocene will not deepen and worsen.

### 1.2.3 Chapter 4: A theory of Earth jurisprudence

In Chapter 4, I present an original interpretation of the philosophy of Earth jurisprudence. While I recognise the limits of jurisprudence (and juridical devices more generally) as a tool for realising radical change, I also contend that speculation about what an alternative ecological concept of law might look like is important. Indeed, our concept of law has played an incredibly important historical role in legal development. For example, the revolutionary consequence of shifting from natural law and legal positivism has been well documented (Berman 1983, 2006). Today, jurisprudence continues to provide the intellectual context within which positive laws are made and interpreted. This remains true, dispute the more overt ways in which power and money influence the functioning of a legal system.

Drawing on Berry's jurisprudential writing, I interpret Earth jurisprudence as a continuation of the project of 'ecological natural law', which was popularised by figures such as Aldo Leopold (1986). According to this interpretation, there exist two types of law that are organised in hierarchical relationship. At the top of the hierarchy is the 'great law', which represents the principle of Earth community and the scientific concept of ecological integrity. Beneath the great law is human law, which represents rules articulated by human authorities, which are consistent with the great law and enacted for the common good of the comprehensive Earth community.

Regarding the interrelationship between these legal categories, two points are critical. First, human law derives its legal quality from the great law. In this function, the great law functions as a kind of informal or 'vernacular law' (Weston & Bollier 2013: 104) and provides the design parameters beyond which a legislature may not cross. This discussion of design parameters is strengthened with reference to the emerging project for Earth democracy, which I contend may provide the positive law framework for Earth jurisprudence. Further to this point, Earth jurisprudence also maintains that a purported law that contravenes the great law is defective and not morally binding on a population. In this instance, Earth jurisprudence offers a legal justification for acts of civil disobedience aimed at reforming a defective law. Moreover, I contend that a purported law might be so contradictory to the great law that civil disobedience is justified regardless of the consequences to a specific government.

## 1.2.4 Chapter 5: Private property revisited

In Chapter 5, I return full circle to the concept of private property and describe how Earth jurisprudence could influence its future development. Rather than discarding private property as a social institution, this chapter presents a reformist analysis that seeks to give private property radically new content. This approach recognises that private property is an indeterminate concept with many potential incarnations. While the institution currently reflects an anthropocentric heritage and liberal rights-based values, it can also be conceived to reflect ecocentric ideas such as the concept of Earth community. To this end, I offer a description of private property as *a relationship between and among members of the Earth community, through tangible or intangible items.*

Under this construction, private property is socially situated and property rights are contingent on their impact on others within the community. Further, obligations and responsibilities are inherent to the institution. These duties represent a deliberate limitation of human freedom, derived from the concept of Earth community and the great potential human beings have to devastate the environment. Finally, the concept of private property offered in this chapter places specific importance on the object of property itself. That is, private property is a relationship facilitated by a specific item or thing. Conceived in this way, the object of a property relationship plays a key role in shaping the types of use rights and responsibilities that attach to a specific item of private property. For land, ownership would shift from the present right-based agenda to an unfolding practice that bends to reflect place and treats the component parts of the Earth as coequal subjects rather than as objects. I conclude by arguing that a concept of private property that overlooks any of these considerations is defective and deserves to be labelled as such.

# Chapter 2

# Anthropocentrism and private property

## 2.1 Introduction

In this chapter, I explore private property as a legal–philosophical concept and consider how it embodies anthropocentric assumptions. Private property is prioritised over other areas of law because it plays a primary role in mediating human relationships with the environment and because it contains some of law's key messages about the environment and our place within it. Furthermore, developing an understanding of the ideas that underpin the institution of private property is critical for its future reform – hence the importance of the arguments to be offered here. The related task of adapting private property toward ecocentric ethics and the legal philosophy of Earth jurisprudence is undertaken in Chapter 5.

In this chapter, I present private property as an indeterminate concept that does not have fixed meaning across place, time or culture.[1] Instead, private property is understood here as a cultural artefact and shaped by economic, religious and philosophical ideas. As C. Edwin Baker (1986: 741) contends: 'Property rights are a cultural creation and a legal conclusion.' From this perspective, private property lacks an in-built unitary structure that can be discovered through descriptive analysis or logical deduction. Thus, rather than presenting an absolute definition of private property, I aim to construct a composite picture or 'collage' of private property ideas and to highlight the cultural norms on which the modern institution is built (Davies 2007: 3).

I begin this chapter by positing that the starting premise for Western theories of private property is human dominion over nature. I trace the origin of this concept in Greek philosophy and consider its application in Roman law. I also consider how this concept was developed by Christian jurists with reference to the myth of *dominium* as depicted in the Bible. Following this analysis, I investigate the influence of the scientific revolution and the scientific method on Western attitudes toward the environment. I also look at

---

1. There is an alternative perspective that holds there is an objective or true concept of property. Richard Epstein (1985: 304), for example, describes private property in essentialist terms, arguing that private property means the 'exclusive rights of possession, use and disposition'.

how theories of private property changed during the industrial revolution to promote economic growth and how property came to be defined as a person–person relationship between human beings. Finally, I investigate how liberal and neoliberal political theory influenced the development of private property. In particular, I demonstrate how private property came to focus on the individual and on the maximisation of choice without the construction of corresponding duties or obligations to the human or ecological community.

## 2.2 Dominion

> If the world was made for us, then it belongs to us and we can do what we damn well please with it. (Quinn 1995: 21)

The fundamental starting premise for Western theories of property is that human beings have dominion over nature and that the environment is the object of human property relationships. An English jurist, Lord Scarman, provides evidence of this premise in the opening chapter of his commentary on English law. Scarman (1975: 59) writes, '[f]or environment, a traditional lawyer reads property.' In support, Eric T. Freyfogle (1993a: 49) comments, '[w]hen lawyers refer to the physical world, to this field and that forest and the next-door city lot, they think and talk in terms of property and ownership.' Moreover, English common law has evolved principally to protect the private property rights and economic interests of property owners (Bates 2002: 20). Such property rights can exist directly over parts of the environment (incorporating both land and non-human animals) or over products derived from the environment that exist in some synthetic form, such as a pen or book. Property conceptualism therefore has extensive reach over material realities.

From the outset, it is important to recognise that the conceptualisation of the environment as human property is a mere cultural construct. It is not the case that human beings are inherently separate from the environment or that nature must out of necessity be understood in an instrumental way. Rather, the anthropocentric reduction of the environment to property is just one of multiple possible ways that human beings have defined their relationship to the natural world throughout human history. Perhaps the simplest way to understand this point is by comparison with another statement on the environment from Tanganekald-Meintangk[2] woman Irene Watson. Watson's comments are in regard to a piece of land near where this book was written and which is currently defined legally as private property. Watson (1999: 9–10) writes:

> To own the land is a remote idea. The indigenous relationship to *ruwe*, the land is more complex. In Western capitalist thought, *ruwe* becomes

---

2. The Tanganekald-Meintangk peoples come from the lower lakes and Coorong region in South Australia.

known as property, a consumable which can be traded or sold. We live as part of the natural world; we are it also. The natural world is our mirror. We take no more than necessary to sustain life; we nurture *ruwe* as we do our self, for we are one. Westerners live on the land taking more than needed, depleting *ruwe* and depleting self. So self can be no more tomorrow. Westerners are separate and alien to *ruwe* . . . all is one, one is all, we are the land, the land is us and the law is in all things. That is the law.[3]

While I do not wish to homogenise indigenous perspectives on the environment, Onondaga Chief Oren Lyons makes a similar point when commenting on the disposition of his people from the area near Syracuse, New York. Lyons (2007: 208) states:

> The idea of land tenure and ownership were brought here. We didn't think that you could buy and sell land. In fact, the ideas of buying and selling were concepts we didn't have. We laughed when they told us they wanted to buy land. And we said, well, how do you buy land? You might as well buy air, or buy water. But we don't laugh anymore, because that is precisely what happened.

How then are we to make sense of the particular description of private property that came to dispossess and colonise aboriginal people around the world? Because private property is a social institution, I suggest that the most instructive approach is to examine some of the larger cultural attitudes that surrounded its development. I begin by considering the philosophical and theological justifications for the foundational notion of human dominion over nature.

### 2.2.1 Philosophical justifications for dominion

> The safest general characterization of the European philosophical tradition is that it consists in a series of footnotes to Plato. (Whitehead 1979, 39)

> I am a man who loves learning, and trees and open spaces cannot teach me a thing, whereas men in town do. (Plato 1997: 230)[4]

---

3. Note that '*ruwe*' means land. While this is an accurate description of private property tendencies, it should also be noted that individual relationships to land within Western culture are far more complex and diverse than a monolithic reading of them would imply (Reid 2000).
4. Socrates' reasoning was in direct and deliberate contrast to the earlier 'natural philosophers' such as Thales and the main rival philosophical school established by Pythagoras in 530 BCE. While little can be said about Pythagoras with any definiteness, it is known that he sought knowledge from studying nature's patterns. Pythagoras also instructed his students on the care of and respect for nature. For example, he encouraged vegetarianism and taught that the souls of dead humans migrated to animals. This teaching sought to establish kinship with nature and is not dissimilar to Eastern religious ideas of reincarnation (Singer 1975: 205–206).

The philosophical origin of human dominion can be traced back to the very root of Western intellectual thought and in particular to the writing of Plato and his pupil Aristotle. Plato is the main historic source of ideas related to 'otherworldliness' in occidental philosophy. It is through him that the conception of an unseen eternal world of ideas[5] gains a foothold in the West. Further, it is from his writings that the belief that the highest good for human beings lies in somehow translocating themselves into such a world has been perennially nourished (Tarnas 1993: 6).

In his classic study of Western metaphysics, Arthur O. Lovejoy traces the origin of the philosophical concept of 'great chain of being' to Plato's concept of plentitude. This concept covers a wide range of premises but I am using it here to refer to the notion that the universe is a *plenum formarum* in which the entire range of conceivable diversity of kinds of living thing is exhaustively exemplified (Lovejoy 1960: 52).[6] Put otherwise, everything that can exist does exist.[7] Plato (1997: 1236) rationalises this conclusion in the following terms: 'the best soul could begrudge existence to nothing that could conceivably possess it and desired that all things should be as like himself as they could be.'

While perhaps benign when read in isolation, the notion of plentitude was strengthened by the concept of 'continuity'[8] formulated by Aristotle. This concept was designed to fuse with the concept of plentitude and to be regarded as logically implied by it (Lovejoy 1960: 55). This combination of concepts led Aristotle to conclude that all quantities (lines, surfaces, solids, etc.) must be continuous in time and space. Importantly, this did not mean that all organisms could be arranged in one ascending and continuous sequence of forms. Aristotle made no attempt to frame any single exclusive scheme of classification for animals or the environment. Nevertheless as Lovejoy (1960: 56) observes, 'any division of creatures with reference to some one determinate attribute manifestly gave rise to a linear series of classes.' And such a series, Aristotle observed, tends to illustrate a shading-off of the properties of one class into those of the next rather than a clear or sharp distinction between them. This minute graduation of differentness is especially evident

---

5. The Platonic idea is the expression of the simple thought that every rightly formed conception has its solid basis in objective reality.

6. Note that the concept of plenitude has also been used to refer to the idea that no genuine potentiality of being can remain unfulfilled and that the great abundance of the creations must be as great as the possibility of existence and commensurate with the productive capacity of a 'perfect' and inexhaustible source.

7. For Plato, the totality of existence reflects nothing less than the sensible counterparts of every one of the Ideas. This is revealed in the dialogue *Parmenides* (1997: 360), in which the character Parmenides reminds the young Socrates that in the 'World of Ideas' all things exist, even things paltry, ridiculous and disgusting.

8. Aristotle (1984: 921) defines continuity as follows: 'Things are said to be continuous whenever there is one and the same limit of both wherein they overlap and which they possess in common.'

at precisely those points which common speech implies the presence of profound and well-defined contrasts. Aristotle (1984: 922) writes:

> Nature proceeds little by little from things lifeless to animal life in such a way that it is impossible to determine the exact line of demarcation, nor on which side thereof an intermediate form should lie. Thus, next after lifeless things in the upward scale comes the plant, and of plants one will differ from another as to its amount of apparent vitality; and, in a word, the whole genus of plants, whilst it is devoid of life as compared with an animal, is endowed with life as compared with other corporeal entities. Indeed, as we just remarked, there is observed in plants a continuous scale of ascent towards the animal. So, in the sea, there are certain objects concerning which one would be at a loss to determine whether they be animal or vegetable.

Just as the Platonic writings were the principles source of 'otherworldliness' and of its opposite in Western philosophy, so the influence of Aristotle is most often recognised as the great representative of a logic that rests on the assumption of the possibility of clear divisions and rigorous classification. Indeed, from the Platonic principle of plentitude, the principle of continuity could be directly deduced: if there is between two given natural species a theoretically possible intermediate type, that type must be substantiated – and so on forevermore. Otherwise, there would be gaps and the universe would not be as full as it might be. This would further imply the 'inadmissible consequence' that the source of creation was not 'good' in the sense that adjective has in Plato's *Timaeus* (1997: 1227).

There are in the Platonic dialogues occasional suggestions that the ideas (and therefore their sensible or physical counterparts) are not all of equal metaphysical rank. However, this tendency toward hierarchically ordered essences remains in Plato only a vague tendency. In spite of Aristotle's recognition of the multiplicity of possible systems of natural classification, it was he who chiefly suggested to naturalists and philosophers of later times the idea of arranging (at least) all animals in a single graded scale according to their 'degree of perfection'. Aristotle constructed two formulations of this hierarchy. The first focused on the degree of development reached by the offspring at birth. From this analysis, he discerned 11 general grades, with humankind at the top and the zoophytes at the bottom (1984: 1136–1137). Furthermore, this basic hierarchy is supplemented by the notion of graduation, which includes clear instrumental values (Lovejoy 1960: 56). That is, the environment is conceived of as being an instrument for human use. The following passage from Aristotle (1984: 1991) illustrates this analysis:

> Plants exist for the sake of animals, the brute beasts for the sake of man – domestic animals for his use and food, wild ones (or at any rate most of them) for food and others accessories of life, such as clothing and various

tools. Since nature makes nothing purposeless or in vain, it is undeniably true that she has made all animals for the sake of man.

Aristotle's (1984: 1991) second formulation organises the hierarchy with regard to the 'powers of soul'. The scale ranges from the 'nutritive' qualities of plants, to the 'rational' attributes of human beings and then 'possibly another kind superior to this' (1984: 659). Importantly, each higher element in the hierarchy possesses all the qualities of those below and an additional differentiating element of their own. The second ranking had great influence on subsequent philosophy and natural history and was used by later intellectuals to justify the anthropocentric worldview. Indeed, Lovejoy (1960: viii) argues that 'Aristotle's hierarchy is one of the most potent and persistent presuppositions in Western thought.' Following Lovejoy's analysis, I suggest that the hierarchical ordering of the environment was profoundly important to the development of classical law and theories of property. While Greek philosophers had written on both topics (Aristotle 1984: 2008–2009; Plato 1997: 550–551) the Roman Stoics undertook the first sophisticated formulation of private property.

Stoicism was developed by Zeno of Citium and his followers from the third century BCE and became the most influential philosophy of the Hellenistic age. A defining feature of Stoicism was its focus on human ethics and the desire expressed by many of its proponents to give human beings some stable belief system in the face of a hostile and chaotic environment (Tarnas 1993: 76). The result of this impulse is a metaphysics that viewed each component part of the environment as permeated by rationality and divinely planned by the organisation of matter. Zeno described this planning in terms of cosmic determinism (Russell 1972: 254). Indeed, Zeno believed that there is no such thing as chance and that the environment was rigidly determined by natural laws. Moral goodness and happiness is achieved (if at all) by replicating that perfect rationality in oneself and by discovering and enacting one's own assigned role in the cosmic scheme of things.

At the lowest physical level, the world consists of two coextensive principles – passive 'matter' and active 'god'. At the lowest observable level, these principles are constituted into the four elements earth, water, air and fire. Air and fire form an active and pervasive life force called *Pneuma* or 'breath', which constitutes the qualities of all bodies, and in an especially rarefied form, serves as the souls of all living things (Sedley 2005: 1002). A lawgiver who was also a beneficent providence ordained the course of nature down to the smallest detail. The whole of the environment was designed to secure certain natural ends that are to be found in the life of human beings. Bertrand Russell (1972: 254) draws out the anthropocentric implications of this metaphysics:

> Everything has a purpose connected with human beings. Some animals are good to eat, some afford tests of courage; even bed bugs are useful, since they help us to wake in the morning and not lie in bed too long.

For Greek Stoics, the supreme power is sometimes called God and sometimes Zeus. Whatever the name, this power is not separate from the world and every human being contains part of the divine fire. The entire environment is part of one single system called nature and the individual life is good or virtuous when human will is directed to ends that are among those of nature. Thus, virtue consists in a *will* that is in agreement with the cosmic and determined order of nature. Russell (1972: 254) elaborates further: 'The wicked, though perforce they obey God's law, do so involuntarily; in the simile of Cleanthes, they are like a dog tied to a car, and compelled to go wherever it goes.'[9]

Roman jurists inherited the worldview and hierarchical ordering of nature from their Stoic forbearers and held that 'virtue consists in a will which is in agreement with Nature' (Russell 1972: 254). In this context, however, 'nature' refers to human nature and not specifically to the natural world. Indeed, human beings were considered to be the measure of virtue and universal truth could be obtained through human reason. This orientation led to the development of natural law jurisprudence or the *jus naturale*. Stoic philosopher Cicero (2008: 105) provides the classic formulation of natural law:

> True law is right reason in agreement with nature; it is of universal application, unchanging and everlasting; it summons to duty by its commands, and averts wrongdoing by its prohibitions . . . It is a sin to try to alter this law, nor is it allowable to attempt to repeal any part of it, and it is impossible to abolish it entirely. We cannot be freed from its obligations by senate or people, and we need not look outside ourselves for an expounder and interpreter of it. And there will not be different laws at Rome and at Athens, or different laws now and in the future, but one eternal and unchangeable law will be valid for all nations and all times, and there will be one master and ruler, that is, God, over us, for he is the author of this law, its promulgator and its enforcing judge.

Cicero describes natural law as possessing three important characteristics. First, his formulation holds that there are universal and immutable 'laws' that are accessible at all times to human lawmakers. Second, the law of nature is a 'higher law' and superior to laws promulgated by political authorities (the *jus commune*). Finally, consistent with Aristotle's idea of continuity, Cicero's formulation holds that all things have natural essences or ends that are directed toward human beings. To discover these ends, human beings are required to use their reflective intellect to draw knowledge, reach conclusions and deduce rational steps about what justice requires (Harris 1996: 7).

---

9. There are obvious difficulties with this philosophy. Most pressing for my current analysis is how one can decide (or will) to be virtuous in the context of a completely deterministic world that limits human freedom.

Roman jurists argued that the natural end of the environment was human good. However, because natural law recognises an inherent relationship between law and morality, Roman jurists also made provision for the moral treatment of the non-human world. For example, the *jus animalium* was a specific category within the *jus naturale* that dealt with non-human animals and recognised that they possessed inherent natural rights (Nash 1989: 16). Commenting on the *just animalium*, Roman jurist Ulpian (cited in Nash 1989: 17) explained that the *jus animalium* was part of the *jus naturale* because the latter included 'that which nature has taught all animals; this law indeed is not peculiar to the human race, but belongs to all animals'.

Despite this express concern for non-human animals, the overwhelming current of Roman jurisprudence was fundamentally human centred. Cicero, for example, is credited with forming the humanist movement and holding overtly anthropocentric ideas. The influence of Aristotle's writing on 'continuity' and 'graduation' are evidenced in the following statement from Cicero (2008a: 159): 'just as a shield-case is made for the sake of a shield and a sheath for the sake of a sword, so everything else except the world was created for the sake of some other thing; thus the corn and fruits produced by the earth were created for the sake of animals, and animals for the sake of man.' Cicero's pupil Seneca (1969: 56) continued this legacy and famously stated: 'To mankind, mankind is holy.' This statement became the slogan for humanism through the renaissance and as legal historian Richard Schlatter (1951: 26) notes, Roman jurists 'wove the philosophy of Cicero and Seneca into law through the concept of dominion'.

Roman jurists did not attempt to define dominion and instead left its meaning to arise from use (Nicholas 1962: 152). During the revival of Roman law during the eleventh century, jurists defined *dominium* as being akin to 'lordship' and further noted that it was a sovereign, ultimate or an absolute right to claim title and thus to possess and enjoy an item (Getzler 1998: 82). Despite such absolute language, *dominium* was qualified in practice. Indeed, Peter Birks (1985: 1) contends that '[n]o community could tolerate ownership literally unrestricted in its content.' As in contemporary law, private property over the environment was limited by the 'equal use, enjoyment and abuse by all other owners of their property' (Nicholas 1962: 154). Furthermore, social, economic and political factors could also limit private ownership for example through taxation or land use restrictions.

Despite the great level of evolution and the increasing sophistication that the Western concept of private property has undergone since the classical period, our law has never moved away from the central underlying Roman idea that the land exists as human property and that humans have dominion over the environment. Indeed, this starting point has become the unquestioned presupposition on which all other theories of property have since been based. Speaking directly with regard to the evolution of property, Joshua Getzler (1998: 81) notes: 'Roman ideas about private and public property provide a kind of DNA of legal ownership, the intellectual structure within which most later legal thought has developed.' In agreement, S.F.C. Milsom (1981: 119) notes that the common law doctrine 'of "seisin" and "right" [were] forever dazzled by the Roman vision of possession and ownership'.

I now consider the influence of Christian theology on the development of Western rationality and the concept of private property. As part of this analysis, I illustrate how Christian myths concerning the divine grant of dominium to human beings, fused with Roman law to form the dominant theory of private property through the Middle Ages and to the nineteenth century.

### 2.2.2 From dominion to dominium

> Christianity is the most anthropocentric religion the world has seen.
> (White 1967: 1203)

The next significant development for the Western theory of private property occurred at the hands of Christian jurists. Following the conversion of Roman Emperor Constantine to Christianity in 313 AD 'clerical jurists combined classical humanist philosophy with Christian myths of the Garden of Eden and the Fall of Man [to make] the standard theory' of property of the medieval church (Schlatter 1951: 26). This combination of conceptualisations was favourable to the early church leaders who had no express desire to amend exiting property arrangements in such a way that would challenge church (Pipes 1999: 10). For them, the concept of dominion 'not only solved this dilemma: it dovetailed neatly with other Christian myths and doctrines' (Schlatter 1951: 35; Humfress 2005: 167–171).[10]

The Roman concept of *dominion* was strengthened and given continued longevity by the Christian idea of *dominium*. Both words share the common etymological root domino, which means to 'rule' or 'power over another' (Onions 1996: 198). The most explicit Christian reference to human dominium over nature is found in Genesis, Chapter 1. Here we are told that God made human beings in his own image and stationed them in a special position in relation to the rest of creation. Moreover, human beings are explicitly given dominium over all things. Genesis 1: 28–31 states:

> Be fruitful and increase in number; fill the earth and subdue it. Rule over the fish of the sea and the birds of the air and over every living creature that moves on the ground. Then God said, I give you every

---

10. In providing this description of the Christian influence on Western rationality, I also acknowledge an alternative branch of theology, which provides a striking critique of this language of mastery and promotes the recognition of ethical responsibilities to the environment. Exemplars of this view can be noted in figures such as St Francis of Assisi (Sorrell 2009), Benedict of Nursia (Dubos 1973), Norman Habel (2010), Ron Engel (1986), Leonardo Boff (1997) and Thomas Berry (1999). This ecological branch of Christianity is evidence of the deep variety of religious experience within the Christian faith. Nevertheless, I contend that it represents a minor thread in the orthodox or mainstream interpretation of Christian scripture.

seed-bearing plant on the face of the whole earth and every tree that has fruit with seed in it. They will be yours for food. And to all the beasts on the earth and all he birds of the air and all the creatures that move on the ground – everything that has the breath of life in it – I give every green plant for food and it was so. (Zondervan 2002: 7)[11]

Religious scholar W. Lee Humphreys comments that in this on this passage, noting that Hebrew linguists have interpreted the operative verbs 'subdue' (*kabash*) and 'dominion' (*radah*) to signify a violent assault or crushing. According to these interpretations, the image 'is that of a conqueror placing his foot on the neck of a defeated enemy, exerting absolute domination' (Humphreys 1971: 67). Theologian Gloria Schaab (2011: 45) supports this interpretation, arguing that church leaders used this passage to limit moral value to human beings. In contrast, the rest of the natural world was positioned as having only 'instrumental value' – that is, as 'valuable solely in terms of what it supplies the human being'.

Further insight can be gained through a reading of the fall of humankind depicted in Genesis 3: 13–19. In this passage, God caught Adam and Eve eating from the forbidden tree. On receiving their confessions, God banished them from the Garden and inflicted hardship on them and the serpent that tricked Eve. Mythologist Joseph Campbell (2002: 59) argues that one of the dominant messages portrayed in this passage is that the environment is something to be condemned. Indeed, in this story we see human beings, God and nature as three *separate* entities in *conflict*. Zen philosopher Daisetz T. Suzuki (1954: 294–295) comments: 'Man is against God, Nature is against God, and Man and Nature are against each other. God's own likeness (Man), God's own creation (Nature) and God himself – all three are at war.' Thomas Berry (cited in Jensen 2004: 37) supports this interpretation of Genesis, arguing:

> There is nothing to indicate a love of existence or a capacity for intimacy with the natural world for its own sake. Not to use it for monetary or even spiritual purposes but to be present in it.

This textual analysis of the development of anthropocentrism in western rationality is strengthened through a consideration of the Abrahamic biblical myths. G.W.F. Hegel provided the most insightful analysis of this point in his early paper 'The Spirit of Christianity' (1971: 182–301). While this paper is predominately read for the insight it provides into the logical structure of Hegel's ethical vision,[12] I limit my consideration to Hegel's contention

---

11. This covenant is restated in Genesis 9: 1–3.
12. At the centre of Hegel's ethical vision is a compelling analysis of the interconnectedness of all life. He argues that to act against another person is to destroy one's own life. In this way, the flourishing and foundering of each is intimately bound up with the flourishing and foundering of all.

that biblical Judaism represents an important moment in the development of Western rationality and our perceived separation from the environment (1971: 182; Bernstein 2003: 395).

It is significant to Hegel's argument that he begins 'The Spirit of Christianity' with the story of Noah and the flood. Hegel interprets this mythological event as a moment of rupture that brought Western consciousness out from the 'state of nature'. He describes the flood as a 'destructive' and 'invincible' force that reveals the indifference of the environment to human ends. Western rationality emerges in response to this event and is generated as a means to human survival against a cold and indifferent natural world (Bernstein 2003: 395).

Following his discussion of the flood, Hegel argues that Western mythology reveals two basic ways or paths through which one can master nature. The first is through something 'real' or material such as a collective practical activity such as building a city or a dam.[13] The second is through 'some thought' such as the invention of the Jewish God (1971: 183). According to Hegel, Noah adopted the second solution by posing the ideal of God to set against the hostile environment and then ascribing reality to that ideal. By adopting this method, Noah gives the ideal of a Jewish God power over material reality. Yet, the mere thought of such a God cannot possibly provide for an actual mastery over the natural world. Hence, a certain type of conceptual deferral or complex machinery must also be built into the experience and the mythology of God.

Hegel scholar Jay Bernstein (2003: 396) describes the mediation of God's relation to nature through his relation to human kind as the 'theological contract'. Bernstein describes the terms of the contract as follows: 'God promises to restrain the forces of nature on the condition that human beings master their nature, nature within, our murderous hearts, by obeying his laws of conduct.' Nature, from this perspective, is reduced to a sign of human obedience to God. Hegel (1971: 187) states this thought unequivocally in his account of Abraham: 'It was through God alone that Abraham came into a mediate relation with the world, the only kind of link with the world possible for him.'

Importantly, Hegel argues that Noah's strategy for mastering nature is ultimately self-defeating. He writes (1971: 184): '[Noah] made a peace of necessity with the foe and thus perpetuated the hostility.' This sentence encapsulates Hegel's contention that nature-dominating rationality is necessarily self-defeating: the logic of causal manipulation and the subjection of our self to an external authority both internalise the conception of nature as other and as something antagonistic. As Bernstein (2003: 397) suggests, '[N]ature knows only one solution: domination and control.'

---

13. This was the solution adopted by Nimrod, son of Noah. In response to the flood, Nimrod is said to have built a 'tower which was to be far higher than the waves and streams could ever rise and in this way to avenge the downfall of his forefathers' (Hegel 1971: 184).

The ideas of domination and control were the central organising principles behind the religious attitude toward property developed by the early Christian church. For these writers, the idea of human dominium over nature constituted an unquestioned assumption or starting premise for their writings. Yet, as with the Roman jurists, the early Christian writers also wrote within the framework of natural law and their writings on property are saturated with a vision of interpersonal human ethics. As early as the third century, Clement of Alexandria advanced an ethic of Christian charity on the grounds that God had bestowed the Earth to human beings in common and that each was to use only what he needed (Schlatter 1951: 36). In accordance with this view, St Ambrose followed Cicero is saying that by nature all property is for the common use of human beings.

While there was divergence of opinion among the early Christian jurists,[14] the orthodox position of the Western Catholic Church was codified by St Thomas Aquinas in his *Summa Theologica*. Aquinas's writings on property reflect a subtle combination of humanist Greek philosophy and Christian theology. Aquinas (1981: 1470) considers the early Christian view that, in a certain sense, 'it was not natural for man to possess external things.' However, he ultimately rejects this position, correctly reasoning that God's original grant of the Earth to human beings in common did not logically preclude private ownership.[15] Drawing on Aristotle,[16] Aquinas gives unequivocal support to the concept of plentitude (1991: 75) and affirms the primacy of human beings and the 'great chain of being'. Aquinas argues (1991: 789) that non-human animals are 'ordered to man's use' and have 'no independent moral standing'. He also draws on Aristotle's *Politics* to argue against holding property in common on the basis that it promotes discord. Indeed, Aquinas (1981: 1471) argues that private property was vital to spiritual growth and served the public good by enabling the giving of alms.

Under the influence of Aquinas, the Christian view of private property shifted from being a 'regrettable but unavoidable reality' to being a theory that was defended with vigour (Pipes 1999: 17). As testimony to Acquinas' enduring influence, in 1329 Pope John XXII (cited in Pipes 1999: 17) drew directly on Aquinas to restate human dominion over nature in a papal edict: 'Property (*dominium*) of man over his possessions does not differ from the property asserted by God over the universe, which He bestowed on man created in his Image.'

14. For example, in *City of God* (2003: 897) St Augustine described property as the creation of the state (as opposed to something natural) and the fruit of sin. Elsewhere he advises Christians not to own property individually and asserts that there will be no private property in paradise.

15. Using a similar logic, Aquinas asks whether human beings should always remain naked just because we were naked in the state of nature.

16. Commenting on the relationship between Aristotle and Aquinas, Ralph McInery (1977: 30) notes: 'It has been said that without Thomas, Aristotle would be mute; it can equally be said that without Aristotle, Thomas would be unintelligible.'

Had the religious interpretation of dominium remained the exclusive possession of theologians, its subsequent influence on law would have been slight. However, from the Middle Ages to the modern era, jurists and political theorists have cited dominion as a justification for private property (Schlatter 1951: 57). The most well-known example is Sir William Blackstone (1796: 2) who defined property as 'that sole and despotic dominion that one man claims and exercises over the external things of the world, in total exclusion of the right of any other individual in the universe'. Blackstone (1796: 2) also justified the institution on the following basis:

> In the beginning of the world, we are informed by holy writ, the all-bountiful Creator gave to man 'dominion over all the earth, and over the fish of the sea, and over the fowl of the air, and over every living thing that moveth upon the earth'. This is the only true and solid foundation of man's dominion over external things, whatever airy metaphysical notions may have been started by fanciful writers upon this subject. The earth, therefore, and all things therein, are the general property of all mankind, exclusive of other beings, from the immediate gift of the Creator.

Under the influence of Christian authors, the idea of human dominion over nature was firmly entrenched (Locke 1970: 14; Raff 2005). This perspective underwent further significant development during the scientific and industrial revolutions. I turn now to consider this period and its consequence for the concept of private property.

## 2.3 The scientific and Industrial Revolutions

During the seventeenth century the notion of human dominium was supplemented by a mechanistic philosophy that described the environment as a fragmented, lifeless, machine (Ehrenfeld 1978; Leiss 1994; Lovejoy 1960; Merchant 1990). The basis for this thinking was the scientific revolution that began at the end of the sixteenth century and continued until the Industrial Revolution in the eighteenth century. Like all major shifts in epistemology, the scientific revolution had a profound impact on the Western worldview. John Bernal (cited in Brown 2007: 36) captures this transition in the following terms: 'The renaissance enabled a scientific revolution which let scholars look at the world in a different light . . . religion, superstition and fear were replaced by reason and knowledge.'

The scientific revolution has a significant impact on all major scientific fields and more fundamentally in the way that scientists conceived and interacted with the natural world. Further, as mechanistic philosophy infiltrated the political class, this shift in perspective came to influence law and the institution of private property (Graham 2011: 28–58; Schlatter 1951: 125).

### 2.3.1 The scientific revolution

Many authors have traced the origin and development of the scientific revolution (Jacob 2009). Because of his influence on the development of scientific method, our investigation begins with Francis Bacon. Bacon was one of the most original and profound of the intellectual reformers of the sixteenth and seventeenth centuries. According to John Milton (2005: 77) Bacon's 'dream was one of power over nature' derived through experiment and embodied in appropriate institutions and used for the amelioration of human life. According to Bacon, this could only be achieved if rational speculation was coupled with the craft skills in the practical arts. This led Bacon to develop a new method of inquiry based on eliminative induction (as opposed to deductive logic or mathematics). As described by Bacon, eliminative induction drew on data extracted from extensive and elaborative constructed natural histories. Unlike the orthodox methods of logical deduction, Bacon hoped that his method would be able to make use of negative as well as positive instances of natural history and thus allow conclusions to be established with certainty.

Bacon's scientific writings were driven by the desire to perfect eliminative induction and to position it as a lasting process for reestablishing the mastery of nature that human beings had enjoyed in the biblical stories (Tarnas 1993: 273). Hans Jonas (1984: 140) supports this interpretation, noting that the intention of Bacon's epistemological method was to 'gain knowledge and power over nature and to utilize power over nature for the improvement of the human lot'. Bacon provides further content to this aim in *The New Atlantis*. Here Bacon (1990: 34–35) argued that 'the purpose' of human society is to acquire 'the Knowledge of Causes, and Secret Motions of Things; and the Enlarging of the bounds of the Humane Empire, to the Effecting of all Things possible'.

Bacon's concern with mastering nature is premised on a perspective that positions the natural world as 'other' and as a mere 'object' for human use. Like his Christian predecessors, Bacon assumed that human beings occupied the central place in a God-created universe. This is made clear in Bacon's (1985: 270–271) interpretation of the myth of Prometheus: 'Prometheus clearly and expressly signified Providence . . . the special and peculiar work of Providence was the creation and constitution of Man.' He argues further:

> The chief aim of the parable seems to be, that Man, if we look to final causes, may be regarded as the centre of the world; in so much that if man were taken away from the world, the rest would seem to be all astray, without aim or purpose . . . and leading to nothing. For the whole world works together in the service of man; and there is nothing from which he does not derive use and fruit . . . insomuch that all things seem to be going about man's business and not their own.

From this perspective, human beings are separate from the environment. Only human beings are 'subjects' and in a position to conduct objective inquiry. In contrast, the natural world is a separate object under investigation. Within this framework it is ontologically impossible to be both subject and object – 'something is either culture or it is nature; human or not human; the inquirer or the object of inquiry' (Graham 2011: 29). Bacon argued that this belief in the centrality of human beings would eventually be carried over into the secular realm and be maintained in practically all narratives of human evolution, even though God would be dispensed with in most scientific accounts of the origin of the universe and of our species.

Importantly for the argument being sketched in this chapter, the dichotomy that Bacon drew between human beings and the environment resulted in violent implications – particularly with regard to the extension of patriarchy in Western rationality (Merchant 1980). Commenting on the goal of his scientific method, Bacon (Farrington 1949: 62)[17] holds: 'My only earthly wish is . . . to stretch the deplorably narrow limits of man's dominion over the universe to their promised bounds . . . putting [nature] on the rack and extracting her secrets . . . storming her strongholds and castles.' At no time did Bacon (Farrington 1949: 62) hide his agenda: 'I come in very truth leading you to nature with all her children to blind her to your service and make her your slave . . . the mechanical inventions of recent years do not merely exert a gentle guidance over Nature's courses, they have the power to conquer and subdue her, to shake her to her foundations.' Elsewhere he notes: 'We have no right to expect nature to come to us . . . Nature must be taken by the forelock, being bald behind' (Farrington 1949: 129). He also warns that delay or more subtle method 'permit one to clutch at nature, never to lay hold of her and capture her' (Farrington 1949: 130).

Bacon's scientific method had a profound impact on the philosophical investigations of René Descartes. Descartes is often called the father of modern philosophy (Garber 2005: 174) and sought to start philosophy anew by breaking with the dominant traditions of the seventeenth century. Descartes (1985: 113) followed Bacon's instruction 'never to accept anything as true if [one] did not have evident knowledge of its truth'. Hence the *Meditations* (2006) begins with a series of arguments intended to cast doubt on everything formerly believed and culminating in the hypothesis of an all-deceiving evil genius, as a device to keep former beliefs returning. The rebuilding of the world begins with the discovery of Descartes' (2006: 13) well-rehearsed *cogito* argument – 'I think, therefore I am.' This 'I' is a self, known only as a thinking thing and it is discoverable independently of the senses.

17. I have cited Farrington for several of Bacon's quotes because his book represents the most authoritative source for the statements reproduced. The essays from which the quotes were derived were not translated as part of Bacon's complete works.

While Descartes provides a fascinating first position for philosophy, what concerns me the most about his argument is the essential hierarchy and division of the world that his argument implies. According to Descartes, rational human beings know their own awareness to be certain and entirely distinct from the external world of material substance. The material world has less certainty and is perceptible only as an object. Thus, *res cogitans* – thinking substance, subjective experience, spirit, consciousness – was understood to be different and separate from *res estensa* – extended substance, the objective world, matter, the physical body, plants and animals, stones and the entire physical universe (2006: 145). Only in human beings did the two realities come together and both the cognitive capacity of human reason and the objective reality and order of the natural world found their common source in God (Garber 2005: 174–175).

According to Descartes, the physical universe was entirely devoid of human qualities. Rather, as purely material objects, all physical phenomena (including non-human animals) could be comprehended as machines – much like the lifelike automata and ingenious machines, clocks, mills and fountains being constructed and enjoyed by seventeenth-century Europeans (2006: 137).[18] God created the universe and defined its mechanical laws, but after that the system moved on its own. Such a substance was best understood in mechanistic terms, reductively analysed into its simplest parts and exactly comprehended in terms of those parts, arrangements and movements. As Descartes (1985: 139) argued: 'The laws of Mechanics are identical with those of Nature.'

Because human beings combine material and spiritual qualities, Descartes argued that we have 'rendered ourselves the lords and possessors of nature' (Descartes 1985: 141).[19] Moreover, he argued that animals were insensible and irrational machines that 'moved like clocks, but could not feel pain' (cited in Nash 1989: 18). Further, in his sixth discourse on method, Descartes (1998: 34) held that 'coercing, torturing, operating upon the body of Nature . . . is not torture [because] Nature's body is an unfeeling, soulless mechanism.' For Descartes, the scientific method was much more than a tool for the attainment of objective truth. He used it to solidify the logic of human mastery over the environment (Graham 2011: 31).

Deprived of any autonomous life force, the non-human world was considered as an instrument for the attainment of human ends. It was also vulnerable

18. This mechanistic description of nature appears first in the writing of Isaac Newton, who argued that the cosmos was like an immense clock whose basic principles and features could be revealed through a reductionist scientific methodology. Using this method, Newton claimed that nature was rendered 'knowable, adjustable [and] manageable . . . it belongs to the people who control it' (cited in Suzuki 1997: 14).

19. Commenting on this statement, Thomas Berry (1991a) held: 'Descartes killed the Earth and all its living beings. For him the natural world was a mechanism. There was no possibility of entering into a communion relationship. Western humans became autistic in relation to the surrounding world.'

to manipulation and exploitation according to human will. Thomas Berry notes:

> Descartes killed the Earth and all its living beings. For him the natural world was a mechanism. There was no possibility of entering into a communion relationship. Western humans became autistic in relation to the surrounding world.

Like all major transformations in thinking, the scientific revolution had a significant impact on the way that Western culture perceived and related to the natural world. Furthermore, Schlatter (1951: 125) argues that the 'new scientific thinking influenced the political writers on property.' Nicole Graham (2011: 38) states this point more boldly, noting: 'The anthropocentric division of the world into nature and culture formed the basis of the modern concept of property in law.'

The historical context within which this perception operated and flourished coincided with the growth of capitalist economies and with the Industrial Revolution. The mechanistic philosophy of the scientific revolution, in particular Descartes' (1998: 34) description of nature as an 'unfeeling, soulless mechanism', provided the perfect intellectual footing for growth economics to flourish. Karl Marx (1992: 512–513 fn 27) picks up on this point, noting that Descartes 'saw with the eyes of the manufacturing period' and that both Bacon and Descartes 'anticipated an alteration in the form of production and the practical subjugation of Nature by Man'.

### 2.3.2 The Industrial Revolution

> The Industrial Revolution's dams, mills, factories and canals used land with increasing intensity, causing damage that more and more frequently extended to neighbouring, increasingly populated lands. Sometimes things went wrong, causing fires, floods and explosions, while pollution and other kinds of damage were inherent in the activities themselves. (Guth 2009: 450)

The Industrial Revolution began at the conclusion of the scientific revolution during the eighteenth century and concluded at the beginning of the twentieth century. This period was characterised by technological advancement, most notably in agriculture, manufacturing, mining and transport. While often neglected in the literature, each of these activities is fundamentally connected to private property, which is the medium that law uses to facilitate land use interactions (Alexander 1999; Freyfogle 2003; Hall, Finkelman & Ely 2004; Horwitz 1977). To analyse the relationship between the Industrial Revolution and private property, I focus on the historical evolution of property in the United States. While jurisdictional and historical differences are acknowledged, the development of private property in the United States provides an important insight into how other Western capitalist systems evolved over the same period. Further, developments in law and jurisprudence from the United States continue to exert significant influence other common law jurisdictions to this day (Freyfogle 2003).

Prior to the Industrial Revolution, property rights in the Unites States were underpinned by an 'explicitly anti-development theory' that limited landowners to what courts regarded as natural use (Horwitz 1977: 32). In the 1879 case *Bryant v Lefever*, the English Common Plea Division explained the notion of 'natural use or incidents' in the following terms:

> What then is the right of land and its owner or occupier? It is to have all natural incidents and advantages as nature would produce them. There is a right to all the light and heat that would come, to all the rain that would fall, to all the wind that would blow, a right that the rain which would pass over the land should not be stopped and made to fall on it, a right that the heat from the sun should not be stopped and reflected on it, a right that the wind should not be checked, but should be able to escape freely; and if it were possible that these rights were interfered with by one having no right, no doubt an action would lie.[20]

The 'natural use' idea of private property equated to strong trespass law, which barred all uncontested entries onto the land and nuisance law that prohibited neighbours from indirectly impairing a neighbour's enjoyment of land. Furthermore, a landowner could not disturb the natural drainage of land or take water from a river to the extent that it 'diminished its quality or quantity' for landowners downstream. Finally, under the doctrine of ancient lights, landowners could halt any construction that interfered with sunlight (Freyfogle 2001b: 4).

It was quickly recognised that this conception of private property stood in the way of economic progress. To increase economic growth, lawmakers were required to 'materially change the meaning of landownership to facilitate . . . intensive land uses' (Freyfogle 2001b: 4). Horwitz (1977: 253) comments that: '[L]aw once conceived of as protective, regulative, paternalistic and above all, a paramount expression of the moral sense of the community, had come to be thought of as facilitative of individual desires and as simply reflective of the existing organisation of economic and political power.'

Fundamental to this shift, was the idea that private property entailed the right to use the land more intensely than had been practised by previous generations. For example, communities who once enjoyed water laws that protected natural flow had these protections removed so that industries could draw more water and even introduce pollutants into the water system. Industrial parties required the right to emit smoke that degraded air quality; to

---

20. Bryant v Lefever, 4 Common Please Division 172 (1879).

make noise that scared livestock and on occasion to emit sparks which had the potential to set wheat fields on fire. Waterwheels disrupted the migration of fish, tall buildings blocked sunlight (Freyfogle 2001b: 4). In essence, the legal concept of private property was reconceptualised to promote market growth 'at the expense of farmers, workers, consumers' (Horwitz 1977: 254) and, of course, the environment.

Over the next 100 years, lawmakers entrenched this shift in positive law, redefining land as a commodity that could be used, exploited and even destroyed to satisfy production and profit. The most important avenue for shaping property rights during this period was the common law. An illustrative case from 1805 was the New York Supreme Court decision in *Palmer v Mulligan*. In this case, Palmer established a sawmill on land held along the Hudson River. Years later, a competitor constructed a dam, 180 metres upstream that altered Palmer's access to the natural flow of water. Palmer sued the competitor, citing case law that protected riparian rights. Two dissenting judges decided that the defendant 'clearly' had no right to obstruct Palmer's riparian right. They held:

> The defendants have clearly . . . no right to obstruct the plaintiffs in the enjoyment of the water. They have an equal right to build a mill on their soil, but they must so use the water, and so construct their dam, as not to annoy their neighbour below in the enjoyment of the same water.

However, the three majority judges decided differently, holding that riparian rights were to give way to cost/benefit economic analysis (Horwitz 1977: 33). On this point, Justice Livingston held that the public benefit 'always attends rivalry and competition' and that Palmer's claim would have the consequence of closing down the defendant's mill. Arguing against this outcome, Livingston held that the public interest was served by allowing all landowners to use their land productively. To side with Palmer would simply grant a monopoly. He noted further that the no harm principle 'should be limited to such cases only where a manifest and serious damage is the result of such use or enjoyment'.[21]

While the reasoning in Palmer is commonly advocated in courts today (Horwitz 1977: 63–108), it represented a dramatic departure from the existing case law of the period. Joseph Guth (2009: 451) argues that this decision was the first time 'the American legal system allowed an enterprise to damage a neighbouring landowner without paying compensation based on an explicit consideration of the relative economic efficiencies of competing uses of land'. Horwitz (1977: 38) argues further that the *Palmer* decision introduced the 'entirely novel view that an explicit consideration of the relative efficiencies of conflicting property uses should be the paramount test of what constitutes legally justified injury'.

---

21. *Palmer v Mulligan* 3 Cai R 307 (1805) at [314].

While it would take many years before courts fully accepted this decision and defined a new legal test to determine this balance, *Palmer* stands firmly for the emerging notion that property implies the right to develop and exploit the land for economic purposes (Horwitz 1977: 37).[22] By the end of the nineteenth century, judges widely accepted Livingston's claim that industrial activity generally produces net social benefit despite increasing environmental harm. Indeed, judges held that society would be better off if everyone accepted this damage rather holding steadfast to the undisturbed and quiet enjoyment of the land. According to Guth (2009: 452), this reasoning was based not on a conclusion about 'economics and the social good' but on the basis of a 'passionate belief in industrialization that was widespread in American society'.

At the beginning of the twentieth century, private property had undergone a radical transformation from being a regrettable but unavoidable institution, to being a primary facilitator of human interaction with the land. The narrative of private property that emerges from this period was that of human dominion over a lifeless, mechanistic machine. The industrial revolution was fuelled partly by this narrative, which it used to justify more intensive forms of land use and the shaping of property rights in pursuit of economic growth.

The concept of private property also continued to perpetuate anthropocentric values during the twentieth century by defining property as a human–human relationship and by placing only minimal emphasis on the object of the property relationship. This development is now considered here, with respect to the writing of John Locke, Jeremy Bentham and Wesley Newcomb Hohfeld and the gradual succession of positivist over natural law descriptions of property.

## 2.4 Separation and fragmentation: Locke, Bentham and Hohfeld

The mechanistic perception of the natural world advanced during the scientific revolution was vital for industrial progress. Improvements in technology enabled human beings to exercise a degree of control and mastery over the environment never previously known in human history. During this same period, the legal–philosophical concept of private property also changed from a focus on the relationship between people and the land to a relationship between and among people. In other words, the dominant conception of property shifted from describing a tangible reality to a dephysicalised description of human interactions (Vandevelde 1980: 333). Graham (2011: 134) describes this shift as follows:

> In legal theory, 'dephysicalisation' means the removal of the physical 'thing' from the property relation and its replacement with an abstract

22. Horwitz (1977: 37) contends that the *Palmer* decision represents 'the beginning of the gradual acceptance of the idea that the ownership of property implies above all the right to develop that property for business purposes'.

'right'. Dephysicalisation describes the shift from the person-thing model of property to the person–person model of property.

The historical foundation of dephysicalisation in English law is located in John Locke's *Two Treatise of Government*. Locke provided the foundational narrative of colonial property law and evaluated non-English societies by reference to their laws, economy and whether they used land as a resource or a 'thing'. Indeed, Locke (1970: 16) argued that the 'cultural development' of a given society is measured by 'its sufficient removal from the common state Nature hath placed it in'.

The book of Genesis was foundational to Locke's theory of property. Consistent with the early church jurists, Locke argued that God had gifted the Earth to humankind as collective property. However, he held that any individual could seize a piece of land from the common stock and make it his own simply by mixing his labour with it. The individual, Locke reasoned, owned himself and his labour. Because of that ownership, he also owned the fruits of his labour. When a person mixed his labour with a physical thing, it was only proper (and morally correct) to allow him to own the thing as well as the value added (1970: 287–288). Inherent to this justification for private property is the view that the environment lacks intrinsic value – it is passive and vulnerable to power. Moreover, Locke relates persons and things to each other only via the process of value adding or wealth maximisation. The underlying presumption is that the environment can only be valued through human interaction (labour, use or ownership) and uncultivated land was waste (1970: 299–302).

It is important to note that Locke's justification for private property was linked to a very specific idea of labour. In the *Second Treatise*, Locke speaks almost exclusively in terms of agrarian farming methods, rather than more intensive labour such as mining, grazing, manufacture or other forms of industry that could theoretically provide an equal claim to proprietorship through labour (Arneil 1994: 603). And yet, with the advent of the Industrial Revolution, it was the proponents of latter forms of labour that most often utilised Locke's writing as a justification for private property. As Macpherson (1962: 204) points out, Locke's justification of private property 'was only needed when and because a moral case had to be made for putting every individual on his own in a market society'. As interpreted by the manufacturing classes, the communal customs of agrarian communities had the least claim to it. Indeed, enclosure and cultivation increased the productive value of the land and were thus promoted as the kinds of labour that justified title.

### 2.4.2 Positive law and Jeremy Bentham

Jeremy Bentham rejected the natural rights justification of property advocated by Locke and others. Instead, he argued that private property could only be justified with regard to positive law: 'Property and law are born together, and die together. Before laws were made, there was no property; take away laws, and property ceases' (1931: 113). He notes further that property is not physical but 'metaphysical, it is a mere conception of the mind' (1978: 41).

These comments reflect a recognition of the diverse number of things that might be considered valuable items of possession. For Bentham (1983: 283), this list includes 'power, reputation and condition in life . . . not forgetting exemption from pain'. Further, Bentham argues that the division of property into 'real' and 'personal' was obsolete and failed to account for a growing economy, wherein land was not the sole source of wealth and power. For example, in Bentham's submission to the Real Property Commission in 1828, he advanced a unified system of property law that was broad enough to include 'newer proprietary rights such as shares in companies and copyright' (cited in Sokol 1994: 287).

Bentham's political philosophy had two significant consequences for the concept of private property. To begin with, by rejecting the natural rights justification of private property and seeking to expand the number of things encompassed by the institution, Bentham promoted a person–person (as opposed to a person–thing) conception. Second, the merging of both personal and real property into one expanded category (based on the person–person model) transformed social wealth from land into a legal right to land. In regard to this second point, Graham (2011: 138) argues that '[I]n effect, what Bentham's theory of property achieved was the separation of land from the idea of property and from the body of law itself by "elevating" the entire basis of property from natural rights to cultural rights.' Real property was no longer fixed to an external reality – it is dephysicalised and exists only in an abstract form (Graham 2011: 138). The abstraction between people and things perpetuated the anthropocentric separation of people from place by defining 'people and culture in opposition to land and nature' (Graham 2011: 139). The thing itself (land in the case of real property) was an object and could only receive as much consideration as was necessary to further human good.

By the mid-eighteenth century, the conception of property as the product of natural law had given way to the 'self-sufficient determination of positive law' (Fitzpatrick 1992: 54) as articulated by the sovereign.[23] As a result, there was no inherent need for property law to have regard to morality or derive its character from humankind's relationship to the Earth. Rather, private property was whatever the legislators decided it was and it came to be directed by instrumental values and the pursuit of social goals (Coyle & Morrow 2004: 96).

The shift toward a positive law conception of property fundamentally altered the 'moral framework' of property rights (Coyle & Morrow 2004: 96). Graham (2011: 140) critiques this shift, arguing that Bentham's repression of the physical and moral aspects of property 'forgets the ground on which it

---

23. Coyle and Morrow (2004: 96) argue that natural rights theories of property 'tended to regard varieties of agrarian communism or agrarian capitalism as the inherent form of property law.'

stands'. By denying these aspects, Bentham's description creates an illusion – what Kevin Gray (1991: 1) described in a different context as 'property in thin air'. Furthermore, the shift toward instrumental positive law meant that property law focused less on environmental considerations and increasingly on providing for the demands of a growing industrial economy. Moreover, the sense that property was a social or community institution was eroded and the responsibility for limiting use rights came increasingly under the purview of the state.

### 2.4.3 Hohfeld's contribution

By later in the nineteenth century, Bentham's dephysicalised conception of property was established as the dominant theoretical discourse. Furthermore, during the 1880s and 1890s, American courts began recognising new property interests and defining property as a right to value, rather than as a right to some tangible item. According to Kenneth Vandevelde (1980: 358), 'legal commentators were acutely aware of the development of the new property' and the commercial potential it embodied.

However, initial determinations regarding the constitution and applicability of dephysicalised property rights were both arbitrary and confusing. Wesley Newcomb Hohfeld (1913, 1917) wrote two seminal articles in response to the general confusion attending the notion of 'rights', an analysis with some relevance for debates concerning the nature of property rights. Consistent with Bentham's analysis, Hohfeld (1913: 24) contends that the law weighs the 'aggregate of abstract legal relations' rather than deferring to 'figurative or fictional' categories. In the context of property specifically, legal rights do not refer to 'a tract of land or chattel' but property 'denotes a right over a determinate thing' (Hohfeld 1913: 22).

For Hohfeld, the term 'right' can be analysed to reveal four fundamental categories of juridical relations. First, the basic term 'right' describes a claim that is correlative to another person's duties. Next, the term 'liberty' (or privilege) means that the holder has no legal duty to refrain from a particular activity. Hohfeldian 'powers' describe the capacity to change legal relationships – for example, through a contract or a will. Finally, 'immunities' correlate with disabilities of another, e.g. constitutional rights correlate with disabilities of the government to act in certain ways (Harris 2002: 83–93; Hohfeld 1913: 25–58). According to Hohfeld, these categories provide the core elements of all legal relationships. They have been reproduced in Table 2.1, together with

*Table 2.1* Hohfeld on rights

| Right | Liability | Power | Immunity |
|-------|-----------|-------|----------|
| Duty | No right | Liability | Disability |

their correlative and opposite concepts. (Note that in this table, correlations are represented vertically and that opposites run diagonally.)

Put together, these items make up Hohfeld's eight fundamental legal conceptions (Munzer 1990: 18). For example, to say that X has private property in land means that others have a correlative duty to respect that right. Further, to say that X has a power means that they can voluntarily change their legal relationship with some other person (i.e. their tenant in the case of a lease agreement) who has a correlative liability. Finally, X may have the immunity from being fined for parking their car in a restricted area while, Y may not have this privilege and so has a disability.

The significance of Hohfeld's analysis for the present discussion is that it continues to have tremendous influence on the legal–philosophical property discourse to the present day. Stephen Munzer (1990: 19) notes that Hohfeld's vocabulary has 'no serious rival of its kind in intellectual clarity, rigor and power.' Indeed, Hohfeld crystallised and entrenched the scholarship of Bentham and Hohfeld can rightly be considered to be the most influential scholar under what Vandevelde (1980: 330) terms the 'new property' – that is the shift from Blackstone's natural law person–thing conception to the positivist person–person conception.

## 2.5 Marx's critique of dephysicalised property

The conceptualisation of private property as a person–person relationship has had significant consequences for the environment. A conception of property that focuses on relations between human persons as owner–possessors significantly diminishes the importance of the subject of the property relationship – or in the traditional view – the 'thing' itself. In the case of land law, a person–person conception is structured in a way that disregards the specific attributes and ecological requirements of the land. Private property is not place based, which means that the same generic rights can be transplanted onto any location and ecosystem (Graham 2011: 190–197). Indeed, this decontextualised relocation of generic property rights can be noted in the appropriation of indigenous lands, which occurred throughout the industrial era – and integral to this process was precisely the displacement of cultures that had developed an intimate relationship to a place and ecologically sensitive habitation practices.

This shift was particularly important in the context of industrial capitalism, which required constant self-expansion into new territories or undeveloped markets (Luxemburg 2003: 348–399; Wallerstein 2011b: 14). Given this context, it is also worth pausing to consider Karl Marx's analysis of how the dephysicalised conception of property facilitated environmental exploitation and advanced industrial capitalism. In presenting this analysis, I do not wish to portray Marx as an environmentalist or as having a sophisticated ecological ethic, for plenty of evidence can be found to contradict such a view (Marx 1992: 820), and indeed a consciously environmentalist position was a rare position to hold in light of the confronting social problems that faced nineteenth-century Europe. Yet, I suggest that Marx's rigorous critique of private property and his analysis of its relationship to environmental problems remain as pertinent today as ever before.

The idea of an unalienated relationship between people and their means of production was central to Marx's critique of capitalism and to his analysis of property fetishism. He first explored this theme in 1842, as a response to the enclosure of the commons, which forced peasant communities off their land in favour of private development (Neeson 1996). In a major Rhineland newspaper (the *Rheinische Zeitung*), Marx wrote a paper entitled 'Debates on the Law on Thefts of Wood', in which he explored the prosecution of peasants who collected wood from the forest to heat their homes and cook food (Marx 1996). While this practice had taken place for countless generations, the growth of industrialisation and the system of private property led to harsh prosecution of those peasants who continued to violate the new property laws.

In the article, Marx lamented how the law had managed to transform into a source of private property that which was once a common and had no market value. Under the new laws, 'wood thieves', who depended on the common stock of the forest for their subsistence, were turned over to the forest owner (whoever had property title) and forced into labour, thereby increasing the profits of the owner (Foster 2000: 67). Such a law, Marx argued turned the ordinary peasant into a 'criminal' or 'enemy of the wood'. The poor were thus denied any relation to place that was unmediated by a dephysicalised system of private property (Marx 1996).

Marx developed the more technical aspects of this analysis throughout his subsequent writing. In particular, he returned to the theme of alienation in *Das Kapital* during a discussion of the duel character of labour as embodied in commodities (1992: 133). In this discussion, Marx looks at some of the universal properties of useful labour (that is – labour that has some social use and demand). He does so because: '[L]abor . . . is a condition of human existence which is independent of all forms of society' (1992: 133). Indeed, he recognises that '[L]abor [is] an eternal natural necessity which mediates the metabolism between man and nature, and therefore human life itself' (1992: 133).

This idea of 'metabolism' with labour as the mediator of human existence and our relationship to nature is foundational to Marx's materialist argument (Foster 2000: 141–177). 'Use values' Marx writes 'are combinations of two elements, the material provided by nature, and labour' (1992: 133). Hence, 'when man engages in production, he can only proceed as nature does herself' (1992: 133). This is an important point for in Marx's analysis – whatever we do must be consistent with natural forces or natural law:

> [W]e can only change the form of the materials. Furthermore, even in this work of modification [we are] constantly helped by natural forces.

> Labour is therefore not the only source of material wealth i.e. the use-value it produces. As William Petty says, labour is the father of material wealth, the earth is its mother. (1992: 133–134)

This gendered metaphor dates back (at least) to Francis Bacon (Merchant 1980). However, what is interesting about Marx's application of the metaphor is that he draws no clear separation between human beings and nature in the labour process. That process is wholly natural and wholly human at the same time. It is construed dialectically as a moment of 'metabolism' in which it is impossible to separate the natural from the human. But within this unity there is also a duality. There is, Marx says 'a process between man and nature, a process by which man through his own actions, mediates and controls the metabolism between himself and nature' (1992: 283). Thus, human beings are active agents in relation to their property:

> Man confronts the materials of nature as a force of nature. He sets in motion the natural forces which belong to his own body, his arms, legs, head and hands in order to appropriate the materials of nature in a form adapted to his own needs. Through this movement he acts upon external nature and changes it, and in this way he simultaneously changes his own nature. (1992: 283)

It is in statements like this that we most readily encounter Marx's dialectical formulation of the integral relationship between human beings and the environment. Marx contends that human beings cannot interact with our property, or transform it, without also transforming ourselves. Conversely, when we change ourselves, or our perceptions, this can lead to dramatic changes in the environment around us. For Marx, this interplay can never be displaced. Instead, the perpetual transformation of individuals and the world is fundamental to understanding the evolution of human societies as well as the evolution of nature itself (Harvey 2010: 112).

Yet, the new forms of dephysicalised property rendered the material character of labour and other interactions both distant and opaque. The new forms of property also needed to be rendered commensurable with the old or tangible forms of property to facilitate trade. This process of comparison effectively dissolved the 'concrete and particular' qualities of the land (Best 1994: 44).

Marx describes this change as being a shift from qualitative value to quantitative value as represented in the money form (1992: 93). Indeed, because the value of dephysicalised property is immaterial, it cannot exist without a means of representation. The monetary system thus becomes a means of tangible expression that makes value the regulator of exchange relations between tangible and intangible property (1992: 142). The uniform language of money and the transformation of tangible things into abstract numbers were essential for the development of capitalist growth economics. Indeed, even after centuries of anthropocentric intellectual thought, it is easier to exploit a dollar figure than a piece of land with unique attributes and ecological functions. A Canadian lumberman evidences this argument in the following statement: 'When I look at trees I see dollar bills' (Jensen 2007: 15).

Marx regarded the dephysicalisation of property as both a cultural and environmental concern. He argued that human abstraction and alienation from the environment were inherently unsustainable (Marx 1975a: 276). Referring back to his writing on the metabolic relationship between human beings and the land, he writes: 'Man lives on nature – [this] means that nature is his body with which he must remain in continuous interchange if he is not to die' (Marx 1975a: 276). This critique ought to profoundly disturb anybody that is seeking to make sense of the deepening environmental crisis.

## 2.6 The liberal (and neoliberal) theory of private property

So far in this chapter, I have sought to establish the relationship between anthropo-centrism and the concept of private property. I have argued that starting point for theories of property is human dominion over nature and I have considered how this notion was captured in early Roman and Christian conceptions of property. I then described how during the scientific revolution the natural world was conceived as a lifeless, mechanistic instrument for human happiness. The integration of these worldviews helped to shape legal scholarship during the Industrial Revolution and ultimately led to the promotion of a person–person or dephysicalised conception of property. The person–person model represents the dominant framework in contemporary property law and acts to promote rights over duties and diminishes any sense of normative commitment to land as place.

During the twentieth century the most significant influence on the theory of private property was liberal political philosophy. Liberalism refers to a heritage of thought about human nature, agency, freedom and value and its bearing on the origin and function of political and legal institutions (Bentham 1969; Manning 1976; Mill 1989; Rawls 1971; Sandel 1984). Today, liberalism has associations with progressive politics and equality. However, the classic meaning emerges from the Latin *liberales*, meaning 'free man' and is best described as a form of political organisation and a set of political values rooted in the primacy of individual liberty (Mill 1989: 16).[24] This exclusive focus on

---

24. John Stuart Mill (1989) represents the most sophisticated and nuanced advocate of liberalism. While he maintains the primary of individual liberty he also worries about what an exclusive focus on liberty will produce in society. In particular, Mill wants us to not only formulate our own ends but also our own understanding of those ends. To achieve this, Mill writes against some of the foundational pillars of Bentham's description of utilitarianism. Mill wants to develop the inner person and our outward capacities for greatness and achievement.

the rights and value of individual human beings means that liberalism can be used as a convenient conduit for anthropocentric ideas. Indeed, while there is nothing to prevent liberal theory from taking an interest in culture, community and the environment, such an interest will always be 'secondary and derivative' (Waldron 2005: 570).

Further to these points, liberals contend that there is something particularly important in allowing individuals to direct their own lives and act on their own terms (Mill 1989: 20). That is, liberals exalt individual freedom, although what exactly this refers to is subject to some controversy (Manning 1976: 56). John Stuart Mill (1989: 16; see also Berlin 2002) provides the classic formulation of negative liberty, arguing that '[T]he only freedom which deserves the name, is that of pursuing our own good in our own way, so long as we do not attempt to deprive others of theirs, or impede their efforts to obtain it.' On this view, freedom flourishes when constraints are removed, and the promotion of autonomy ought to be the central concern of political authorities. Positive conceptions of liberty, by the same token, provide the State with a much greater role and promote the idea that freedom is something to be achieved or brought about by effective education and by the creation of favourable social conditions (Waldron 2005: 572).

The twin pillars of individualism and freedom have exerted significant influence on the contemporary concept of private property.[25] Indeed, private property is *the* key mechanism through which liberals promote their platforms of individual freedom and choice (Waldron 1988: 31–40). Paul Babie (2010a: 531) explains further: 'In order for life to have meaning, some control over the use of goods and resources is necessary; private property is liberalism's means of ensuring that individuals enjoy choice over goods and resources so as to allow them to fulfil their life project.'

Consistent with Hohfeld's analysis, the liberal theory of private property is a person–person relationship. Place or physicality continues to be cast aside as irrelevant. With regard to the specific rights that constitute the liberal conception, theorists commonly draw on the work of Anthony Honoré (1961). Commenting on the relationship between the theoretical accounts of Hohfeld and Honoré, Munzer notes: 'if one is to use Hohfeld's vocabulary to elaborate the sophisticated conception of property, it will help to conjoin it with an analysis of private property suggested by AM Honoré' (1990: 22).

Honoré argued that private property is more complicated than simply holding a 'right' or 'dominion' over a thing. Indeed, private property is more accurately conceived of as being a bundle of rights, liabilities, powers and duties (1961: 84). In regard to any potential item of property, the bundle could include any of the following standard incidents: 'rights to possess, use, manage and receive income; the powers to transfer, waive, exclude and

---

25. Naffine (2013: 1) contends that the image of the 'fully independent individual' that is projected by liberalism is a 'Weberian ideal type'. See further Weber (1971).

abandon; the liberties to consume or destroy; immunity from expropriation; the duty not to use harmfully; and liability for execution to satisfy a court judgement' (Munzer 1990: 22).

Under this conception, private property includes (at a minimum) what Margaret Jane Radin terms the 'liberal triad' of use, exclusivity, and alienability (1993: 121). Owners may have different sticks relative to their particular property right and individual sticks can be disaggregated or added to the bundle (Singer 2000: 8–10). Furthermore, Honoré does not claim that the 'standard incidents' are inherent or intrinsic to the concept of private property. Indeed, Honoré is explicit that his description relates specifically to the 'liberal concept of full individual ownership' (1961: 84). The Hohfeld–Honoré combination reveals that the rights attained by property holders (whatever those rights are) provide individuals with the power to act in certain ways in relation to the rights of other people or groups of people. Indeed, private property 'amounts to the decision-making authority of the holder of that right' (Baker 1986: 742–743) and can be used to exercise control over things and over the lives of other people.

The specific environmental and social consequences of the liberal conception of private property have been detailed in the context of industrial farming practices (Burdon 2010a), climate change (Babie 2010b) landscape fragmentation (Freyfogle 2002a) and wildlife law (Freyfogle & Goble 2009). Theorists within each of these areas have expressed concern that a conception of private property that focuses exclusively on individual freedom fails to account for the vast network of social and ecological relationships within which human beings exist within. Joseph William Singer captures this concern in his term 'ownership model'. He describes this idea as follows:

> We presume that most uses of property are self-regulating, in that only the owner is legitimately interested and others have no legitimate claims to control what the owner does with his own property. Substantial freedom to control one's property without interference by government regulation is believed to promote both individual autonomy and economic efficiency. (2000: 3)

This model is taken for granted in mainstream property theory. For example, Jeremy Waldron notes that the 'organising idea' of property is ownership and that it is for 'a certain specified person (rather than for anyone else or for society as a whole) to determine how a specified resource is to be used' (2005: 60). More strikingly, libertarian property theorists such as Richard Epstein argue that private property means the 'exclusive rights of possession, use, and disposition' over a particular resource (1985: 2). Further, Epstein argues that individual freedom should not be interfered with by the state, except in very rare circumstances such as war or natural disaster (Epstein 1998: 187).

In law and economics discourse, the ownership model is taken as scripture and property relationships are conceived as operating through the 'hidden hand' of the market. Most theorists within this discipline begin from the assumption that all of nature should be privately owned and that owners should be provided freedom to use their property as they desire, or to exchange it at will (Singer 2000: 4). For example, legal economist Richard Posner argues that 'if every valuable (meaning scarce as well as desired) resource were owned by someone (universality), ownership connotes the unqualified power to exclude everybody else from using the resource (exclusivity) as well as to use it oneself, and ownership rights were freely transferable or as lawyers say alienable (transferable), value would be maximized' (1986: 32).

Consistent with other free market capitalists, Posner argues further that freedom and wealth maximisation are best achieved 'when goods and other resources are in the hands of those who value them most, and someone values a good more only if he or she is both willing and able to pay more in money to have it' (1979: 103). According to this view, the regulation of property rights is inefficient, limits the freedom of property owners, decreases business investment, reduces jobs and may end up having a negative impact on people overall. Regulation is only justified when the markets work imperfectly or when government intervention is more expedient than market solutions (Posner 1986: 32–33).

The image of private property that emerges from this discourse is of an institution designed to reflect liberal values and protect individual freedom – which increasingly has come to mean market freedom (Harvey 2007: 6). This freedom is exerted over the environment without inherent concern for either the ecological or the human community. Singer argues that within this framework, 'the owner has a host of powers and can use the property in almost any way' they like (2000: 30). This power can be limited when it causes harm to other people or if it infringes the freedom of others to do the same. However, it is clear that the liberal theory of private property focuses on securing choice and freedom to satisfy individual desires. This aspect of the 'ownership model' has been described variously as 'self-regarding behaviour' or 'preference satisfaction' (Singer 2000: 13). J.W. Harris (1996: 30–31) elaborates on this characterisation:

> The rules of [a] property institution are premised on the assumption that, *prima facie*, [a] person is entirely free to do what he will with his own, whether by way of use, abuse, or transfer . . . [h]e may also, within the terms of the relevant property institution, defend any use or exercise of power by pointing out that, as owner, he was at liberty to suit himself.

Sovereign states have increasingly adopted and enforced the liberal ownership model since the transition from Keynesian to neoliberal economics in the 1970s. This shift toward neoliberal economics has resulted in greater disparities between the rich and the poor, uneven geographical development and hyper environmental exploitation (Harvey 2007: 152–183). Singer offers an explanation of these themes, noting that 'by conceiving property as ownership, we invite owners to use their property without regard to the needs of others' (2000: 6). Put otherwise, we invite (and in fact reward) people to 'consider their self-interest alone – to act as if no one existed but themselves' (Singer 2000: 6). Conceived in this way, ownership and obligation are opposites. Indeed, the ownership model ownership 'abhors obligation' because obligations limit ownership and individual freedom (Singer 2000: 6).[26]

The liberal (and neoliberal) concept of property is morally deficient and works to alienate human beings from society and from the natural world. However, as will be demonstrated in detail in the next chapter, human beings do not live alone and property choices cannot be exercised in isolation. Indeed, all tangible items of property are (in one way or another) derived from nature and our property choices have very real and immediate impacts on our community and the environment. Demystifying the anthropocentric narrative that currently dominates legal discourse and coming to terms with our interconnected reality with nature is the foremost task for current and future property discourse.

## 2.7 Conclusion

In this chapter, I have argued that the contemporary concept of private property is anthropocentric and is contributing to environmental harm. To establish this argument, I described private property as being an indeterminate concept that reflects the social and cultural values from which it has emerged. Using this description, I then explored significant historical periods in the development of private property.

I began by positing that the starting premise for Western theories of private property is human dominion over the environment. This idea has its roots in Greek Stoic philosophy and Christian theology. It became entrenched in Roman law and was later developed by Christian jurists with reference to the biblical grant of dominium over 'creation' to human beings. During the scientific revolution the environment was interpreted as being a lifeless machine and a scientific method was developed that entrenched a human/nature dichotomy. This perception was integral to the Industrial Revolution and helped to facilitate increased environmental exploitation. The resulting increase in economic power led to the deliberate removal of ancient natural law protections for the community, and the environment was made vulnerable to the reformulation of private property constructed as a dephysicalised person–person relationship. Finally, I considered the influence of liberal and

26. On the excess of neoliberal market rationality and the privatisation of public property, see Sandel (2012).

neoliberal discourse on private property. I argued that the liberal 'ownership model' perpetuates an anthropocentric worldview by inviting owners to exercise their property rights as though they existed in isolation from nature and from the human community. I argued that this model is socially and environmentally harmful.

In the next chapter, I demonstrate that anthropocentrism does not represent a credible or scientifically valid worldview. In its place, I offer an ecocentric understanding of the environment and the place of human beings within it. In contrast to anthropocentrism, the ecocentric paradigm holds that human beings are interconnected and dependent on a comprehensive community that includes both living and nonliving entities. The paradigm also contends that the Earth is composed of a community of subjects and not objects to be used and exploited. Following this introductory analysis, I consider how law, as an evolving social institution, can adapt to reflect the concept of Earth community. I do this by considering an alternative cultural narrative proposed by Thomas Berry and also by considering the role of social movements in actively challenging and changing the law. This discussion lays the foundations for Chapter 4, which seeks to outline an ecocentric legal philosophy called Earth jurisprudence. This philosophy is then used to construct an alternative concept of private property in Chapter 5.

# Chapter 3

# Earth community: narrative and action

A community is an intimate relationship with all living things both animate and inanimate. (Bell 2003: 80)

## 3.1 Introduction

In Chapter 2, I argued that the dominant concept of private property in Western culture perpetuates an outdated and environmentally harmful anthropocentric worldview. To establish this premise, I presented private property as an indeterminate concept and explored its construction in antiquity, the scientific revolution and in contemporary political and economic theory. This chapter builds on this discussion to advance an alternative focus for law based on Thomas Berry's ecocentric concept of Earth community. As described in the introduction, the concept of Earth community positions human beings as one interconnected part of a broader community of life. Moreover, the concept of Earth community maintains that all parts of the Earth are subjects and have inherent value.

In this chapter, I critically explore the paradigm of Earth community with respect to a range of scientific disciplines, including quantum physics, ecology and Gaia theory. While not without controversy, I contend that the findings of contemporary science are so significant that we have undergone a second Copernican revolution (Suzuki 1997: 12–15). Indeed, just as Nicholas Copernicus demonstrated that the Earth was not at the centre of the universe, contemporary science has demonstrated that human beings are not at the centre of the Earth community. More specifically, human beings are not the arbiters of all meaning and our relinquishment of epistemic mastery over nature provides the basis for a new intimacy with the Earth. Berry (1988: 18) comments on this point:

If our science has gone through its difficulties, it has cured itself out of its own resources. Science has given us a new revelatory experience. It is now giving us a new intimacy with the earth.

Before outlining the scientific bases for the concept of Earth community, I wish to make two preliminary comments. First, the analysis of scientific principles presented in this chapter is necessarily general and directed toward scientific ideas rather than mathematical formulae (Latour 2013: 7). The intention is to take a generalist perspective[1] and to assimilate a variety of leading voices from the scientific community that describe nature in terms of relationship and community. Second, this chapter acknowledges the critique of the scientific method and the importance of arguments against positing science as the only valid source of knowledge. Certainly, as Jerome Revetz (1971) and Thomas Nagel (1992) have illustrated, science is not purely objective and is profoundly shaped by value commitments and biases. Further, the scientific method does not reveal 'truth'. It provides limited and approximate descriptions of fact. Put otherwise – the scientific method advances through preliminary findings to a series of more suitable and subtle questions that seek to reach deeper into the essence of an entity or phenomenon.

My decision to rely on science to describe the concept of Earth community is based on its power as a persuasive mode of communication in Western culture. Indeed, detached from mechanistic assumptions, science is a powerful tool for investigating the physical world – it is also the distinctive discovery of our Western culture. Speaking in support of this point, Freya Matthews (1994: 49) comments that '[w]e may be discontented or disappointed with its findings, and we may wish to supplement scientific method with other investigative techniques, but if a new worldview is to attain legitimacy and take root in this culture, it must ultimately have the sanction of science.'

Following its description of Earth community, this chapter will contend that it is not enough simply to put forward an alternative worldview and assume that it will influence a legal system. Instead, an explanation must also be provided that outlines how this worldview can become assimilated and entrenched broadly within law. As part of this discussion, I will consider two methods for catalysing legal change.

The first is the 'new story' proposed by Thomas Berry and Brian Swimme (1994). The function of the 'new story' is to offer a functional and scientific cosmology for the contemporary world. Rather than perpetuating anthropocentric values, the 'new story' is premised on the idea of Earth community and seeks to provide the foundation for a paradigm shift in human ethics and law. Following this, I will consider theories of legal change arising out of the growing literature on law and social movements (McCann 2006a). Drawing on that literature and developing it in the context of this book, I consider the

---

1. Commenting on the benefit of a generalist approach, see Mumford (1967: 16): 'The generalist has a special office, that of bringing together widely separate fields, presently fenced in by specialists, into a larger common area, visible only from the air. Only by forfeiting the detail can the overall pattern be seen, though once that pattern is visible new details, unseen even by the thorough and competent field workers may become visible.'

global movement for Earth jurisprudence and other ecological approaches to law and governance. I will argue that this movement (or something like it) will need to expand, to organise and to politicise if anything resembling the vision of Earth jurisprudence is to emerge and influence the future direction of our global society. The essential contention here is that our legal system will not reflect ecocentric ethics until such an ethic is deeply rooted and allowed to thrive within the population itself.

## 3.2 Paradigm shift: Earth community

> After a time of decay comes the turning point (Capra 1983: 5)

The notion of 'paradigm shift' was coined by Thomas Kuhn in the context of describing scientific development. Kuhn (1996: 76) argues that a paradigm can only work 'so long as the tools a paradigm supplies continue to prove capable of solving the problems it defines'. Paradigms succeed because they provide a vision or worldview that is consistent with dominant intellectual thought and because they are physically possible or practical. According to Kuhn, a paradigm reaches crisis when alternative ideas place doubt on the existing paradigm and present a more plausible framework of meaning and suggest a more viable mode of future practice. The process from paradigm crisis to paradigm shift occurs in discontinuous, revolutionary breaks (1962: 77). Importantly, Kuhn (1996: 172–173) maintains that a paradigm shift does not necessarily equate to progress or movement towards perfection or improvement. Rather, a paradigm shift is a matter of adaptation and a function of time and place. That is, it succeeds only within particular social (or natural) conditions and is intimately connected with cultural values, thoughts and perceptions (1996: 172–173).

Today, it is common to use Kuhn's theory to describe broader cultural transformations. 'Accordingly', physicist Fritjof Capra (1996: 5) contends, 'what we are seeing is a shift of paradigms not only within science, but also in the larger social arena.' Following Capra, I argue that the anthropocentric paradigm that has characterised the Western idea of private property is in a period of crisis and needs to be replaced by a sustainable ecocentric paradigm. The decline of anthropocentrism is being brought about by a growing recognition of its contribution toward environmental harm and also by the intellectual understanding that it no longer represents an accurate description of the relationship between human beings and the environment. For Kuhn, the questioning and critique of dominant paradigms is the necessary first step for their replacement. It is only when a paradigm reaches it limitations that the full extent of its characteristics emerges (Capra 1985: 12).

During a paradigm shift, the new paradigm first emerges in outline. Kuhn describes a pre-paradigm period where there are different schools of thought, different worldviews and value systems in co-existence. The new paradigm

establishes itself only when a synthesis is produced that is sufficiently attractive to a large enough number of people in the community (1996: 78). A
new paradigm can only be said to exist once a community shares it broadly.
In this sense, a paradigm is different from a worldview, which can be held by
a single person.

While it would be too great a statement to suggest that the concept of Earth
community (as described in the introduction) has received broad acceptance
in society, I contend that some of its fundamental tenets enjoy broad acceptance and are supported by the best available science. With these claims in
mind, I will now critically examine the scientific foundations to the concept
of Earth community as it is described in quantum physics, ecology and Gaia
theory. This detail provides the necessary foundations for the second part of
this chapter, in which I discuss how Western culture and ideas of law can shift
to reflect an ecocentric paradigm.

### 3.2.1 Quantum physics

The concept of Earth community is supported (at the conceptual level) by
evidence concerning the micro-scale of existence offered by quantum physics and advancements in knowledge made during the 1920s. Prior to this
time, the dominant paradigm in science was influenced by the Cartesian
description of the natural world developed during the scientific revolution.
As discussed in Chapter 2, this method was premised on anthropocentric
reductionism, posited a sharp dichotomy between subject and object, and
described the environment as a lifeless mechanism. Under this method, it
was held that parts of nature, including genes or particles, could be separated
from their surroundings and studied in isolation. It was further believed that
all physical phenomena could be reduced to the properties of hard and solid
material particles (Capra 1996: 30).

This understanding of matter began to dislodge during the early twentieth century when physicists investigated more deeply into the structure of
matter. During these investigations, scientists discovered several phenomena
connected with the structure of atoms (such as X-rays and radioactivity) that
could not be explained using the terms of traditional physics. For example,
the alpha particles[2] that emanate from radioactive atoms were used as high-
speed projectiles in a 'cosmic game of marbles' and fired at the atoms (1983:
76). This experiment enabled scientists to draw inferences about the atom's
structure from the way in which the projectiles were deflected.

This exploration brought scientists unexpected findings and face to face
with a new reality that shifted the foundations of their existing worldview
(Heisenberg 1962). They found that solid material objects appear to dissolve at

---

2. Alpha particles consist of two protons and two neutrons bound together into a particle identical to a
   helium nucleus, which is produced in the process of alpha decay.

the subatomic level into smaller particles and waves. Under the then dominant existing paradigm, this discovery created a paradox – subatomic phenomena appeared as both a particle (solid) and a wave (fluid). How could they be both?

In time, the scientists broke away from orthodox thinking by reasoning that atomic particles are both particles and waves – that is, they act like a particle in some instances and like a wave in others. Capra (1983: 79) explains: 'while [the sub-atomic entity] acts like a particle, it is capable of developing its wave nature at the expense of its particle nature and vice versa, thus undergoing continual transformations from particle to wave and from wave to particle.' From this observation, physicists reasoned that subatomic particles are best described in terms of connectivity and interconnectedness. They do not have meaning as isolated entities and can only be understood as relations among various processes of observation and measurement. Put another way, 'subatomic particles are not things, but interconnections between things' (Capra 1983: 79).

This new understanding forced physicists to revise existing ways of understanding matter. In their struggle to grasp this new reality, physicists became painfully aware that existing concepts, language and their method were all inadequate to describe and explore this new paradigm. Chief investigator of these experiments, Werner Heisenberg (1962: 32) notes that at this time there did not exist a common language or means of expression between those who still held to the old paradigm and those who were beginning to integrate the new worldview ushered in by quantum physics. For many, the problem was not just intellectual, but like all significant paradigm shifts, it involved a deep emotional and existential experience. Heisenberg (1962: 50) describes this experience as follows: 'I remember a discussion with [Niels] Bohr which went through many hours till very late at night and ended almost in despair; and when at the end of the discussion I went alone for a walk in the neighbouring park I repeated to myself again and again the question: Can nature possibly be so absurd as it seemed to us in these atomic experiments?'

It took physicists time to realise that the paradoxes they encountered were a result of trying to apply traditional concepts to describe atomic phenomena. Once this was understood, they began to ask the 'right' questions and as Heisenberg (1962: 67) notes, 'they somehow got into the spirit of the quantum theory.' To move forward, the physicists had to change their whole way of thinking and find entirely new concepts and research processes. Eventually, they worked through the crisis and were rewarded by deep insights into the nature of matter and of nature itself. However, even after the mathematics of quantum theory was developed, its conceptual framework was not easy to accept. Indeed, after thousands of years of anthropocentric and mechanistic thinking the researchers found their view of reality 'truly shattering' (Capra 1983: 76). To quote Heisenberg (1967: 53) again: 'The violent reaction to the recent development of modern physics can only be understood when one realises that here the foundation of physics have started moving; and that this motion has caused the feeling that the ground would be cut from science.'

To adapt to this new paradigm, Heisenberg formulated the principle of indeterminacy, which holds that no atomic phenomenon has any intrinsic properties independent of its environment. The properties it exhibits depend on 'the apparatus it is forced to interact with' (Heisenberg 1962: 53). Thus the measurement of phenomena cannot be separated from, and indeed are influenced by, their environment. From a metaphysical perspective, this means that all phenomena are indeterminate and probalistic at base. Following Heisenberg, Niels Bohr complemented this finding with his principle of complementarity (Folse 1985: 63). Bohr considered that particle and wave pictures represented two complementary descriptions of the same reality – each of them only partly correct and having limited application (Folse 1985: 87). Yet, both pictures are needed to provide a robust account of the atomic reality, and both are to be applied within the limits of precise mathematical formula constructed in Heisenberg's uncertainty principle.

In summary, the resolution of the particle/wave paradigm crisis forced physicists to accept a new understanding of matter. Their experiments demonstrated that at the subatomic level 'matter does not exist with certainty at definite places', but rather shows 'tendencies to exist' (Capra 1983: 79). Furthermore, atomic events do not occur with certainty at definite times and in definite ways, but rather show 'tendencies to occur' (Capra 1983: 79). Consistent with the concept of Earth community, these findings demonstrate that there is no such thing as a solid and separate object. Instead, the patterns observed in physics point more directly to probabilities of interconnections rather than to concrete 'things'. As Heisenberg (1962: 139) notes: 'The world thus appears as a complicated tissue of events, in which connections of different kinds alternate or overlap or combine and thereby determine the texture of the whole.'

At a micro-level, the paradigm shift in quantum physics provides some of the best evidence in support of the interconnectedness of both living and nonliving nature. My argument now turns towards transitioning from anthropocentrism to ecocentrism, strengthened by the science of ecology. While the dispassionate scientific method of ecology has been called into question (Evernden 1999: 5–22), it has become the discipline that most informs our understanding of interconnectedness and most visibly reflects the notion of Earth community.

### 3.2.2 Ecology

The word ecology derives from the Greek *oikos*, meaning 'house' or 'place to live in'. Literally, ecology is the study of organisms 'at home' (Odum 1971: 3). Ecology is concerned with studying the relationship between organisms or groups of organisms with their environment or as the 'science of the interrelations between living organisms and their environment' (Odum 1971: 3). Because ecology is concerned especially with the biology of groups of organisms and with functional processes on and in land, oceans and fresh water, it is also proper to define ecology as 'the study of the structure and function of nature, *it being understood that mankind is a part of nature*' (Odum 1971: 3; emphasis added). In support of this assertion, Eugene Odum (1971: 8) defines the concept of ecosystem as follows:

> Living organisms and the nonliving (abiotic) environment are insepara-
> bly interrelated and interact upon each other. Any unit that includes all
> of the organisms (i.e. the community) in a given area interacting with the
> physical environment so that a flow of energy leads to clearly defined tro-
> phic structure, biotic diversity and material cycles (i.e. exchange materials
> between living and nonliving parts) within the system is an ecological
> system or an ecosystem.

Odum's definition is necessarily broad and seeks to draw attention to the obligatory relationships, interdependence and causal relationships that exist in nature. Further, in direct contrast to the anthropocentric paradigm, the concept of ecosystem expressly positions human beings as one 'unit of organ-isms' or as part of the ecological community. This concept shifts our under-standing of nature from a hierarchy with humans on top, to 'an assemblage of organisms, bound into a functional whole by their mutual relationships' (Capra 1996: 33–34).

A further achievement of ecology is the understanding that most organ-isms are not only members of ecological communities, but are also 'complex ecosystems themselves' and contain a 'host of smaller organisms' that are autonomous and yet integrated into the larger whole (Capra 1996: 33–34). Neil Evernden (1999: 39) provides a useful example of this point in regard to human beings:

> [Humans] have long known that we exist in close alliance with some
> other species, such as the intestinal bacteria that assist our digestive
> efforts. But now it appears that some of the organelles in our cells
> are quite as independent as the chloroplasts in plants. Mitochondria, the
> energy providing structures within each cell, replicate independently of
> the cell and are composed of RNA which is dissimilar to that of the rest
> of the cell . . . the mitochondria move into the cells like colonists and
> continue their separate existence within. We cannot exist without them,
> and yet they may not strictly be 'us'. Does this mean that we must regard
> ourselves as colonies?

Outside of the human body, our interdependence is clearer still. Consider the following thought experiment.[3] Imagine that you are walking in a forest

---

3. This narrative has been adapted from Ian Lowe cited in Suzuki (1997: 16).

that you are familiar with. Enter the forest and feel the cool air provided by the canopy overhead. Walk over and sit at the base of one of the large trees that stand before you. Your nose is alerted to a strong smell at the base of the tree. You reach down and pick up a truffle that is growing freely among some of the other trees of the forest. You observe that trees with truffles at their base are larger and greener than those without. This is because truffles extract water and minerals from the soil and dispense them over the roots of their host. While you reflect on this reciprocal relationship, a longfooted poteroo[4] hops into view and stops to rest beside you. It bends down to eat the truffles and before leaving excretes on the base of another nearby tree. The spores of the truffle, now coated in rich organic matter can begin to regenerate and thereby enhance the overall health of the forest. Here the human being, poteroo, truffle and eucalypt – four very different species of mammal, fungus and plant are all bound together in a remarkable web of interdependence. In this thought experiment, for example, the human being is not separate from nature, but represents a further layer of interconnectedness, for at the most basic level, you, the human participant are breathing air produced by the forest and returning carbon dioxide to it. Your shoes may carry seeds in the cleats to be dropped elsewhere. You may also pick the truffles for cooking and return the waste to the soil to further enrich its quality. This is just one very simplified example of how an ecological or biotic community works as relationality. A parallel term often used in German or Russian literature is *biogeocoenosis*, which translated means 'life and Earth function together' (Odum 1997: 30).

To help assimilate this interconnected understanding of the environment, some scientists have adopted the language of network and systems theory. In direct contrast to mechanistic science, systems theory seeks to describe the world in terms of relationships and integration. Consistent with the findings of quantum physics, systems theory describes the environment as an integrated whole and posits that the properties of nature cannot be reduced to smaller or isolated units (Bertalanffy 1968: 37; Odum 1997: 29). Indeed, while it is possible to discern individual parts in a system, these parts are not isolated and the composition of the whole is always distinct from the sum of its parts (Begon 1996: 677). Rather than concentrating on basic building blocks or basic substances, the systems approach highlights principles of organisation. Examples of systems abound in nature: they can be noted in the mitochondria in human cells, the complex interaction of a forest and even within social systems such as an anthill, beehive or a human city (Capra 1983: 266, 1994: 334).

The view of living systems as networks has provided a more accurate representation of ecosystems than the so-called hierarchies of nature (Burns 1991). Indeed, since living systems (at all levels) are networks, we can visualise them

---

4. An Australian marsupial now classified as rare.

as 'webs of relationships' interacting in a network fashion with other systems. Capra (1983: 266) provides a useful explanation on this point:

> [W]e can picture an ecosystem schematically as a network with a few nodes. Each node represents an organism, which means that each node, when magnified, appears itself as a network. Each node in the new network may represent an organ, which in turn will appear as a network when magnified, and so on.

In this example, each scale of network reveals itself as smaller networks. The concept of Holon, developed by Arthur Koestler (1967), provides another way to understand this point.[5] Koestler describes a Holon as something that is simultaneously a whole and a part. Each aspect of a Holon has two opposite tendencies – 'an integrative tendency to function as part of the larger whole and a self-assertive tendency to preserve its individual autonomy' (Koestler 1967: 201). In social and biological systems alike, each Holon must assert its individuality so that the system's order is maintained. Further, each Holon must also submit to the demands of the whole in order to make the system viable (Swimme 1998: 166–167). These dual tendencies are opposite and complementary, just as in any healthy system (individual, social or ecological) where there is a balance between integration and self-assertion (Capra 1983: 43).

The network perspective has become increasingly central to ecology. As Bernard Patten (1991: 288) notes: 'Ecology is networks . . . to understand ecosystems ultimately will be to understand networks.' Further, the ecosystem concept has been the key to advances in the scientific understanding of the relationship between human beings and nature. These advances unsettle the subject/object dichotomy promoted by the anthropocentric paradigm and illustrate clearly the integral interconnectedness and interdependence of all nature. This point is further supported by the concept of autopoesis and by Gaia science. I turn now to consider how these descriptions of nature support the concept Earth community.

### 3.2.3 Autopoiesis and Gaia theory

> Earth is no more a planet-sized chunk of rock inhabited with life than your body is a skeleton infested with cells. (Margulis & Sagan 1995: 28)

To put it as starkly as possible, I would claim that those who intend to survive the coming cataclysms of climate on hope and faith, or who square off against it armed only with the results of externalized and universal knowledge

---

5. Ken Wilber (1995: 35–78) also uses the concept of Holon in his description of integral ecology.

are doomed. The age of such faiths is over. I hope to show that it is by facing Gaia, that wholly secularized and earthbound set of processes, that there is a dim possibility that we could 'let the Spirit renew the Face of the Earth'. (Latour 2013: 9)

Autopoiesis is the central concept in systems and network descriptions of nature. Humberto Maturana and Francisco Varela define autopoiesis to mean self-organisation and production (Lyon 2004: 21).[6] This concept is related to the physiological principle of homeostasis, which is the regulatory system whereby organisms maintain a stable internal environment despite external environmental fluctuations (Lyon 2004: 29). Circular causation is the key to understanding living systems and the flow or transformation of matter and energy that sustains life. Without this function, 'organic beings do not self-maintain – they are not alive' (Margulis & Sagan 1995: 23).

The human body is one example of an autopoietic system. Every five days our stomach is relined; the cells in our liver regenerate every two months; our skin replaces itself every six weeks; and every year over 98 percent of our body's atoms are replaced (Margulis & Sagan 1995: 23).[7] This continuous replacement metabolism is a sign of life. Maturana (1970: 2) argues that '[L]iving systems . . . [are] organised in a closed causal circular process that allows for evolutionary change in the way the circularity is maintained, but not for the loss of the circularity itself.' Since all changes in the system take place within this basic circularity, the components that specify the circular organisation are also maintained and produced by the system.[8]

Autopoietic descriptions have been extensively made at the micro/cellular level. Alongside these accounts, scientists have extended the principle of autopoiesis to the Earth and its atmosphere (Lovelock & Margulis 1974). The Earth is autopoietic *in the sense* that it maintains itself at a relatively constant homeostatic equilibrium. While still hotly debated (Schneider & Boston 1991), there is plenty of evidence to support this point. To take just one example – standard astrophysical models of the evolution of stars illustrate that the sun was once cooler than it is now. The sun's radiance has increased by 30 percent since life first emerged on Earth. While this increase in luminosity should have dramatically increased the surface temperature of the Earth, fossils from ancient life confirm that the temperature of the planet has remained relatively stable (Margulis & Sagan 1995: 26–29). In response, Lyn Margulis and Dorian Sagan (1995: 27) argue that 'the temperature of the

---

6. Note that sometimes autopoiesis is termed 'operational closure' (Maturana & Varela 1980).
7. Only cells, organisms made from cells and the biosphere made of organisms can metabolise and are thus autopoietic. While DNA and viruses can reproduce, they are not autopoietic (Margulis & Sagan 1995: 23).
8. Note that while Maturana did not enjoy great popularity in his lifetime, many of his findings have been validated by independent research. On the relationship between Maturana and subsequent developments, see Lyon (2004).

entire biosphere has been self-maintained . . . life seems to have succeeded in cooling the planetary surface to counter the overheating sun.' Indeed, life forms have 'prolonged their own survival' by removing atmospheric greenhouse gases that trap heat and by changing their surface colour and form by retaining water and growing slime (Margulis & Sagan 1995: 26).

Ivanovick Vernadsky (1992) was the first to study how this mechanism operates. Drawing on the earlier work of Vasilievich Dokuchaev (1879) and Edward Suess (1924), Vernadsky portrayed living matter as a geological force – indeed 'the greatest of all geological forces' (cited in Margulis & Sagan 2007: 1999). His research illustrated that the 'biosphere of the Earth was . . . an integral dynamic system controlled by life' and that the 'leading factor which transforms the face of the Earth is life' (Lapo 1979: 29). In the present terminology, the biosphere of the Earth constitutes a cybernetic system that promotes self-regulation. Commenting on the significance of this discovery, Andrey Lapo (1979: 29) notes:

> Vernadsky saw one of the most characteristic manifestations of the orderliness of the biosphere in the presence of an ozone shield which is located above the biosphere and absorbs ultraviolet radiation deleterious to life (for us this is the most dramatic manifestation of self-regulation of the Earth's biosphere as the cybernetic system). The composition of the gaseous envelope of our planet is fully regulated by life.

Vernadsky maintained that living matter totally penetrated (and thus became involved in) what were superficially 'inanimate' processes such as weathering, water flow, and wind circulation. As interconnected members of this living system, human beings also play a role in altering and mobilising the concentrate of chemical elements of the Earth. Indeed, Vernadsky (1992: 56) viewed human beings as constituting a 'new phase in biogeochemical evolution'. Since Vernadsky, the terraforming capability of living organisms has been subject to increased investigation. As noted in the introductory chapter, this analysis has received support with scientists such as Paul Crutzen calling for formal recognition of the term 'anthropocene' to describe the new epoch in which human beings have become a geological force.

Vernadsky also rejected the standard classification of animal, vegetable and mineral used by his contemporaries and refused to classify and fragment the Earth's natural phenomena (1992: 2000). Consistent with contemporary systems thinking, Vernadsky conceived life as 'far less a thing with properties' than as a 'happening, a process' (1992: 56). Controversially, Vernadsky eschewed philosophical, historical and religious notions of what was and what was not alive. Instead, he described the 'everywhereness of life' (1992: 56) in seemingly inanimate processes of geology, water and wind. He described minerals as he would organisms – calling them 'living matter' (1992: 56).

This broad definition of life enabled Vernadsky to extend the scope of his research beyond biology. His focus turned to the Earth's crust – more specifically to myriad beings whose reproduction and growth influence matter on a global scale (Margulis & Sagan 1995: 45). In describing this process, Vernadsky contrasted life with gravity and noted that while gravity pulls material vertically toward the Earth's centre, life moves matter horizontally across the surface. Further, Vernadsky argued that a special 'thinking' layer of organised matter grew and changed the Earth's surface (Margulis & Sagan 1995: 45). To describe this, Vernadsky adopted the term 'nöosphere', from the Greek *nöos* or mind.[9] For Vernadsky, the nöosphere referred to humanity and technology as an integral part of the planetary biosphere. The nöosphere became central to demonstrating the role of life in shaping the planet and the importance of understanding the terraforming potential of all species with consciousness.

Vernadsky's investigations enabled James Lovelock and Lynn Margulis to develop Gaia theory. While Vernadsky described both organisms and minerals as being 'living matter', Gaia theory describes Earth's surface in its entirety as being 'alive' (Lovelock & Margulis 1974: 471). Every evolutionist admits that humans have adjusted their environments to suit their needs. What makes Lovelock's and Margulis' argument unique is that they extend this technical ingenuity to every single agent, no matter how small.[10] Lovelock's (1979: 18) explains further: 'The entire range of living matter on Earth from whales to viruses and from oaks to algae could be regarded as constituting a single living entity capable of maintaining the Earth's atmosphere to suit its overall needs and endowed with faculties and powers far beyond those of its constituent parts.' Lovelock (1979: 18) defined Gaia as '[A] complex entity involving the Earth's biosphere, atmosphere, oceans, and soil; the totality constituting a feedback of cybernetic systems which seeks an optimal physical and chemical environment for life on this planet.'

Gaia theory emerged from the realisation that biomass modifies atmospheric conditions to achieve suitable homeostasis for the biosphere. The research of Lovelock and Margulis illustrated that the Earth possesses a cybernetic and homeostatic feedback system that operates automatically (without consciousness) by the biota, leading to a broad stabilisation of the Earth's chemical composition and global temperature. From this initial hypothesis, Lovelock claimed the existence of a 'global control system' of ocean salinity, atmosphere composition and surface temperature.[11] In explaining this point, Lovelock (1991: 36) notes:

> Seen in all its shining beauty against the deep darkness of space, the Earth looks very much alive. This impression of life is real. Only a planet with

9. Note that this term was later adopted by French philosopher and Jesuit priest Teilhard de Chardin who, in turn, had tremendous influence on the thinking of Thomas Berry. Vernadsky was an atheist and pictured life on Earth as a global chemical reaction. In contrast, Teilhard (1977) took the nöosphere to be a vehicle for achieving a global spiritual transformation.
10. This claim is also made by Timothy Morton (2013) with reference to object-oriented ontology.
11. This hypothesis is controversial and subject to continued critique. See Kirchner (2002) and Schneider (2004).

abundant life and able to retain its water and regulate its unique atmosphere and climate could appear so different from its sister planets, Mars and Venus, both of which are dead. Of course the Earth is not alive like an animal, able to reproduce itself and have its progeny evolve in competition with other animals. It is a Superorganism, alive like the great ecosystems or some giant tree, the largest life form we yet know. I think it wrong of science to deny the status of life intermediate between inanimate matter and a sentient organism, yet greater and longer lived than most organisms.

As expounded by Margulis, however, Gaia theory is less anthropomorphic. Margulis notes that 'the temperature of the planet, the oxidation state and other chemistry of all of the gases of the lower atmosphere (except helium, argon, and other nonreactive ones) are produced and maintained by the sum of life' (2007). Importantly, Margulis emphasises that Gaia theory is a biological idea and rejects the term 'organism' in her interpretation. Consistent with other criticisms of the theory (Gould 1997: 106), Margulis argues that reference to such terms is a misinterpretation and aimed at achieving political goals. She (1997) contends:

> Lovelock's position is to let the people believe that Earth is an organism, because if they think it is just a pile of rocks they kick it, ignore it, and mistreat it. If they think Earth is an organism, they'll tend to treat it with respect. To me, this is a helpful cop-out, not science.[12]

Despite this difference between their accounts, Lovelock and Margulis agree on the fundamental principles of Gaia science and in particular that nature's interconnected systems play a critical role in regulating the internal consistency of Earth. It is this function that gives rise to the notion that Earth is autopoietic, rather than the broader range of factors common to living organisms and noted by Maturana and Varela. Indeed, just as relations among the body's cells regulate temperature and blood chemistry, so planetary regulation occurs in response to interaction among the Earth's living inhabitants. From this perspective, 'life does not exist on Earth's surface, so much as it *is* Earth's surface' (Margulis & Sagan 1995: 28). This is not a metaphysical or spiritual claim, but arguably one of the most important scientific discoveries of the last century. Moreover, Bruno Latour (2013: 8) describes Gaia theory as 'the most secular figure of the Earth ever explored by political theory'[13] and positions

12. Margulis' interpretation of Gaia as a scientific or biological idea is supported by Bruno Latour (2011: 9) who notes: 'Gaia is a scientific concept. It would be of no interest if it were associated in your mind with some vague mystical entity such as Aywa, the networky Gaia of the planet Pandora in Cameron's *Avatar*. Even though Lovelock has long been a heterodox scientist and remains largely a maverick, the real interest of the concept he assembled from bits and pieces, is that it is assembled from bits and pieces, most of them coming from scientific disciplines.'
13. Latour's (2013: 59) claim that Gaia is a secular concept is based on the following reasoning: '[I]f the adjective "secular" means "involving no outside cause or spiritual basis" and thus fully "of this world" then Lovelock's intuition can be called *fully secular*' (emphasis in original).

his own secular interpretation as the 'only entity able to mobilize in a new way science, politics and theology'.

Gaia theory represents an important branch of Berry's concept of Earth community. Like Lovelock, Berry (2009: 113) was comfortable with mythic and symbolic interpretations of science – indeed Berry wrote that 'the more primordial realities can only be spoken of in a symbolic manner.' Berry also refused the description of Earth as an inert, dead world of objects to be exploited by humans: 'We need to think of the planet as a single, unique, articulated subject to be understood in a story both scientific and mythic' (2009: 114). He explained what he meant by speaking of the Earth as a living planet in terms that both included and went beyond Gaia theory:

> This term, in my own understanding, is used, neither literally nor simply metaphorically, but as analogy, somewhat similar in its structure to the analogy expressed when we say that we 'see', an expression used primarily of physical sight but also used of intellectual understanding. A proportional relationship is expressed . . . The common quality is that of subjective presence of one form to another. In this experience, the identity of each is enhanced, not diminished. (2009: 115)

Commenting further, Berry reiterates that human existence is both derived and sustained through mutual relationships between each component of the Earth (1994: 243). As evidenced by Gaia theory, this expressly includes both living and nonliving entities. From this perspective, it does not make sense to separate human beings from nature. Rather, the Earth is a single integral community that includes human beings, non-human animals and inanimate entities.

### 3.2.4 A critique of Gaia theory and the mesh

Before concluding this section, I wish to give some attention to one recent objection to Gaia theory raised by the influential 'object-oriented ontologist'[14] Timothy Morton. For Morton (2009: 1) the concept of 'nature' is an obstacle to truly ecological thinking: 'Strange as it may sound, the idea of nature is getting in the way of properly ecological forms of culture, philosophy, politics and art.' Morton (2011) summarises his objection as follows:

> Nature is this 'thing' that is always over there somewhere. I can see bunny rabbits and mountains. But I cannot see nature; it is always somewhere

---

14. Object-oriented ontology opposes the view that objects conform to the mind of the subject and, in turn, become products of human cognition. In contrast, object-oriented philosophers maintain that objects exist independently of human perception and are not ontologically exhausted by their relations with humans or other objects.

else. So when I look for it I don't find it. The psychoanalytic word for that is the 'big other' . . . Most mental illness comes from when you realise that there is no 'big other'. Big other is not watching you. So you fill the void with some kind of fantasy. This is called the schizophrenic defence. There is a sudden loss of reality, so you hallucinate to fill that gap. I think that nature is a kind of construct that is designed to fill a kind of gap and I think it is no accident that it emerges in the first phase of industrial capitalism, the late 18th century.[15]

Thus for Morton, nature is a cultural fiction that abstracts from the intimacy that we already have with non-human beings both within and outside of social space. Following this reasoning, Morton contends that the concept of 'totality' or 'holism' is another fiction that does not really exist. Indeed, he contends: 'There is no totality, it is always some kind of retroactive construct that we make and is superimposed onto things' (2011).

Moreover, Morton suggests that Gaia theory is really a form of mechanism in disguise. He mounts this critique by drawing on the work of (ir)reductionists, such as Bruno Latour (1999: 43–44), who contend that human beings are not reducible downwards into smaller pieces or upwards into larger wholes. The same applies to other nonhuman beings from plankton, to viruses and to wilderness areas. For Morton, Gaia theory violates this principle of non-reducibility, and has the consequence of rendering the larger whole 'more real' and thus more important than its component parts.

As a result of this reasoning Morton contends that Gaia theory views the loss of single species as irrelevant. Stepping into the shoes of a Gaia advocate, Morton (2011) proclaims: 'Oh well people will do their thing, and will screw up the planet, but nature or Gaia . . . will fix it after we have gone. Gaia will always replace us with something better.' Morton likens this to the detachment one might feel when replacing a tyre or small part of a car. In both instances, it is the totality that is important and the individual parts are akin to replicable components in a machine. Indeed, he contends: 'If my car is more real than the parts in my car, then the parts in my car are less relevant and replicable' (2011).

Morton's critique of Gaia theory draws on an argument advanced by Murray Bookchin during his fiery debate with deep ecologist Dave Foreman (1999). For Bookchin, a holistic description of the Earth contained the seeds of its own terminal contradictions. Indeed, he argued that holism represented a 'deadening abstraction' of humanity from its evolutionary history and its place in the natural world (1987: 11). For Bookchin, seeing humanity as just being one part of a larger whole tells us nothing about humanity's unique evolution from the natural world or how humanity came to be so ecologically

15. Morton's analysis draws heavily on Žižek (2009: 420–462).

destructive. Neither does it say anything specific about humanity's future role. Moreover, to define this ultimate 'self-realisation' as the attainment of an undefined 'organic whole' is, for Bookchin (1987: 9), to erase 'all the rich and meaningful distinctions that exist not only between animal and plant communities but above all between nonhuman and human communities.' Indeed, Bookchin (1987: 11) argued that 'a "Self" so cosmic that it has to be capitalized is no real self at all.' Rather it is 'a category as vague, faceless and depersonalized as the very patriarchal image of "man" that dissolves our uniqueness and rationality' (1987: 11).

For both Bookchin and Morton, holism also has the propensity to perpetuate an anti-human form of environmental ethics, which views humanity as a virus that should be eradicated for the wellbeing of the whole. This can be witnessed in Lovelock's *Gaia: The Practical Science of Planetary Medicine* (56) where he tries to persuade humans that they are no more than Gaia's disease – the 'people's plague'. Proponents of deep ecology have made similar arguments, most notably when Earth First! activist Dave Foreman (Devall 1985: 4) characterised the 1984 Ethiopian famine in terms of 'nature seek[ing] its own balance' and recommended that the international community 'let the people just starve there.'

These arguments mirror other Malthusian justifications for population control practices and fail to differentiate between the victims and perpetrators of ecological harm (Bookchin 1999: 30–31). Indeed, from his perspective, one cannot fully appreciate an ecological crisis without a more nuanced critique of hierarchy that includes an analysis of anthropocentrism, racism and economics.

Advocates of holism should be cognisant of this anti-human branch of environmental ethics. However, the mechanistic detachment that Morton ascribes to adherents of Gaia theory is not a necessary or logical conclusion. On the contrary, a far more common perspective for advocates of Gaia theory is that nature as a whole is valuable and worth protecting. From this perspective, each component part of the environment needs to be protected for the health and future flourishing of the Earth community. And indeed, this alternative interpretation of holism has inspired a generation of environmental activists who sacrificed a great deal to protect parts of the environment (Shabecoff 2003). To lump all advocates of holism into one group, or even to suggest that adherents to an anti-human branch of environmental ethic are in the majority, does a great disservice to those who embrace Gaia theory as a genuinely egalitarian and ecocentric ethic.

Having outlined Morton's objection to holism, I will conclude this section with a brief note concerning the alternative ecological perspective that he advocates. As already noted, Morton contends that concepts such as nature must be understood as being secondary to the genuine intimacy that we have with non-human beings. Furthermore, rather than seeing human beings as part of a whole, Morton prefers to the term 'collectivism' and contends that we human beings should see ourselves as *co-existing* with discrete beings (2011). This, he suggests, retains the principle of interconnectedness but dispenses with what he considers the 'weird' and 'politically objectionable' connotations that pertain to terms such as 'nature' or 'holism' (2011).

The distinction that Morton is drawing between collectivism and holism is greater than mere semantics and in many ways takes us back to some of the points raised earlier during the discussion of ecological science. Morton, however, bases his argument for collectivism not in ecology, but in a close reading of Charles Darwin's *The Origin of Species*. As interpreted by Morton, Darwin's description of animals often slides from specific life forms in the 'entangled bank' to the general pool of life (2012: 19).[16] In other words, Darwin eschews the notion of 'species' as a fixed and definite placeholder for categorisation. 'It is' Morton (2011: 19) contends, 'as if we are already seeing the life-forms blurred and morphed in time, like watching the flow of turbulent currents in a stream – already, that is, before we get the generalisations that make even this picture seem like a crisp and vivid snapshot.'

Indeed, the 'punch line of [Darwin's] book is that there are no species and there is no origin' (Morton 2011). One cannot specify the origin of a chimp and furthermore, the species chimpanzee is just a collection of discrete individuals that express DNA. There is also no strong ontological difference between a species and a variant of the species and a species and a monstrosity. In other words, Morton contends that 'in some way, all life forms are a kind of monstrous collage made up of other life forms and there is no real coherency' (Morton 2009: 60–66). It is from this basis that Morton (2011) contends we should begin the project of rethinking our ecological ethics and politics and not on the basis of what he calls a 'fictional whole'.

Morton has also developed his analysis of collectivism with reference to what he calls 'the mesh'. While it would be easy to interpret this term with reference to the concept of interconnectedness, it is clear that Morton has something more fantastic in mind. Drawing on his own Buddhist worldview, Morton uses the term 'mesh' to describe the 'infinite connections and infinitesimal differences' (2009: 30) of the entire universe. He contends that the mesh is both non-local and non-temporal and has ramifications that flow 'all the way through the universe' (2011). In this sense, it expresses a much greater collectivism than conventional ecological science. In language that

---

16. See, for example, Darwin (2003: 395–396): 'It is interesting to contemplate an entangled bank, clothed with many plants of many kinds, with birds singing on the bushes, with various insects flitting about, and with worms crawling through the damp earth, and to reflect that these elaborately constructed forms, so different from each other, and dependent on each other in so complex a manner, have all been produced by laws acting around us. These laws, taken in the largest sense, being Growth with Reproduction; Inheritance . . .; Variability, from the indirect and direct action of the conditions of life, and from use and disuse; a Ratio of Increase so high as to lead to a Struggle for Life, and as a consequent to Natural Selection, entailing Divergence of Character and the Extinction of less-improved forms.'

virtually mirrors Berry's analysis of intersubjective space detailed in the introduction, Morton (2009: 33–34) notes:

> Nothing is complete in itself. Consider symbiosis. A tree includes fungi and lichen. Lichen is two life forms interacting – a fungus and a bacteria [sic] . . . seeds and pollen have birds and bees to circulate them. Animal and fungal cells include mitochondria, energy cells (organelles) that are evolved bacteria taking refuge from a (for them) toxically oxygenated world . . . Our stomachs contain benign bacteria and harmless amoebae . . . Even DNA is subject to symbiosis, coevolution, parasitism, conflict and cooperation. We consist of organs without bodies, like the grin of the Cheshire Cat.

Thus for Morton, there are real entities that co-exist with other beings. All life forms are the mesh, and 'so are all the dead ones, as are their habitats, which are also made up of living and nonliving beings' (2009: 29). Every single life form is literally familiar and genetically related. The mesh is also nonhierarchical and 'cannot be ranked in a single file' (2009: 29). Additionally, each point in the mesh 'is both the center and edge of a system of points, so there is no absolute center or edge' (2009: 29).

What I find interesting about Morton's writing is the unique way in which he expresses an alternative ecological worldview. His intervention into the debate about the relationship between human beings and nature is welcome and indicates the healthy vitality that one encounters in disciplines that are still dynamic and whose participants are striving toward a deeper understanding of the complexities of their subject matter.

And yet in articulating his ecological thought, I also contend that Morton does not adequately distinguish his own philosophy from the holistic theories that he critiques. Given the explicit influence of Buddhism on his writing this is perhaps not surprising. Morton also neglects to state clearly why his concept 'the mesh' is more politically stable or demonstrable than the secular description of Gaia offered in this chapter. At base, I think that these shortcomings reflect a subtle (yet important) misunderstanding that Morton makes in his presentation of Gaia theory. Specifically, I contend that he misunderstands the dynamic particularities at play in Gaia theory and overstates the extent to which its proponents are fixated on the cybernetic whole.

For Lovelock and Margulis, the anatomy of Gaia is composed of particularities. Each organism on Earth acts to modify its ecological community so as to render the chances of its own survival more probable. The concept of Gaia 'captures the distributed intentionality of all the agents that are modifying their surroundings to suits themselves better' (Latour 2013: 67). This reflects a generous distribution of intentionality and results not in one whole or complete providential being but in a 'mess' that reflects the chaotic world that we all inhabit (Latour 2013: 68).

In this respect, Gaia theory is completely compatible with the Darwinian narratives that Morton advocates – each particular organism is working for itself and not for some overarching good. Moreover, for both Lovelock and Margulis, Gaia theory evaporates fixed notions such as 'species' and the 'environment'. Since all living things follow their intentions and modify themselves and their neighbours, it impossible to differentiate with any certainty the environment to which an organism adapts and the point where the adaptive process starts. Timothy M. Lenton (1998: 440) describes this point as follows:

> Gaia theory aims to be consistent with evolutionary biology and views the evolution of organisms and their material environment as so closely coupled that they form a single, indivisible process. Organisms possess environment altering traits because the benefit that these traits confer (or fitness of the organisms) outweigh the cost in energy to the individual.

In this passage, Lenton captures a peculiar beauty in Gaia theory – the inside and outside of fixed all boundaries is subverted. This is not because all of nature is connected in a great chain of being as Aristotle proposed. But rather because the coupling of the activity generated from one organism manipulating another and being manipulated in turn, defines 'waves of action' that do not respect traditional boundaries and are not happening at a fixed scale (Latour: 2013: 69). These waves are the real actors and their interconnections should be followed without sticking to the fixed boundaries of isolated individuals within an environment. Indeed, Latour (2013: 69) contends that those waves are the 'real brush strokes with which Lovelock hopes to paint Gaia's face'.

## 3.3 Cultural and legal change

The description of contemporary science just introduced presents an account of the Earth that is characterised by interconnectedness. In direct contrast to the anthropocentric paradigm, the concept of Earth community seeks to transcend the subject/object dichotomy and to place human beings firmly within the web of life. Contemporary science illustrates that human beings are intimately connected to, and dependent on, the Earth. There is no evidence in such an account to support the anthropocentric worldview and its assertion that nature exists to satisfy human preferences. Instead, human beings co-exist with other organisms and perhaps as a 'subsystem of the Earth system' (Berry 2009: 95–96). For this reason, Berry (2009: 96) argues that there are compelling grounds for rational individuals to recognise the Earth community as being primary in human affairs:

> [T]he planet Earth constitutes a single integral community. It lives or dies, is honoured or degraded, as a single interrelated reality. As regards

the future, it can be said quite simply that the human community and the natural world will go into the future as a single . . . community or we will both experience disaster on the way.

Statements of this kind have found their way into the object sections of domestic legislation[17] and into international documents such as the Earth Charter (Engel & Mackey: 2011). However, there remains a psychological and material problem about how most effectively to catalyse cultural and legal change. It is this problem that I take up in the second part of this chapter. To begin, I will consider the role of cultural narrative or story in displacing harmful hierarchical notions such as anthropocentrism. I do this with regard to the 'new story' initiated by Berry (1978) and later developed by Brian Swimme and Mary-Evelyn Tucker (2011). My rationale for rooting my discussion in the writing of Berry is because of his foundational work on an alternative cultural narrative and also because of his centrality to the theory of Earth jurisprudence. Indeed, a consideration of Berry's cosmological writing will provide a necessary introduction to how his legal writing can be interpreted and applied.

This part of the analysis draws partially on the analysis of law and culture provided in the introduction of this book. Indeed, if Hall (Hall and Karsten 2009: 379) is correct that law has developed over time to reflect the grand narratives and values held by past generations, then it follows that the future of law can be influenced by the values and narratives of present and future generations also. Put another way, Hall's description of law implies that if anthropocentric values and assumptions were to change, then this *could play a role* in catalysing legal change.

Yet, a shift in law is only one element of broad social change and cannot adequately capture the complexities inherit in transitioning society toward Berry's vision of an ecocentric era. This limitation is equally applicable to any deterministic social theory. Karl Marx, for example, is often accused of technological determinism or of class struggle determinism (Cohen 1978). Other theorists place the nature dictates argument (Diamond 2005), the process of production (Holloway 2002), changes in lifestyle or consumption (Hawken 2007) or ideology (Klein 2008) as being sufficient to cause social change. Certainly, an exclusive focus on any one of these factors in isolation is insufficient. In practice, major social transformations occur through a dialectic of transformations that develop unevenly in space and time. A deterministic stance fails to capture the dynamic features of social life and misrepresents the conditions necessary for broad social change (Harvey 2010: 196).

While Marx is often painted as a deterministic social thinker, I contend that he offers a compelling analysis of the complexities of social change. For

17. For an excellent overview of legislation around the world, see UKELA (2010).

example, in volume one of *Das Kapital* (1992: 494–495 fn 4), Marx argues that social change is predicated by a complex interplay of six identifiable conceptual spheres:[18] technology, relation to nature, the process of production, the production and reproduction of daily life, social relations and mental conceptions of the world (Harvey 2010: 124–139, 2011: 189–212).[19]

The positioning of his enumeration of these spheres is prior to a lengthy examination of how the dominant technological organisational forms of capitalism were put in place. In context, Marx is grasping with the origin of the factory system and the rise of a machine tool industry as autonomous business dedicated to innovating new technologies. Throughout the chapter, Marx co-evolves his six identified spheres and describes how they develop unevenly to accommodate and consolidate the dynamic character of a capitalist mode of production. While there is no substitute for reading the text itself, Harvey (2011: 127) provides a useful summary of their interplay:

> Mental conceptions of production as an art were displaced by scientific understandings and the conscious design of new technologies. Class, gender and family relations shifted as workers were increasingly reduced to the status of flexible appendages to the machine rather than as individuals endowed with the unique skills of the artisan. At the same time, capitalists mobilised new technologies and organisations forms as weapons in class struggle against labour . . . the entry of a large number of women into the labour force, then as now, had all sorts of social ramifications. This brought forth other institutional changes, notably the educational clauses in the Factory Act of 1848 . . . New organisational forms (the corporate factory) promoted new technologies under new institutional arrangements that had ramifications for social relations and the relation to nature.

Each of these spheres is subject to continual renewal and transformation, both in interaction with the other spheres and through their own unique internal dynamic. The relation between each of the spheres is not causal but dialectical. As such the whole configuration 'constitutes a socio-ecological totality' (Harvey 2011: 128). Furthermore, history provides numerous examples where explosive development in one of these spheres positions that element at the vanguard of social change. For example, strong social activism around women's rights or environmental harm have taken on a dominant role in the co-evolutionary process and put pressure on the other spheres in the totality.

18. After a brief engagement with Darwin's theory of evolution, Marx (1992: 494 fn 4) comments that 'technology reveals the active relation of man to nature, the direct process of production of his life and thereby it also lays bare the process of the social relations of his life and of the mental conceptions that flow from these relations.'
19. To these six elements, Harvey adds 'institutional arrangements' (2011: 126).

In the light of this analysis, after first considering the role of mental ideas in social and legal change, I will turn to consider the sphere of social relations or social movements. I will contend that social movements are currently playing a vanguard role in the struggle toward a more just and environmentally sustainable world. The current movement for Earth jurisprudence is identified later as being as one part of this broader movement. Furthermore, I will contend that social movements provide an essential material base for any project directed toward establishing an ecocentric era out of the shell of the anthropocene – a vital supplement to Berry's 'new story'.

### 3.3.1 The new story

Thomas Berry positioned the medium of story as a method to shift Western culture from an anthropocentric worldview to the concept of Earth community. His approach was influenced by his training as a passionist priest and by his belief in the material significance of cosmology in ensuring cultural vitality, transformation and survival (Eaton 2001: 1). Berry argued that all societies live with some form of narrative that shapes and guides personal and collective action and interactions. Outside this story (be it scientific or religious), he argued that there is no context in which human life can function in a meaningful way (1988: 111). Berry's ideas for a 'new story' began in the early 1970s, following the emergence of public discourse on the environmental crisis. He summarises the roots of his work as follows:

> I studied history and philosophy to find out and test how people found meaning. I wanted to go back through the whole human tradition and test the whole process, because it was obvious from the beginning, going into religious life, that the process was not working . . . our modern world was not working. Christianity in this sense is not working . . . Religion is assuming no responsibility for the state of the Earth or the fate of the Earth . . . somehow, when I was quite young, I saw the beginning of biocide and genocide. (cited in Dunn, Clarke & Lonergan 1991: 143–144)

Berry first published 'The New Story' in 1978 as part of the inaugural *Teilhard Studies* journal. Berry's 'New Story' was revised and published again in 1988 in his classic book *The Dream of the Earth*. Berry (1988: 123) opens the essay by contending:

> It is all a question of story. We are in trouble now because we do not have a good story. We are in between stories. The old story, the account of how the world came to be and how we fit into it, is no longer effective. Yet we have not learned a new story.

The traditional myths of Western culture have sustained generations of human beings. As discussed in Chapter 2 with reference to Christian theology, cosmology has played a key role in shaping our mental perceptions of the environment. It should also be clear from this discussion that mythology does not always promote harmony or make people behave in a moral way. Instead, the traditional stories of Western culture have provided a 'context in which life could function in a meaningful manner' (1988: 123). Berry critiques anthropocentric theology and philosophy on the basis that it has become dysfunctional and has remained stagnant in response to contemporary knowledge about the relationship between human beings and the Earth community. In response, Berry argued that '[w]e need something that will supply in our times what was supplied formerly by our traditional religious story . . . we need a story that will educate us, a story that will heal, guide and discipline us' (1998: 124).

In developing a 'new story', Berry was deeply influenced by Italian philosopher Giambattista Vico (1976; Berry 1949, 1989). Vico's most significant influence on Berry was in regard to his methodology as a cultural historian. Vico's writing enjoyed a renaissance during the 1960s as branches of cultural theory shifted from the isolation and description of unit ideas to the linking of 'intellectually satisfying concepts' over history to see how thought itself is 'shaped by changes in our mindset' (Hutton 1985: 74).

For example, Vico describes historical periods in terms of large, sweeping categories. Through this macrophase approach, Vico identifies three historical periods – the age of the Gods, the age of the heroes and the age of humans (Bergin & Fisch 1970: xi). Briefly, the first period is characterised by theocratic government and 'primitive' mythology. The second period is characterised by aristocratic government, slavery and broad class conflict. Finally, during the third age, democracies appear and the power of reason and human rights emerge. Corresponding to each age are different laws, customs, arts, languages and forms of economics. Furthermore, at each stage, a different human faculty operates, namely 'sensation, imagination and intellect' respectively (cited in Tucker 2006: 154).

Vico contends that this cycle recurs during human history as we shift from 'savage' to 'civilized' states and from 'myth' to 'rationality' (1976: 34). The role of poetry, natural wisdom and intuition are crucial for this transition and for the establishment of nations. Vico (1976: 34) describes transition in terms of 'barbarism and reflection' and argues that in passing through phases, history moves toward 'a creative barbarism of sense.' Vico's description of people in the state of barbarism has obvious parallels to the egoistic way that developed Western countries are currently behaving with reference to the environmental crisis (Burdon 2013b). He writes:

> Such people, like so many beasts, have fallen into the custom of each man thinking only of his own private interests and have reached the extreme of delicacy, or better pride, in which like wild animals they bristle and lash out at the slightest displeasure. Thus no matter how great the throng and press of their bodies, they live like wild beasts in deep solitude of spirit and will. (1976: 381)

The clearest indication of Berry's alignment with Vico's approach lies not only in his consistent construal of history in terms of recognisable ages, but also in his characterisation of these ages in terms of decline followed by deep intellectual change (1988: 39–40). Berry's first delineation of the eras of human history proposed four phases: the tribal–shamanic, the religious–cultural, the scientific–technological and the ecological or 'Ecozoic' (1981: 12). Consistent with Vico, Berry associated a predominant mode of human thought and activity within each of these periods. The tribal–shamanic was characterised by human focus on 'the ultimate mystery of the universe' and 'creativity in the expression of this sensitivity' (1988: 39). The religious cultural period or classical period saw an increase in social stratification, sacrificial rituals, articulated theologies and spiritual disciplines in cultures that are now considered the great civilizations of the world. During the scientific–technological period Western culture concentrated on rational objectivity and technological progress (1988: 39).

While recognising the positive aspects of the present period, Berry's description is akin to Vico's in accentuating its negative aspects. He describes the barbarism of the present age where our relationship to nature is being repressed by an overriding anthropocentric worldview. In contrast, for Berry, the critical feature of the emerging ecological age is a paradigm shift in human consciousness toward relationship with nature and recognition of the Earth community. This shift is far greater than a rationalist response or an attempt at a technocratic fix (Berry 1981b, 1988: 50–69). It is a paradigm shift in human perception and associated values. Berry (1988: 201) writes:

> The achievements [modern scientific, industrial, rational] which are sometimes designated as the full realization of the human mode of being, have a certain tendency to disintegrate in the manner then we are presently experiencing. Giambattista Vico . . . considered that the eighteenth century was the period when a second barbarism, a barbarism of refinement, erupted in the civilizational enterprise. A new descent into a more primitive state must then come about, a new reimmersion in the natural forces out of which our cultural achievements came about.

Unlike Vico, however, Berry did not seek to construct a 'new science' through which to study human culture. Instead, Berry articulated a vision and attempted to persuade people to think and to act in what he saw as a respectful and mutually beneficial way towards nature and each other. Berry also believed that Western culture would only go through a paradigm shift if the principles underlying the ecological age were presented in a broadly accessible way. To this end, he argued that historical development was more than a cumulative rational process. As Anne-Marie Dalton (1999: 21) suggests: 'Human action is driven by a complex interaction of emotion, practical judgment and communal interaction accessible to each generation on the basis of our common humanity and encapsulated in the enduring language, symbols and artistic expression of any culture.' Berry, likewise, sees that, despite the fluctuations of time, the medium of story has remained a constant and powerful mode of communication throughout human history. He argues further that story has the ability to connect the 'paradigmatic structure of the depth of the human psyche to the human context of cultural narrative' (1992: 228).

To command reasoned loyalty from modern society, Berry's 'new story' is told in the language of science and mathematical cosmology – disciplines that Berry considered to be 'inherently mythic' (cited in Dalton 1999: 84). The story's content covers many of the scientific insights presented in this chapter – but Berry's 'new story' is also far broader than human history and the delineation of periods noted above. It assumes that the Earth and the universe itself emerged in a succession of events and that these events lend themselves to a narrative explanation.[20]

The 'new story' begins with the 'flaring forth' of the primordial fireball and the stages of early evolution, as they are presently understood and accepted by most scientists. It then proceeds onto the formation of the planets and the geographical and biological developments on planet Earth. Here, the story traces the evolution of pre-life forms and the emergence of life, up to and including human life.[21] In this sense, the 'new story' is also a history. Importantly, by extending the narrative beyond human history, Berry is also making an important comment on anthropocentrism and on the premise that the Earth exists for human beings. Brian Swimme and Matthew Fox (1982: 22) comment that '[T]o consider human history in isolation is equivalent to expecting to find the full meaning of a novel on its last page.' This, I suggest, is an accurate analogy, for as biologist Jayne Benyus (2007) argues:

> *Homo sapiens* are an incredibly young species, we don't think of ourselves as young, but we are. We came very late in the calendar year of the Earth. If the Earth calendar started on January 1 and now we are at December 31st, humans got here at fifteen minutes before midnight on December 31 and all of recorded history has blinked by in the last sixty seconds.

Berry's 'new story' marks a shift away from human history towards the comprehensive history of the universe, and in that choice communicates the idea that human beings are but one part of a greater process. Furthermore, and perhaps most importantly for Berry, the 'new story' is not finished. Rather, the Earth is part of an irreversible emergent process. To make this point, Berry draws on the work of French Jesuit, Teilhard de Chardin and, in particular, on

20. In more poetic fashion, Berry often referred to this quality of the emerging universe as the universe itself telling the story. See Dunn, Clarke and Lonergan (1991: 132).
21. For a visual representation, see the film put together by Brian Swimme and Mary Evelyn Tucker, *Journey of the Universe* (2011): http:// www.journeyoftheuniverse.org/.

his appreciation of developmental time (Tucker 2006: 154). Chardin (1968: 193) constantly noted that since Darwin's origin of species we have gained awareness that the Earth is not static in development, but is a continually unfolding cosmogenesis. Teilhard suggests that this perspective provides a distinctive realisation regarding our place in the universe:

> For our age to have become conscious of evolution means something very different from and much more than having discovered one further fact . . . It means (as happens with a child when he acquires the sense of perspective) that we have become alive to a new dimension. The idea of evolution is not, as sometimes said, a mere hypothesis, but a condition of all experience. (1968: 193)

For Berry, the 'new story' is the primary context for understanding the immensity of cosmogenesis. He argues that we do not live in a 'spatial mode of consciousness', in which time is experienced as a 'seasonal renewing sequence of realities that keep their basic identify in accord with the Platonic archetypal world' (1999: 26). Instead, we live in a 'cosmogenesis'. That is, in a 'universe ever coming into being through an irreversible sequence of transformations moving, in the larger arc of development, from a lesser to a greater order of complexity and from a lesser to greater consciousness' (1999: 26). As the reality of developmental time is assimilated in Western culture, Berry felt that its assimilation would lead to a greater understanding of human connectedness to nature. He contends:

> The human emerges not only as an Earthling, but also as a worldling. We bear the universe in our being as the universe bears us in its being. The two have a total presence to each other and to that deeper mystery out of which both the universe and ourselves have emerged. (1988: 132)[22]

For Berry, the idea of cosmogenesis and the recognition that the knowledge we now possess about the universe can be understood and described in narrative telling was the 'single greatest achievement of the entire scientific venture from Copernicus to the present' (1992: 236). Importantly, the idea that there is a story of the universe in historical sequence and measurable time was unknown prior to the twentieth century (Berry & Swimme 1992: 236).

---

22. The subjective presence of things to each other is arguable one of the most distinctive aspects of Berry's thought. Again, he was influenced by the writing of Chardin (1960: 92) who writes: 'In the Divine Milieu all the elements of the universe touch each other by that which is most inward and ultimate in them.' Commenting on this point, Berry (1988: 135) writes: 'The reality and value of the interior subjective numinous aspect of the entire cosmic order is being appreciated as the basic condition in which the story makes any sense at all.'

In earlier periods, there was a sense that human beings were passing through certain stages of intellectual development, described by Auguste Comte (1988) as the religious, metaphysical and positivist phases. There was also a perception of social evolution toward more acceptable social institutions and community life, articulated by writers such as Charles Fourier (Fourier, Jones & Patterson 1996) and later by Marx (1992). Finally, there was an awareness of the biological development and evolution of species described by Charles Darwin (2003) and an outline of the sequence of geological formation of the Earth by Charles Lyell (Lyell & Secord 1998). However, none of these important insights gave any indication that the universe itself was evolving in an identifiable sequence of irreversible transformations.

To conclude, Berry's 'new story' provides a tool for shifting Western culture away from anthropocentrism and toward the notion of Earth community. While the articulation of a modern story has broad value, its specific application is to provide the basis for more a reciprocal and mutually enhancing relationship with nature. If the 'new story' formed the basis of culture, Berry hoped, people would be moved to act according to the values it carried – principally, the idea of Earth community. In that sense, the story would supply a functional cosmology for a 'viable human existence' within the limitations of the natural world. Speaking to this point, Mary Evelyn-Tucker (2006: 154) contends that:

> [t]he new story provides context and perspective for implementing the specific kinds of social, political and economic changes that will be needed to sustain and foster life on this planet . . . [t]he assumption is that, when one's worldview shifts to comprehend the interrelatedness of all life, one's ethics likewise will be affected to encourage human justice and environmental sustainability.

### 3.3.2 Legal change and the global movement for Earth jurisprudence

While some version of Berry's 'new story' is arguably necessary for human society to transition to an ecocentric era, it is not sufficient. We cannot simply propose an alternative story and hope that it will be adopted by diverse cultures and legal systems around the world. Further to these points, it must also be recognised that global industrial capitalism will not stop destroying the planet at the mere pronouncement (or even the widespread acceptance) of a coherent ecocentric cosmology. Instead, some explanation must be given as to how ideals such as Earth community could become broadly accepted and infused in law.

The theoretical underpinning of this part of my analysis is social constructionism (Berger & Luckmann 1966), which holds that the meaning of concepts, including legal concepts, is the product of evolving social practices and values rather than a reflection of an unchanging, objective reality. In adopting this theoretical position, however, I will be staying clear of the highly abstract debates that dominate this field and will concentrate instead on how and why, as a practical matter, socially constructed legal concepts acquire meaning and how those meanings change.

As noted by Marx, social relations and social activism represent a fundamental material element of social and legal change. Yet despite the clear importance of this element, it was recently noted that 'legal scholars seem largely oblivious to the existence of social science literature on social movements' (Rubin 2001: 2). Further to this, Michael McCann (2006b: 17) has written that the '[R]igorous study of law and social movements has been a surprisingly limited and marginal intellectual endeavor in the legal academy.' McCann (2006a: xi) also observes that social movement specialists 'have rarely directly analysed whether, or to what extent, law does or does not matter for the struggles at stake'. The lack of cross-pollination is unfortunate. In particular, advocates for Earth jurisprudence would benefit greatly from a more nuanced 'approach for understanding the origin and meaning of legal concepts' (Rubin 2001: 3) as well as how legal concepts change and adapt in the face of social pressure.

Before going any further, I need to clarify what I mean by the term 'social movement'. A broad definition is adequate for present purposes, and a good place to start is Sidney Tarrow's (1983: 7) frequently cited definition: 'Social movements are groups possessing a purposive organization, whose leaders identify their goals with the preferences of an unmobilized constituency which they attempt to mobilize direct action in relation to a target of influence in the political system.' The political scientist, Charles Tilly, suggests that a social movement is a sustained series of interactions between power holders and persons speaking on behalf of a constituency lacking formal representation, 'in the course of which those persons make publically visible demands for changes in the destruction or exercise of power, and back those demands with public demonstrations of support' (1984: 306). Finally, a further nuance is added by McCann (2006a: xiv), who states that 'social movements aim for a broader scope and political transformation than do more conventional political activities.' Thus, while social movements may press for tangible, short-term goals, they can also be 'animated by more radical aspirational visions of a different, better society' (2006a: xiv).

It is in the light of these characterisations of social movements that I position the global movement for Earth jurisprudence as a form of global social movement.[23] The Earth jurisprudence movement consists of decentralised networks of both incorporated and unofficial groups of individuals who employ a wide range of tactics to advance their cause (Cullinan 2011a:

---

23. In Australia, this movement is most visibly represented in the Australian Wild Law Alliance: http://www.wildlaw.org.au/.

178–191, 2011b: 12–23). While great variations exists across the globe, the activities being undertaken include public education, academic conferences, media campaigns and social networking, as well as more disruptive tactics, such as protests and marches, which are intended to halt or to upset certain existing social practices.

Consistent with other popular social movements, the movement for Earth jurisprudence also seeks to make – through this wide range of techniques and actions – structural impacts on the political and legal system. One particularly clear example can be used to concretise the praxis of Earth jurisprudence advocates and activists: rights for nature activism.[24] While I do not have space to detail this activity in full, the tangible positive law results of this campaign are quite stunning (Burdon 2010b, 2011c, 2012b; Western & Bollier 2013). In brief, as the direct result of local community organising and activism (Linzey 2010), over 30 municipalities in the United States have now drafted and adopted rights of nature ordinances to help protect local ecosystems from industries such as coal mining, water bottling and gas drilling (fracking).[25] This has been mirrored at the international level, with Ecuador adopting rights for nature provisions in its national constitution[26] and Bolivia passing similar legislation at the national level.[27] More recently, in New Zealand the Whanganui River was granted legal personhood and the local *iwi*[28] was recognised as having standing to sue on behalf of the river (Shuttleworth 2012).

Leaving to one side tactical, practical and philosophical issues that these examples have raised (Burdon 2010b, 2012b, 2014; Western & Bollier 2013: 68–76), the current advocacy for the rights of nature has highlighted a key lesson for mobilising cultural and legal change. Indeed, what interests me most about these developments is not the precise content of the laws generated by them, but the fact that such laws have arisen from popular struggle – that is from the bottom up – as legislatures respond to social movement pressure. This is important, because it reveals that groups of people have organised and

24. See, in particular, the Global Alliance for the Rights of Nature: http://www.therightsofnature.org/.
25. For example, in 2008 the township of Barnstead, New Hampshire, adopted an ordinance that reads: 'Natural communities and ecosystems possess inalienable and fundamental rights to exist and flourish within the Town of Barnstead.'
26. Article 1 of the Constitution reads: 'Nature or *Pachamama*, where life is reproduced and exists, has the right to exist, persist, maintain and regenerate its vital cycles, structure, functions and its processes in evolution. Every person, people, community or nationality, will be able to demand the recognitions of rights for nature before the public organisms.'
27. This law states that 'Mother Earth is a living dynamic system made up of the undivided community of all living beings, who are all interconnected, interdependent and complementary, sharing a common destiny.' It goes onto grant nature legal rights, specifically the 'rights to life, regeneration, biodiversity, water, clean air, balance, and restoration.' Bolivia's law mandates a fundamental ecological reorientation of Bolivia's economy and society, requiring all existing and future laws to adapt to the 'Mother Earth Law' and accept the ecological limits set by nature.
28. The word *iwi* means 'peoples' or 'nations'.

worked cooperatively to identify a tangible solution to a specific problem, express ownership of the idea and to construct a particular understanding of its meaning that matches their own unique history, geography and problem. Further, such groups have gained practice in building networks of solidarity, participating in democracy and the confidence that comes from political victory. Each of these attributes can assist the people concerned to play an ongoing role in governance and in ensuring that the laws are interpreted and applied in a way that is consistent with what they intended. Moreover, such collective and individual experience provides the foundation for making bolder demands that have the power to address root causes and to institute alternative social, legal and economic forms.

Thus, I contend that, alongside seeking change in individual and social mental ideas and constructs concerning the environment, collaborative struggle is essential for the production of meaningful and long-term cultural and legal change.[29] Moreover, community empowerment and ownership of laws cannot be handed to the community via the standard top-down legislative process. Instead, there is a need for grassroots social movement engagement and activism. In the final analysis, laws and legal rights are empty signifiers, in the sense that their meaning is open to disputation and rival claims. Of particular importance in giving rights meaning is the question of how rights come into existence – a factor related to the issue of which communities or institutions influence the ways in which rights are filled with meaning. Indeed, interpretive power and the issue of rights genesis are always intimately related because even semantic torsion in the interpretation of an existing right can be seen as birthing a 'new' right or even a new order of rights (Baxi 2006). This intimacy between interpretation and genesis is evident, arguably, in the reality, common today, of the power that financiers and corporations have to influence the political and judicial process in order to ensure that their own interests are protected – a process in which 'new' forms of corporate right emerge – such as the right of US corporations to influence electoral campaigns (*Citizens United*). But then, since rights remain interpretively open – semantic placeholders – advocates for Earth jurisprudence, environmentalists and anti-capitalists can also make arguments filling rights with meaning, and aimed at shifting the underlying orientation of orders of rights. Part of this agonistic process is the need to confront the question of whose rights are being identified, while recognising, as Marx (1992: 344) contends, that 'between equal rights force decides'. Accordingly, the definition and interpretation of the law or right is itself an object of continuing struggle and as David Harvey (2012: xv) recognises, 'that struggle has to proceed concomitantly with the struggle to materialise it'.

29. In this aspect, I concur with Western and Bollier (2013: 112–120) in their contention that 'the greatest promise lies in "bottom-up" or grassroots-driven approaches, especially those that are inclusive and cross-sectoral.'

Within this struggle to material rights meanings lies an important lesson for the Earth jurisprudence movement. A 'new story' alone will not suffice. Indeed, while some legislative gains have been made, I nonetheless contend that the movement will need to expand, organise and politicise, if anything resembling an ecocentric era is to emerge in law through democratic processes. It is the 'grassroots' or 'bottom-up' theory of legal transformation that has been central to every significant legal development for the expansion of rights or moral consideration (Zinn 2005). Contrary to Berry's contention, no version of an ecocentric era will emerge simply through a transformation of mental ideas. Rather, organisation and struggle are also necessary for effecting lasting legal change and must be situated in dialectical tension with the five additional spheres identified by Marx.[30]

## 3.4 Conclusion

In this chapter, I presented an alternative paradigm for law based on the concept of Earth community. In direct contrast to the existing anthropocentric paradigm of law, the concept of Earth community holds that human beings are deeply connected to and dependent on the Earth. Indeed, this chapter posits the human community as one part of a comprehensive community that includes other life forms and inanimate subjects: the environment does not exist simply to satisfy the needs and preferences of human beings. It has its own distinct history, reality and function in the processes of Earth.

The concept of Earth community was supported with reference to three distinct areas of science. At the micro-level, quantum physics illustrates that subatomic particles are best explained in terms of interconnectedness. Matter does not have meaning when fragmented and is best understood in context and in terms of relationship. This finding was supported further with reference to the discipline of ecology: the concept of ecosystem holds that living organisms and the abiotic environment are inseparably interrelated. To help articulate this concept, ecologists have adopted the language of network and systems theory, which describes the environment in terms of relationship and integration. Finally, the integral interconnected functioning of the Earth was supported by the concepts of autopoiesis and of Gaia theory: the Earth is said to be autopoietic in the sense that the combined functioning of its living and nonliving components maintains a consistent homeostatic equilibrium. Following this, I discussed an important objection to holism, presented by Timothy Morton and supplemented by my discussion with reference to his ecological concept of 'the mesh'. While none of these branches of inquiry should be conflated or understood as presenting a singular description of reality, it is apparent from the discussion in this chapter that they each re-enforce

30. Perhaps the most comprehensive analysis of what a sophisticated ecological society might look like has been sketched out by Bookchin (1987, 1990, 1996).

the foundational claim of Earth jurisprudence – that human beings exist as but one part of a broader Earth community.

Following this, I argued that for the principle of Earth community to influence law there must be a mechanism for it to become entrenched in culture. I addressed this issue first with reference to alternative cosmology or story presented by Berry. Berry's 'new story' presents a sweeping historical narrative, beginning with the primordial fireball at the beginning of the universe and continuing on to the present. It is told in the language of science and mathematical cosmology, and unlike the traditional stories of Western culture (which have put forward an anthropocentric worldview), is premised on the principle of Earth community. In constructing a 'new story', Berry hoped to facilitate a mutually enhancing human–Earth relationship. He hoped that the 'new story' would shift human values and ethics and then inform human social institutions including our law.

Drawing on Marx's sociological analysis, I then argued, however, for a more complex and multidimensional theory of social change – one invoking the need for the co-evolution of mental ideas such as the 'new story' with changes in technology, our relationship to nature, the process of production, the production and reproduction of daily life and social relations. While a more robust analysis would account for each of these spheres, I focused on the role of social relations or social movements as a particularly strategic vanguard for effecting legal change. I argued that the global movement for Earth jurisprudence represents a necessary condition for any realisation of Berry's ecocentric era – but that to actualise this goal, the movement will need to politicise, organise and engage in robust struggle to realise their goals.

I turn now to consider how our law can respond to the paradigm of Earth community. In Chapter 4, I outline an alternative theory of law proposed by Berry, called Earth jurisprudence. Earth jurisprudence represents an alternative to the dominant anthropocentric philosophy of legal positivism and seeks to make the concept of Earth community integral to our law. Following this discussion, in Chapter 5, I consider the application of Earth jurisprudence to our property system and to the idea of private property itself.

# Chapter 4

# A theory of Earth jurisprudence

> Although we are integral with the complex of life communities, we have never been willing to recognize this in law, economics, morality, education or in other areas of the human endeavour. (Berry 1988: 21)

## 4.1 Introduction

In this chapter, I leave the wonder of cosmology and the hubris of social struggle behind and engage with the analytic tradition of jurisprudence. While I recognise the limits of jurisprudence as a tool for realising broad social change, I also contend that speculation about what an alternative ecological concept of law might look like is important. Speaking figuratively, jurisprudence is the soul or the imagination of positive law. It sets its tone, establishes its patterns of reference and provides the intellectual context within which laws are made and interpreted. I contend that this is true, dispute the more overt ways in which power and money influence the functioning of a legal system. With this in mind, my principal concern in this chapter is to interpret and develop Berry's fragmentary juridical writing and advance a theory of Earth jurisprudence.

In the first part of this chapter, I provide an overview of the literature and arguments made by the leading advocates for Earth jurisprudence. Drawing on this literature, I situate Earth jurisprudence within the broad structure of natural law philosophy. Following this, I describe the legal categories of Earth jurisprudence. I contend that it is possible to discern from Berry's writing an argument for the existence of two kinds of 'law' organised in a hierarchy. At the apex is the 'great law', which represents the principle of Earth community and is measured with reference to the scientific concept of ecological integrity. Beneath the great law is human law, defined as rules articulated by human authorities that are consistent with the great law and enacted for the comprehensive common good.

The interrelationship between the great law and human law is also discussed. Specifically, I interpret Berry as contending that human law derives its legal quality and authority from the great law. The great law can be manifest in positive law instruments such as national constitutions but it also exists in the unofficial or 'vernacular law' of a community. In either manifestation, the great law acts as a bedrock standard or measure for human law. Moreover, laws that contravene the great law and risk the health and future flourishing of the Earth community are considered to be a corruption of law and do not attain legal quality. A defective law is not morally binding on a population and citizens have a moral justification for civil disobedience aimed at reforming the law.[1]

The theory of Earth jurisprudence described in this chapter provides the foundation for Chapter 5, which considers the implications of Earth community for property law and the concept of private property.

## 4.2 What is Earth jurisprudence?

Earth jurisprudence is an emerging philosophy of law, proposed by Thomas Berry in 2001 (Cullinan 2011b: 12–23). Its origin can be explained in a number of ways. One account explains it as a response to the present environmental crisis described in the introduction. It can also be considered a form of critical legal theory. In this regard, advocates of Earth jurisprudence would subscribe to the early principles of critical legal studies, in particular, its critique of law in legitimising particular social relations and illegitimate hierarchies.[2] Earth jurisprudence is also, necessarily, a development from the environmental movement and environmental philosophy more generally. What unites its proponents is a belief that society and the legal order reflect a harmful and outdated anthropocentric worldview. Earth jurisprudence analyses the contribution of law in constructing, maintaining and perpetuating anthropocentrism and looks at ways in which this orientation can be undermined and ultimately eliminated.

1. In offering this interpretation, I acknowledge the formulation of Earth jurisprudence provided by Cormac Cullinan (2003: 84). As described in more detail later, Cullinan describes Earth jurisprudence with reference to the great jurisprudence, which refers to the fundamental laws or principles that govern how the universe functions. For Cullinan, Earth jurisprudence can be seen as a special case of the great jurisprudence, applying universal principles to the governmental, societal and biological processes of Earth. When universal principles are represented in state law, Cullinan describes the prescriptions as 'wild law'. My interpretation of Earth jurisprudence differs from Cullinan's and draws principally from the writing of Berry (1999, 2006) and Aquinas (1997). As described in this chapter, the 'great law' focuses on identifiable ecological concepts such as ecological integrity rather than on universal principles of the universe. Moreover, because I explicitly theorise Earth jurisprudence as a kind of natural law theory, I situate the great law as an immediate measure of legal quality. This necessarily gives rise to challenges concerning legal authority and justifications for civil disobedience. Finally, my interpretation of Earth jurisprudence contends that human law is a project with a purpose and links human law to the attainment of the common good for each aspect of the Earth community.
2. Note that advocates of critical legal studies said very little about the environment.

As progenitor, Berry is primary amongst advocates for Earth jurisprudence. Berry was a persistent critic of the anthropocentric paradigm and its prevalence in western law. In his important essay, 'Legal Conditions for Earth Survival' (2006: 107–112), he argues that the present legal system 'is supporting exploitation rather than protecting the natural world from destruction by a relentless industrial economy;. Berry also critiques legal positivism on the basis that it posits 'abstract' categories or doctrines as the highest authority in human society. He notes: '[H]umans [have] become self-validating, both as individuals and as a political community' and no longer act with reference to a higher power 'either in heaven or on [E]arth' (Cullinan 2003: 13). Berry also critiques contemporary notions of private property as a mechanism that authorises human exploitation of nature (1999: 61–62) and the non-recognition of rights outside the human community (1999: 5, 2006: 107–112, 150–151).

In 1987, Berry set about describing how human society could shift both its idea of law and its legal system in response to the 'new story' described in Chapter 3 of this book. Most of his remarks are broad, as witnessed in his early paper 'The Viable Human' (1987: 5–6):

> The basic orientation of the common law tradition is toward personal rights and toward the natural world as existing for human use. There is no provision for recognition of nonhuman beings as subjects having legal rights . . . the naïve assumption that the natural world exists solely to be possessed and used by humans for their unlimited advantage cannot be accepted . . . To achieve a viable human–Earth community, a new legal system must take as its primary task to articulate the conditions for the integral functioning of the Earth process, with special reference to a mutually enhancing human–Earth relationship.

The idea of 'mutual enhancement' is fundamental to Earth jurisprudence. As argued in Chapter 3, human beings are deeply connected and dependent on the environment. The idea that human good can be achieved at the expense of the larger Earth community is an illusion. Instead, the health and flourishing of the Earth community is a prerequisite for human existence. This necessitates a shift from the anthropocentric notion that nature exists for human use and toward the facilitation of 'mutually enhancing' human–Earth interactions (Berry 1999: 3). Further, Earth jurisprudence considers the principle of Earth community as both relevant and necessary to our idea of law.

While not explicit, it is possible to discern from the writings of Berry an argument for the existence of two types of 'law' that are organised in hierarchical relationship. The first order of law is great law, which refers to the principle of Earth community. The second order of law is human law, which represents binding prescriptions, articulated by human authorities, which are consistent with the great law and enacted for the common good of the comprehensive Earth community.

Two matters typify the interrelation between the great law and human law. First, human law derives its legal quality and power to bind in conscience from the great law. Because human beings exist as one part of an interconnected and mutually dependent community, only a prescription directed to the comprehensive common good has the quality of law. In decisions concerning the environment or human–Earth interactions, it is appropriate to construct human law with reference to the great law. For other matters, the legislator has broad freedom and lawmaking authority. Second, any law that transgresses the great law can be considered a corruption of law and not morally binding on a population.

It will be clear to anyone familiar with legal philosophy that the basic structure and relationship between these different types of law share resemblance to the Thomist and neo-Thomist natural law traditions. Lynda Warren (2006: 13) comments on this resemblance:

> At first sight, the similarities seem obvious. The classical doctrine of Natural Law is based on the existence of a body of law – Natural Law – that is universal and immutable. It has been described as a higher law against which the morality of 'ordinary' laws can be judged. This higher law is discoverable by humans through a process of reason.

Many advocates of Earth jurisprudence, however, are dismissive of natural law philosophy and have expressed concern about becoming locked in the unproductive rivalry between positivism and natural law (Bosselmann 1995: 236).[3] However, while this rivalry has traditionally occupied much territory in legal philosophy, it must be stated that there is no necessary conflict between the two ideas. As Margaret Davies (2008: 79) points out: '[I]t all depends on what view of natural law and positivism is taken.' For example, someone who advocates the position that an immoral rule created by parliament is not really law is putting forward a perspective that is incompatible with the view that rules obtains their legal status only when articulated by an authoritative legislative body. Further, a person who advocates for objective morality is putting forward a position that is directly inconsistent with the view that morality is arbitrary or relative. However, these are not the only ways that the relationship between natural law and positivism can be understood (Beyleveld & Brownsword 1985).

An alternative version of the relationship between natural law and positivism, from the perspective of the natural lawyer, is that an unjust law is still a law, but that lawmakers ought to follow the natural law. In this interpretation there is no necessary relationship between law and morality but conformity is strongly recommended. The existence of objective morality is defended, but

---

3. Commenting on this point, Bosselmann (1995: 236) notes: 'Structurally the ecocentric orientation of values is a turning towards the ideas of Natural law. In this context some authors point towards understanding in a natural-law sense. I do not believe that it is necessary to revert in this way, nor that it could be of any help – considering the unproductive rivalry between positivism and Natural law.'

it is also accepted that lawmakers can make unjust prescriptions and that the state will enforce them. This sort of natural law theory is not incompatible with positivism, since it is accepted that the two systems can co-exist as laws (MacCormick 1992). It is just that the natural law is regarded as 'higher' and in need of implementation.

A second major criticism that advocates of Earth jurisprudence have made against adopting a natural law framework is that the anthropocentric and patriarchal legacy of the latter makes it a poor, and potentially confusing, point of comparison for explaining an ecocentric legal philosophy (Cullinan 2003: 77). This criticism is undeniably potent for many strands of the Thomist and neo-Thomist natural law traditions. However, it must also be stated that natural law comes in many shapes and sizes in addition to the Thomistic interpretation.

Perhaps the most relevant to the present chapter is Aldo Leopold's natural law environmental ethic, which is articulated in 'The Land Ethic' (1986; see also Engel 2010; Rolston III 1986). In this paper, Leopold advances arguments from personal experience, scientific observation and theory and inductive (as well as deductive) reasoning for the ontological reality and moral intimacy of ecological integrity (Engel 2010: 35) – or what Leonardo Boff calls 'the dignity of Earth' (Boff 1997: 87). Consider for example this syllogism in which Leopold (1986: 262–263) derives 'ought' from 'is':

1  All ethics rest upon a single premise: that the individual is a member of a community of interdependent parts.
2  We are all members of the land community.
3  Therefore, we need to exercise the same constraints on our relation to the other members of the land community – soils, waters, plants and animals – as we do in our relation to other people.
4  Thus, the land ethic: a thing is right when it tends to preserve the integrity, stability and beauty of the biotic community. It is wrong when it tends otherwise.[4]

Following Leopold, Arne Næss continued the tradition of natural law environmental ethics in 'The Shallow and the Deep, Long-Range Ecology Movement' (1973). Here Næss set forth an argument for 'intrinsic value' as the root for human duties of respect toward the environment. Further, in 1979, Hans Jonas published *The Imperative of Responsibility*, arguing on clear natural law grounds that only an ethic grounded in the inherent intentionality of each organism's 'yes' to life could be strong enough to convince humanity to take actions necessary for environmental protection (Engel 2010: 35).

Following this tradition in environmental ethics, I contend that Berry's juridical writing and the legal categories he describes are most accurately articulated within a natural law framework. In particular, Berry's advocacy

4. This syllogism was formulated by Engel (2010: 35).

for ecocentric ideas becoming inherent to our idea of law and his recognition of 'higher laws' cannot be fully accommodated from within the constraints of legal positivism or any other self-referential concept of law. Further, following the reasoning of feminist theologian Carol Christ, I suggest that we should not simply abandon a negative word or concept. Rather, we should attempt to find new meaning in the term or else the 'the mind will revert back to familiar structures at times of crisis, bafflement or defeat' (Christ 1979: 275). Thus, while the Thomist natural law tradition has historically been used for anthropocentric and patriarchal goals, this paper attempts to employ its broad framework for ecocentric goals.

I turn now to articulate in more detail the legal categories proposed by Berry. Because Berry only left fragmentary comments about the content of these categories, I will interpret his analysis with reference to the writing of his intellectual mentor – St Thomas Aquinas. For reasons that I hope to demonstrate, I contend that this comparative reading of Berry provides the greatest insight into what he meant by 'Earth jurisprudence'. I also contend that a comparative reading most adequately situates Berry's writing in the intellectual context from which it emerged.

## 4.3 The legal categories of earth jurisprudence

In 1934 William Nathan Berry entered a Catholic monastery of the passionist order. On being ordained as a priest in 1942 he chose the name Thomas in honour of a Catholic priest in the Dominican order, Thomas Aquinas. The influence of Aquinas on Berry's intellectual development has been chronicled by many authors (Fox 2011: 16–31) and is acknowledged frequently by Berry himself (1999: vii). What has not yet been studied is the influence of Aquinas on Berry's legal writing. In this section, I illustrate that the framework of law developed by Aquinas – in particular, his regard for 'higher laws' – exerted a tremendous influence on the outline of Earth jurisprudence offered by Berry.

The natural law tradition represents the most significant jurisprudential legacy left by Aquinas and has inspired generations of neo-Thomist theorists (Bix 2004: 9). For Aquinas, the term 'law' has analogous application and does not have consistent meaning with each use (McInerny 1966: vi). His legal theory encompasses four types of law, organised in a hierarchy. At the apex is eternal law, which comprises God-given rules or divine providence, which govern all nature (McInerny 1966: ix). The second order is natural law, which is that portion of eternal law that one can discover through a special process of reasoning, involving intuition and deduction, outlined by Greek authors (Harris 2004: 8). Divine law refers to the law of God as revealed in scripture. Human law sits at the bottom of this ordering and consists of rules, supported by reason and articulated by lawmakers for the common good of human society.

Speaking to this ordering, Ralph McInerny (1956: vi) comments: '[t]o speak of God's governance of the universe as a "law" and of the guidelines we can discern in our nature as to what we ought to do as "laws" can puzzle us because what the term "law", principally means is a directive of our acts issued by "someone in authority". Nonetheless, it is clear from Aquinas' discussion in Question 90 of the *Summa Theologica* on the 'essence of law' that human positive law is at the forefront of his mind when using the term 'law' (McInerny 1998: 611). Indeed, in Question 90, article 4, Aquinas (1996: 10–11) defines law as 'nothing else than an ordinance of reason for the common good, made by him who has care of the community, and promulgated'. The relationship between Aquinas's hierarchy and that proposed by Earth jurisprudence is outlined in Table 4.1.

In a very basic way, Table 4.1 illustrates the structural relationship between Earth jurisprudence and Aquinas's theory of natural law. Both adopt a higher view of law and describe the consequences of contradicting their unique focus. The categories of eternal law and divine law are absent from this discussion. Aquinas (1996: 29) describes divine law as revelation revealed in Christian scripture. This reference point was deliberately absent from Berry's analysis[5] and is unnecessary for a secular description of Earth jurisprudence. For Aquinas, eternal law represents the source or foundation for the other types of law. He (1996: 46) describes eternal law in Question 93, article 4, as 'the very Idea of the government of things in God the Ruler of the Universe'. Put otherwise, it is the divine system of government, providence, the divine plan and the timeless universal order, which act as the measure for all other laws. Because of his religious background, one might reasonably inquire into whether Berry would have included reference to eternal law in a more detailed study of Earth jurisprudence. I think that there is some evidence in support of this point.[6] However, answering this question is beyond the scope of this chapter and unnecessary for the secular description of Earth jurisprudence that I wish to outline.

*Table 4.1* Natural law and Earth jurisprudence

| Natural law | Earth jurisprudence |
| --- | --- |
| Eternal law (providence) | n/a |
| Natural law | The great law |
| Divine law | n/a |
| Human law | Human law |

5. Berry (1996) argued: '[W]e need to put the Bible on the shelf for twenty years until we learn to read the scripture of life.' Berry (1999: 71) argued further that 'the only effective program available as our primary guide toward a viable human mode of being is the program offered by the Earth itself.'

6. Evidence for this possibility can be noted in Berry's (1988: 20) argument for recognising and acting in accord with the universal logos, which he regarded as 'the ultimate form of human wisdom'. The term 'logos' can be traced back to ancient Greece and the philosophy of Heraclitus. Heraclitus introduced the term logos to describe a similar immanent conception of divine intelligence and the rational principles governing the universe. Logos is relevant to the present discussion, because as Lloyd Weinreb (1987: 56) notes: 'Eternal Law is little more than a Christianised version of Logos and the Platonic vision of a universe ordered with a view to the excellence and preservation of the whole.'

### 4.3.1 The great law

In my interpretation of Earth jurisprudence, the great law represents the eco-logical conception of community articulated by Berry. More specifically, I interpret it to refer to human interconnectedness with nature and the eco-logical integrity of the Earth community. In this respect, the term 'nature' in Earth jurisprudence has a different focus to the way the term is interpreted in Thomist theories of natural law – in which 'nature' refers specifically to 'universal truths' that are derived from human reason.

In response, Berry (2006: 20) argues that human society should broaden its present focus from human beings to recognise the 'supremacy of the already existing Earth governance of the planet as a single, interconnected com-munity'. Berry (1999: 64) contends that an orientation toward the natural world should animate all human activities and upholds 'Earth' as our pri-mary teacher and lawgiver. Importantly, constructing this argument, Berry does not theorise 'nature' or the Earth community in a romantic or altruistic way.[7] Central to his analysis is the amoral status of nature and the fatal con-sequences that follow from transgressing ecological limits (Berry 1999: 4).

Cormac Cullinan's book *Wild Law* represents the first attempt to concretise Berry's writing in traditional legal form. Here Cullinan (2003: 84) describes the great law[8] broadly as 'laws or principles that govern how the universe functions' and notes that they are 'timeless and unified in the sense that they all have the same source'. This law is manifest in the universe itself and can be witnessed in the 'phenomenon of gravity', 'the alignment of the planets', the 'growth of planets' and the 'cycles of night and day' (Cullinan 2003: 84).

Cullinan is not alone in his desire to see human law confirm to so-called 'laws of nature'. Klaus Bosselmann (1995: 73) for example looks forward to the day when 'we may be able to bring the laws of society and the laws of nature into reconciliation.'[9] However, before continuing, it is important to pause and consider whether theorising Earth jurisprudence with reference to the 'laws of nature' is a practicable reference point for human law. Specifically, we need to inquire into exactly what is a 'law of nature'?

A careful investigation into the scientific literature reveals that there is a complete lack of agreement on this seemingly simple question (Armstrong 1983; Curd 1998: 805). In response, two mutually opposed philosophi-cal accounts have been developed. The first, termed *necessitarian*, contends that there are real necessities in nature, over and above the regularities that they allegedly produce and that law statements are descriptions of these

---

7. Note the fascinating critical literature on the use and abuse of the term 'nature' (Code 2006; Evernden 1992).
8. Cullinan (2003: 84) uses the term 'great jurisprudence' rather than great law. For reasons of clarity and consistency, I will use the latter term throughout.
9. See also Robinson (2010: 8): 'We are still far from realizing the objective of confirming human laws to the laws of nature.' See also Weston and Bach (2009).

necessities. The second account, *regularists*, posit that there are no necessities but only regularities – that is correlations and patterns – and that laws are descriptions of regularities (Curd 1998: 805).

Both philosophical accounts address four interrelated issues: (i) semantics of the meaning of law statements; (ii) metaphysical questions concerning the 'fact' to which law statements refer; (iii) epistemological questions pertaining to the basis on which claims of knowledge of a law are justified; and (iv) explanations of the various role of scientific laws (Hooker 2005: 550). In answering these questions, both philosophical accounts encounter distinct difficulties. C.A. Hooker (2005: 550) provides a pertinent example:

> [I]f there are necessities in nature, as the first account claims, how exactly do we identify them: how can we tell which of the inductively confirmed regularities are laws? On the other hand, if there are only regularities, as the second account claims, does this mean that our intuitions and scientific practices are awry and that there really is no distinction between laws and accidental generalizations?

Compounding the puzzles emphasised by this comment is the wide variety of laws supplied by current science and the complexity of the relationship between those laws, regularities and causes. Beyond this is a nagging uncertainty about the relevance of such laws to human law. How, for instance, can Newton's law of motion or Boyle's law of mass and pressure meaningfully assist in the drafting of legislation? Of what possible importance are they to an institution that seeks to govern human relationships and behaviour? Through what mechanism are certain laws prioritised over others? In response, I contend that even if agreement can be reached concerning what constitutes a law of nature, it is difficult to see how this broad focus can assist human lawmakers or jurisprudential questions related to our concept of law.

Rather than describing the great law with reference to universal laws of nature, I contend that the great law should be limited to ecological science and measured with respect to the concepts such as ecological integrity.[10] This approach seeks to strengthen the relationship between science and law by prescribing normative standards that are directly referable to verifiable information.

The term 'ecological integrity' emerged as an ethical concept as part of Aldo Leopold's classic 'land ethic' (1986) and has been recognised in legislative instruments such as the US Clean Water Act (1972).[11] Broadly, ecological

10. A version of this position is advanced by Andrew Kimbrell (2008: 5), who argues: '[W]e can now bolster the teleological tenets of Natural Law with the profound insights offered by modern ecology, effectively marrying Natural Law with the Law of Nature.' Alternatives have also been considered – see, for example, Maloney (2014), who measures the great law with reference to Rockström's (2009) concept of 'planetary boundaries'.
11. Section 101(a) has its objective 'to restore and maintain the chemical, physical, and biological integrity of the Nation's waters'.

integrity calls for a relational model of the global and the local, whereby the global is constituted by the unique character of each of its diverse member localities and the relationships they have to one another and to the Earth as a whole. So stated, ecological integrity provides the standard and base line for planetary civilization, at global, multilateral and local scales. It is descriptive of the fundamental character of a healthy and sustainable civilization and biosphere and it is prescriptive for the ethics and governance policies we need to adapt if we are to enter an ecocentric era.

As described by Laura Westra (2005: 574), the generic concept of integrity 'connotes a valuable whole, the state of being whole or undiminished, unimpaired, or in perfect condition'. Because of the extent of human exploitation of the environment, wild nature provides the paradigmatic example of ecological integrity.

Among the most important aspects of ecological integrity are, first, the autopoietic capacities of life to regenerate and evolve over time at a specific location (Swimme & Berry 1992: 75–77). Thus, integrity provides a place-based analysis of the evolutionary and biogeographical process of an ecosystem (Angermeier & Karr 1994). A second aspect concerns the requirements that are needed to maintain native ecosystems (Karr & Chu 1999). Climatic conditions and other biophysical phenomena can also be analysed as interconnected ecological systems. A third aspect is that ecological integrity is both 'valued and valuable as it bridges the concerns of science and public policy' (Westra 2000: 20). To bridge the chasm between science and public policy, models such as the multimetric Index of Biological Integrity allows scientists to provide an approximate description of the extent to which systems deviate from verifiable integrity levels calibrated from a baseline condition of wild nature (Karr 1996: 96). Degradation or loss of integrity is thus comprised of any human-induced positive or negative divergence from this baseline standard (Westra 2000: 21). Finally, if given appropriate legal status, 'ecological integrity' recognises the intrinsic value of ecosystems and can help curb the excess of human development and exploitation of nature.

Ecological integrity presents a threefold ethical demand; (i) the value of autonomy, the value of each entity and locality for itself; (ii) the value of relationality, the value of diverse entities and localities of the world for each other; and (iii) the value of global Earth community, the systemic value of the world as the objective totality of the activities and relationships of all entities and localities and as the necessary supportive matrix for all of them. If we are to achieve a relationship between the global and the local that claims and restores ecological integrity, we must act simultaneously at the local, multilateral and global scales.

My transition from the descriptive science of ecological integrity to the prescriptive language of ethical demands requires further unpacking. Indeed, the route from description to prescription is one of the most precarious paths in moral philosophy and any who so move will inevitably be accused of the 'naturalistic fallacy'.[12] David Hume (2002: 302) outlined this fallacy as follows:

> In every system of morality, which I have hitherto met with, I have always remark'd, that the author proceeds from some time in the ordinary way of reasoning, and established the being of a God, or makes observations concerning human affairs; when of a sudden I am surpriz'd to find, that instead of the usual copulations of propositions, *is*, and *is not*, I meet with no proposition that is not connected with an ought, or an ought not. This change is imperceptible, but is, however, of the last consequence. For as this *ought* or *ought not*, express some new relation or affirmation, 'tis necessary that it shou'd be observ'd and explain'd; and at the same time that a reason should be given, for what seems altogether inconceivable, how this new relation can be a deduction from others, which are entirely different from it.

In this passage, Hume is making a logical point – an assertion about the relationship between propositions. His intention is to deprive natural law philosophers of that 'most revered philosophical weapon' (Harris 2002: 13) the deductive syllogism.[13]

Since Hume, few would defend the following syllogism: (i) All of nature is interconnected; (ii) humans are part of nature; (iii) therefore humans *ought* to behave in a manner that recognises this interconnection. Here the conclusion contains a copula not contained in the premises, namely, 'ought'. While there might be hundreds of reasons for recognising and responding to this interconnection, logical deduction is not one of them. Peter Singer (1981: 79) explains this reasoning with reference to the ethics of self-preservation:

> [T]he fact that the bull is charging does not, by itself entail the recommendation: 'Run!' It is only against the background of my presumed desire to live that the recommendation follows. If I intend to commit suicide in a manner that my insurance company will think is an accident, no such recommendation applies.[14]

The same might also be said with reference to the environmental crisis. It does not *logically* follow from the fact that the world is teetering on the edge of ecological catastrophe that human beings ought to change their behaviour.

---

12. See also Attfield (1994: 127–134). Attfield notes at 128 that the fact/value gap in considering ecological principles might also be bridged by an implicit position such as 'you ought to preserve the integrity of the ecosystem.'
13. A syllogism is a logical argument comprising of three parts: (i) a major premise; (ii) a minor premise; and (iii) a conclusion.
14. For a partial critique of Singer, see Lyon (2011).

It is only against the background of our presumed desire to live in a safe and sustainable world that the recommendation follows.[15] Human survival is, after all, an option and not a predestined certainty.

To avoid the pitfalls of this argument, Earth jurisprudence seeks to take the first steps toward normative conclusions and to rely on human will and rationality to bridge the naturalistic fallacy. As Holmes Rolston III (1986: 15) contends, '[T]o break an ecological law means, then, to disregard its implications in regard to an antecedent moral ought.' This stance retains discretion and the lawmaking authority of human beings. However, it also seeks to provide 'reasons for action' to compel human beings to consciously align human law with the great law to ensure that ecological integrity is respected and ultimately protected.

### 4.3.2 Human law

In Question 90, article 4, Aquinas (1956: 10–11) defines human law as 'an ordinance of reason for the common good, made by him who has care of the community, and promulgated'.

The description of human law advanced in Earth jurisprudence shares many of these elements. For example, my description of Earth jurisprudence follows Aquinas in defining the common good, not with reference to a utilitarian calculus but with respect to the securing of conditions that tend to favour the health and future flourishing of a community.[16] However, two points of refinement need to be briefly outlined: (i) in Earth jurisprudence, the 'common good' is understood with reference to the wellbeing of the comprehensive Earth community and not simply its human component (Berry 2006: 149). While this view encourages human flourishing, it also limits the ambit of liberty to actions that are consistent with the flourishing of the Earth community. In this sense, Earth jurisprudence is intimately concerned with ecological integrity and the flourishing of the environment; and (ii) Aquinas' appeal to reason is supplemented by the use of scientific description. As articulated in Earth jurisprudence, acknowledging these standards in one's deliberations is part of what it means to be reasonable.

Drawing on these points, I define human law as being rules, supported by the great law, which are articulated by human authorities for the common good of the comprehensive whole. As indicated in the discussion earlier, this definition does not contradict the conceptual claims of legal positivism. Indeed, Earth jurisprudence retains the presumptive authority of human beings to make binding prescriptions for the community. Further,

---

15. The presumption toward human survival has been challenged by Freud (1989), who posited the existence of a 'death instinct' in human beings.
16. Note that Aquinas defined the common good in similar terms. The utilitarian description of natural law is exemplified in neo-Thomist writers such as John Finnis (1980: 193).

Earth jurisprudence does not contest the benefit of positive law in achieving social/common goods that require the deployment of state power or the co-ordination of public behaviour. The dividing line between Earth jurisprudence and legal positivism rests on several fine distinctions, which nonetheless carry theoretical significance.

The most obvious difference between Earth jurisprudence and positivism is the appeal to a 'higher law' that is ordered above human law. Further, Earth jurisprudence argues that human law ought to be described as a project with a purpose. This purposive description of law is consistent with that offered by Aquinas and secular natural law theorist Lon Fuller (1964: 53). Aquinas (1956: 6) for example comments in Question 90, article 2:

> [S]ince the law is chiefly ordained to the common good, any other precept in regard to some individual work, must needs be devoid of the nature of a law, save in so far as it regards the common good. Therefore every law is ordained to the common good.

This statement is supported by Fuller (1964: 123), who argues that the central purpose of law is human flourishing and for people to coexist and cooperate within society.[17] On this account, human law cannot truly be understood without understanding the ideal or 'common good' towards which it is striving. However, while natural law philosophy defines the parameters of community by exclusive reference to human beings (Finnis 1980: 134–161), the focus of Earth jurisprudence is on the comprehensive Earth community.

As noted in the introduction to this chapter, it is not clear that the purposive interpretation of human law advanced in Earth jurisprudence contradicts legal positivism in any way that positivists would wish to deny. Indeed, if notions of purpose and the common good form an important element of legal development, as is often admitted, then it is difficult to see the justification for taking an exclusive attitude (Freeman 2008: 50). As argued by Fuller (1956: 697), to exclude the ideal from a theory of law on the basis of a 'separation of description and evaluation' is to miss the point entirely. Certainly, the social practice and institution of law, 'is by its nature a striving towards' ideals such as the common good (Fuller 1956: 697).

From this perspective, legal authorities are not entirely free to create law without constraints. They must acknowledge and respond to factors that have consequence for law's purpose – the attainment of the comprehensive common good. To be clear, not every human law will be affected by this standard. For example, Earth jurisprudence does not have an obvious or direct relationship to criminal law or contract law. Further, unlike the Thomist tradition

---

17. Note that for Fuller the telos of law is order. This is in contrast to the Thomist and Neo-Thomist tradition, which is more concerned with the common good of human beings.

of natural law philosophy, Earth jurisprudence does not seek to enter broad ethical discourse and advance opinion on sexual preference or on matters concerning life and death. Instead, Earth jurisprudence is concerned primarily with matters concerning the environment and human–Earth interactions. It has obvious implications for property law, environmental law, planning law, natural resource management, and conservation heritage, to name a few. Furthermore, insofar as environmental degradation is linked to human exploitation, Earth jurisprudence has the potential to provide the jurisprudential foundation for human rights law (an area that has traditionally been defended on anthropocentric grounds).

Once one takes a purposive or functional approach to law, important consequences follow regarding laws that contravene this standard. These are considered in the next section, which argues that the great law acts as a standard for human law and as a measure for legal quality. Further, purported laws that are inconsistent with the great law are considered defective and not morally binding on a population. In this regard, Earth jurisprudence provides a legal justification for challenging the authority of law and engaging in civil disobedience.

## 4.4 The interaction between the great law and human law

So far, this chapter has outlined the legal categories great law and human law. It described great law with reference to the ecocentric principle of Earth community. Human law was described as rules passed by human authorities that are consistent with the great law and are enacted for the good of the Earth community as a whole. Regarding the interaction between these two categories of law, two points are discussed and analysed in this section. First, only prescriptions that are consistent with the great law and directed toward the comprehensive common good have the quality of law. Second, any purported law that is in conflict with the great law is regarded as defective or a mere corruption of law and not morally binding on a populace. In this instance, Earth jurisprudence provides a justification for civil disobedience. I consider these points in turn.

### 4.4.1 Legal quality

Earth jurisprudence requires human law to be articulated with reference to the great law. Cullinan (2003: 84–85) supports this interpretation, holding that the great law should be understood as being the 'design parameters within which those . . . engaged in developing Earth Jurisprudence for the human species must operate.' This approach requires lawmakers to respect the great law and to enact legislation that recognises the ecological integrity of the environment as a bedrock value and limit for human law. Because the great law requires interpretation, there are likely to be a range of rules that are consistent with the great law rather than one correct application. Further, the rules actually chosen by lawmakers need not coincide with the rules that specific individuals within that community would have chosen (Finnis 1980: 289). The community need not even regard the laws as sensible or desirable.[18] However, by advocating a necessary connection between human law and the great law, Earth jurisprudence seeks to ensure that environmental ideas are not imposed from the outside in an ad hoc or limited way. Instead, the great law is inherent to our concept of law and provides an immediate measure of legal quality.

In one of his final essays, Berry (2003: 13–14) outlined how his expanded understanding of community could set the design parameters for human law. He argued that the prologue of national constitutions should begin by recognising that human existence and wellbeing is 'dependent on the well-being of the larger Earth community' and that 'care of this larger Earth community is a primary obligation of the nation being founded.'

These comments recognise the critical role of primary governance documents for implementing the broad changes required by Earth jurisprudence. They are also consistent with other proposals for an eco-constitutional state (Eckersley 2004), the recognition of the rights of nature in national constitutions (Burdon 2010b; Weston & Bollier 2013: 57–67) and attempts in international law to formulate a covenant for ecological governance (Engel 2010; Engel & Mackey 2011).

Today, the most significant political movement that is advocating radical changes to human governance mechanisms is the Project for Earth Democracy (Shiva 2005).[19] Distilled to a sentence – the project is an attempt to fuse ecocentric ethics with deeper forms of democracy and public participation (Burdon 2013a). This orientation is explicitly antagonistic to the existing state–capitalist governance structure that dominates much of the world.[20] According to Bosselmann (2010: 103), Earth democracy 'requires a shift from economics to ecology realizing their common ground i.e. the

18. For example, the rule might place limits on economic growth.
19. Many ecological writers are not prepared or sufficiently interested to engage in a principled discussion of democratic theory. For example, Arne Næss, who took leave from the University of Oslo to work with Richard McKeon on the UNESCO study of democracy, found over 315 meanings of democracy in Western history. As a result, he describes democracy as arbitrary and meaning whatever people want it to mean (Næss et al. 1956).
20. Berry (1999: 132) was profoundly concerned by how states have been eclipsed by transnational corporations: 'The nation-states have become subservient to the economic corporations. The corporations now function on a scale beyond any national boundaries. They have drawn the entire Earth into their control. The globalization of the human project as well as the globalization of the Earth economy is now reaching limits that will define the future in a new and decisive manner, for beyond the Earth no further expansion is possible in any effective manner.'

Earth our home'. Existing forms of governance were designed and exist to promote human wellbeing and economic growth. Under this structure, environmental governance is a small concern or an 'add-on or a minimalist, shallow program . . . the poor cousin of economic governance' (Bosselmann 2010: 103).

The Project for Earth Democracy maintains that decisions made by the collective via participatory democracy will reflect both community and ecological interests better than decisions made by corporate executives or by members of parliament operating within existing state–capitalist structures (Burdon 2013a). Properly conceived, democracy is about securing the conditions that make it possible for ordinary people to better their lives by becoming political beings or what Bosselmann (2010: 105) calls ecological citizens. What is at stake is whether citizens can become empowered to recognise that their concerns are best addressed and protected under a governance structure governed by principles of commonality, ecological integrity, equality and fairness; a governance model in which taking part in politics becomes a way of staking out and sharing in a common life and cultivating a deep respect and relationship with the broader Earth community.

The principles just stated conform to what Ron Engel (2010: 28) calls a 'thick interpretation of the democratic ideal'.[21] According to Engel, the long tradition of natural law and natural rights and their evolving metaphysical foundations have characteristically provided the philosophical and ethical grounding for what he calls the 'democratic way of life'. Far from being free-standing or historically contingent, Engel (2010: 29) argues that the central driving purpose or ideal of democratic governance is 'true, authentic, real' because it is a 'universal experience, grounded in human nature and in the creativity that drives the cosmos'. According to this perspective, the moral ends of human action are grounded in the constitution of nature itself, so that contrary to the aforementioned 'naturalistic fallacy' it is possible for a rigorous and rational analysis of human experience to derive what 'ought' to be from what 'is' or as Rolston III (1986: 12–29) argues, to 'discover them together'. Alfred North Whitehead (1938: 151) described the essence of natural law account of democracy well when he wrote:

> The basis of democracy is the common fact of value-experience, as constituting the essential nature of each pulsation of actuality. Everything has some value for itself, for others, and for the whole. This characterizes the meaning of actuality. By reason of this character, constituting reality, the conception of morals arises. We have no right to deface the value-experience which is the very essence of the universe.

---

21. These interpretations, by contrast, include what is variously called 'procedural democracy', 'liberal democracy' or simply the 'democratic process' (Engel 2010: 28).

Arguably, the most sophisticated articulation of Earth democracy is the International Earth Charter.[22] And yet it is clear that Berry and other proponents of Earth jurisprudence are advancing a theoretical argument that cannot be contained within a positive law or civil society document. Indeed, Earth jurisprudence claims that the great law is prior to state law and that it cannot be created or revoked by human beings. Moreover, even if the great law is unrecognised or repressed by the state, it exists as an unofficial law and is recognised informally by many people in society. In this sense, the great law is a source of moral legitimacy and power in its own right.

This point about the multiple forms of law has been recently theorised by Weston and Bollier (2013). The authors (2013: 111 fn 126) critique Cullinan's interpretation of Earth jurisprudence (or wild law) on that grounds that it is 'too tied' to 'Austinian positivism that insists that law, to be law, requires the apparatus of the state, everything else being merely "positive morality"'. Rather than bind themselves to the formalities of positive law and state sanctioned governance structures, Weston and Bollier advocate the concept of 'vernacular law'.[23] They also recognise that their use of the term 'vernacular law' approximates Cullinan's description of wild law (2013: 111).

The term 'vernacular law' is an umbrella concept that captures the realm of unofficial law emanating from people's everyday perspectives and social interactions. It captures ideas such as 'informal', 'customary', 'grassroots', 'indigenous', 'common' and 'local law'. More specifically, Weston (1976: 117) contends that vernacular law is a socially based law that emerges from peoples 'pushing and pulling through reciprocal claim and mutual tolerance in daily competition for power, wealth, respect and other cherished values'. While most legal philosophers would describe this process in terms of social norms rather than law,[24] Weston and Bollier (2013: 33) justify their use of the term on the basis that 'law does not live by executives, legislators and judges alone.' An emphasis on the state as the centrepiece of law misdirects our attention from the full meaning and realm of law. Reismann (1999: 3) explains: 'The law of the state may be important, but law, real law, is found in all human relations, from the simplest, briefest encounter between two people to the most inclusive and permanent type of interaction.'

Alongside the great law, there are many other variants of vernacular law. It exists in the 'horizontal and voluntarist' sphere of international law and in the

---

22. Douglas Sturm (2000) proposes that the Earth Charter is a summons to a new ecocentric era, when the vision of the sacredness of human life and a universal human community is incorporated into the vision of an even more comprehensive universal community that encapsulates the community of life. Engel (2014) provides a powerful critique of the Earth Charter for moving away from the natural law traditional and revolutionary principles such as equality.

23. See also the survey of customary law provided by Renteln (1995), and Reismann (1999), who adopts the term 'microlaw'.

24. H.L.A. Hart (1961), for example, would decry this description on the basis that there is no union of primary and secondary rules.

'vertical and compulsory national legal orders' where codes of conduct and behaviour regulate many aspects of social life – church cannons and sports rules are obvious examples (Weston & Bollier 2013: 33). While unofficial in the eyes of the centralised state, these variants of law provide a critical process for testing the legitimacy of state law and also for reforming it to meet new social and ecological needs. Commenting on this point Weston and Bollier (2013: 107) contend that 'from time to time, when the State and/or its State Law fails to meet the needs, wants, and expectations of the peoples whom they are supposed to serve, then . . . "microlegal adjustments" [e.g. assertions of vernacular law] may be the necessary instruments of change.'

One clear example of this was the Great Charter of Magna Carta, which was forced on King John of England in 1215 in response to his ruinous foreign policy and tyrannical rule (Linebaugh 2009; Weston & Bollier 2013: 107–108). Yet, assertions of vernacular law need not be so dramatic. With respect to the great law, one pertinent example can be noted in 2007 when former vice president of the United States Al Gore stated: 'I can't understand why there aren't rings of young people blocking bulldozers, and preventing them from constructing coal-fired power plants' (Leonard 2007). These comments were followed in a 2008 address to the Clinton Global Initiative: 'If you're a young person looking at the future of this planet and looking at what is being done right now, and not done, I believe we have reached the state where it is time for civil disobedience to prevent the construction of new coal plants that do not have carbon capture and sequestration' (Nichols 2008).

In the example raised by Gore, we can presume that the proponent in question has applied for and received the relevant legal permits and licenses to carry out construction of a coal plant. Consistent with other large-scale projects, there has likely been some form of community consultation, opportunity for public comment and negotiation with stakeholders. However, because of the known ecological damage caused by coal-fired power plants and the risk they pose to the long-term common good, Gore questions the legitimacy of the project. More than this, he expresses his dismay that individuals are not positively breaking the law to stop the development.

To understand these comments it is useful to refer once more to the natural law tradition. From this perspective, it is possible to interpret Gore's statements in (at least) three different ways. First, as saying that the law authorising the construction of a coal fired power plant has the potential to cause such great harm to the Earth community that there is no *moral* obligation to obey that law.[25] Second, that the law in question is not *legally valid* or that there is

---

25. While this is a legitimate interpretation of Gore's statement, it says nothing about the nature of law. It is also contrary to the goal of Earth jurisprudence, which is to recognise the great law as integral to law. Other adherents to natural law philosophy would similarly reject this 'moral reading', on the basis that it trivialises the natural law perspective. As Murphy (2006: 10) observes, interpreting natural law as a claim about the justifiability of disobeying unjust laws, 'is excruciatingly uninteresting, a claim that almost everyone in the history of moral and political philosophy has accepted, and thus is not much worth discussing'.

no law at all. Finally, that the law is legally valid but that it is not law in the *true* sense of the word. That is, because the law is strongly contrary to ecological integrity, it is *defective as law*. Mark C. Murphy (2007: 44) elaborates on the use of the term 'defective':

> To say that something is defective is to say that it belongs to a certain kind and there are certain standards of perfection that are internal to it (that are intrinsic to it, that necessarily belong to) members of that kind. To be an alarm clock just is, in part, to be the sort of thing that if it cannot sound an alarm when one wishes to be awakened, it is defective. But something can be an alarm clock even if it cannot sound an alarm: it might be broken, or poorly constructed, or whatever.

According to the third interpretation of Gore's statement, law has certain standards that are internal to it and a failure to meet these standards renders a purported law defective. Consistent with the purposive description of human law detailed earlier, I consider this third interpretation to be most consistent with Berry's philosophical worldview. From this perspective, Earth jurisprudence advocates a particular methodological approach. It suggests that theorising about law should not be a neutral exercise that fails to have appropriate regard for the common good of the comprehensive Earth community. Moreover, when human law diverges from the great law, the latter can be used (like other variations of vernacular law) as a 'vital wellspring for making State Law more responsive' to human and ecological needs (Weston & Bollier 2013: 33, 106). This function inevitably raises issues concerned with civil disobedience, which I turn now to consider.

### 4.4.2 Corruptions and civil disobedience

As detailed in the previous section, Earth jurisprudence maintains that human laws that are inconsistent with the great law are defective and are not morally binding by virtue of their own legal quality. This gives rise to issues concerning the authority of law and civil disobedience (Bedau 1991; Wellmann & Simmons 2005). Consistent with the description of social movements given in Chapter 3, I define civil disobedience conservatively as a public, non-violent, conscientious yet political act contrary to law that is conducted with the aim of bringing about a change in the law or in the policies of government (Rawls 1999: 320). As should be clear from the previous sections, I do not believe that citizens have an automatic obligation to obey the law (Singer 1973: 3).[26] Rather, as ecological citizens, our fidelity to law arises from the consistency between human law and the great law. Describing human law in this way removes the self-validating nature of legal positivism (Berry 2003: 13) and

26. For an alternative position, see Green (1907).

considers the good of the Earth community as integral to the authority of law to bind a population in conscience.

Among the objections to describing legal authority as contingent, are appeals to avoiding bad example, civil disturbance or the weakening of an otherwise just legal system (Green 1907; Singer 1973: 105–132). Natural law writers such as Aquinas (1981: 356) adopted this position and argued that an unjust law ought to be obeyed in circumstances such as taxation or to 'avoid scandal'. This objection can also be stated in consequentialist terms whereby one is asked to consider the potentially negative consequences that may follow for a society in which people disobey the law. Thomas Hobbes (1999: 143) represents the classical source for this proposition, arguing that 'perpetual war of every man against his neighbour' was the condition of a lawless society. Finnis (1980: 356) makes this argument in terms of 'collateral obligation':

> It may be the case, for example, that if I am seen by fellow citizens to be disobeying or disregarding this 'law', the effectiveness of other laws, and/ or the general respect of citizens for the authority of a generally desirable ruler or Constitution, will probably be weakened, with probable bad consequences for the common good. Does not this collateral fact create a moral obligation?

Such arguments of principle tend to ignore empirical evidence, which suggests that actual examples of concerted civil disobedience do not produce a weakening of bonds to comply with other legislation (Dworkin 1968: 14; Singer 1973: 136–147). Instead, civil disobedience tends to be targeted and focused rather than indiscriminate and violent (Singer 1973: 136–147). Far from weakening a democratic state, political protest is a basic human right and a hallmark of a functioning democracy (Burdon 2012b). Political protest is also an important part of ensuring the accountability of those in power and is justified by the role it plays in bringing publicity to or perhaps a fair hearing of a particular issue Russell 1969: 141–142. Civil disobedience may also provide a method for compelling lawmakers to reconsider a purported law (Singer 1973: 84).

In the context of Earth jurisprudence, it may be the case that a lawmaker may act or fail to act with regard to the consequences that a purported law might have for the common good of the Earth community. A recent example of this is the controversy surrounding the approval process of the Keystone pipeline in the United States that seeks to transport oil from the Athabasca oil sands region in northeastern Alberta, Canada, to the Gulf Coast of Texas. In this example, civil disobedience that aims to make lawmakers reconsider their actions is a potential method for realising environmental goals and aligning human law with the great law. Further, in jurisdictions that provide discretion for prosecutors, the test of legal quality advocated by Earth jurisprudence may be used to guide those responsible for implementing the law concerning when protests ought to be tolerated – both morally and pragmatically (Dworkin 1968: 14; Fairweather 1999: 108–112).

A purported law that is inconsistent with the great law may, depending on the specific circumstances, be so serious that civil disobedience is justified regardless of the consequences to government. The justification for this position is tied to the primacy of the Earth community in the theory of Earth jurisprudence. Indeed, if a purported law is so insensitive to the great law that it places the lives of human beings and other components of the Earth community in jeopardy, it is difficult to see the rationale for privileging the maintenance of a human political institution. Weston and Bollier (2013: 109) support this point, asserting that '[R]evolutions often occur precisely because State Law refuses to make necessary accommodations with Vernacular Law.'

It is not difficult to take this abstract statement and apply it to instances of the present environmental crisis outlined in the introduction to this book. If governments fail to take necessary action to prevent runaway climate change or continue to approve industrial practices that degrade ecosystem or species biodiversity, then on what grounds is their own authority assured? Further, could the actions of protestors who resist government action/inaction be considered morally legitimate and not deserving of punishment? Certainly, these are complex questions and deserving of more attention than can be allocated in this chapter.[27] However, at its base Earth jurisprudence maintains that we must question the value and legitimacy of any law that surpasses the ecological limits of the environment to satisfy the needs of one species. Such an action is unsustainable and risks the common good and future flourishing of the interconnected Earth community.

## 4.5 Conclusion

In this chapter, I offered an interpretation of the concept of law presented in Earth jurisprudence. I also undertook analytical investigation into its legal categories and considered how they interact with each other. It was my intention to ground my exposition in the juridical writing of Berry and also extend his contribution with reference to more orthodox jurisprudence.

I began by describing Earth jurisprudence as a theory of natural law. Drawing on Berry, I posited the existence of two kinds of 'law', organised in a hierarchy. At the apex is the great law, which represents the principle of Earth community. Below the great law is human law, which represents

---

27. I acknowledge that the application of this reasoning to 'hard cases' is likely to be subject to considerable debate. Indeed, whether in a particular case our presumed obligation to obey the law can be outweighed is not something that can be determined in the abstract. As Singer (1973: 64) comments: 'to expect any work of theory to give answers to such questions is to expect more than theory alone can give.'

rules articulated by human authorities that are consistent with the great law and enacted for the common good of the comprehensive Earth community. Human law was also described as purposive rather than neutral or value free. The stated purpose of human law is to secure conditions that favour the health and future flourishing of the Earth community. On this account, human law cannot truly be understood without reference to the ideal or common good toward which it is striving.

Regarding the interaction between legal categories, I argued that human law derives its legal quality from the great law. Further, that a purported law that is in conflict with the great law is defective and not morally binding on a populace. Defective laws, while still enforceable by the state, are considered not 'true' laws or as law 'in the fullest sense'. Earth jurisprudence does not seek to invalidate human law. Rather, it provides a rational basis for the activities of legislators and a guide to deciding whether one has a moral obligation to obey. Purported laws that neglect or contravene this standard can (in theory) provide a justification for civil disobedience. Civil disobedience can further be justified because of the role it can play in bringing publicity or a fair hearing to an issue and also as a means of encouraging lawmakers to amend a defective law.

Having outlined a theory of Earth jurisprudence, I return full circle to the concept of private property outlined in Chapter 2. As discussed, the dominant or orthodox contemporary description of private property reflects an outdated and environmentally harmful anthropocentric paradigm. Recognising the foundational role that legal philosophy plays in the development of legal concepts, Chapter 5 presents an ecocentric theory of private property that is consistent with the philosophy of Earth jurisprudence.

# Chapter 5

# Private property revisited

## 5.1 Introduction

Earth jurisprudence is an ecocentric theory of law that seeks to reflect contemporary ontology, metaphysics and science. Unlike orthodox legal theories, Earth jurisprudence is founded in the premise that human beings are one part of a broader Earth community. It also argues that situating human laws within the physical context of the Earth's system enhances the health and future flourishing of this comprehensive community. To this end, Earth jurisprudence links human law to a 'higher' great law. It also argues that human law is purposive and ought to be directed toward the common good of the entire Earth community and not just human or corporate interests. According to this interpretation of Earth jurisprudence, ecocentric ethics are inherent to law and not something imposed externally by legislators in an ad hoc or limited way.

In this chapter, I build on this discussion to present an alternative description of private property that is consistent with the philosophy of Earth jurisprudence. In the first part of the chapter, I consider a critique put forward by some advocates of Earth jurisprudence (as well as many eco-socialists) that private property is inconsistent with ecocentric ethics and ought to be discarded as a social institution. While sympathetic to this argument and their goals for extending the reach of common property systems, I contend that a more nuanced understanding of private property is required – one that articulates its benefits and also acknowledges the possibility of internally restructuring the institution.

To this end, I present a reformist agenda that seeks to give private property radically new content. My approach draws on the indeterminate description of private property advanced in Chapter 2. As noted, private property is not a static or fixed concept – it is an evolving social institution. The contemporary liberal statement describes private property as a bundle of rights, liabilities, powers and duties (Honoré 1961: 107). According to this view, private property is not a single, determinate right and different 'sticks' within the bundle can be added or removed to serve different ends. Thus, while the current bundle of sticks reflects anthropocentric values, I contend that the bundle can be reconciled with the great law.

To this end, I describe private property as a *relationship* between members of the Earth community, through tangible or intangible items. To be consistent with the philosophy of Earth jurisprudence, I contend that the concept of private property must be reconceptualised to respond to three interconnected factors.

First, that private property is a human constructed social institution that is *limited* by government and community norms. This analysis reconceptualises the notion of autonomy, moving it from individualism towards being fully understood as socially situated and argues that property rights ought to be rendered contingent on their impact on others within the community. Second, that *nonreciprocal obligations and responsibilities* are inherent to the concept of private property. The existence of such duties arise in response to the concept of Earth community and because of the ability human beings have to cause great devastation to nature. Third, that private property should *respond* directly to the 'thing' itself that is the subject matter of a private property relationship. Put otherwise, private property needs to be understood as a human relationship that is *facilitated* by a specific item with unique attributes. Conceived in this way, the object of a property relationship plays a key role in shaping the types of use rights and responsibilities that attach to private property.

Taken together, I contend that these three conceptual shifts would redirect landownership from the current right-based framework described in Chapter 2 to an unfolding practice that adapts to place and treats nature as a subject rather than an object. I conclude this section with the contention that a theory of private property that overlooks any of these three considerations is defective according to the philosophy of Earth jurisprudence and, therefore, not morally binding on a populace

## 5.2 Contested terrain

Some advocates for Earth jurisprudence have argued that private property is incompatible with any transition toward an ecocentric paradigm (Cullinan 2003: 169–170; Fitz-Henry 2011; Linzey 2005). For this transition to be successful, they argue, private property needs to be abolished as social institution and nature recognised as having personhood. The abolition of private property would mark the final liberation of nature and free it from its shackles in precisely the same way that African American slaves were liberated from their bonds. Even alternative allocation and distribution mechanisms such as common property are sometimes seen as antithetical to this goal. Thomas Linzey (2011), for example, warns against building an 'environmental movement by regulating how common property is used' rather than 'envisioning a system in which ecosystems have independent interests of their own'.

A variation of this argument is also made amongst eco-socialists who oppose private ownership over the means of production (Foster 2007; Kovel 2007). A classic source for this perspective is the anarchist writer Pierre-Joseph Proudhon (1970) who remarked that 'property is theft' and held that it lends itself to abuse and exploitation. Eco-socialists also draw on Marx, beginning with his 'Economic and Philosophic Manuscripts'. In this text, Marx describes the transition from private property to 'association'. The abolition of the monopoly of private property in land, Marx (1975b: 320) argues would be realised through 'association' which when applied to the land:

> [R]etains the benefits of large landed property from an economic point of view and realizes for the first time the tendency inherent in the division of land, namely equality. At the same time association restores man's intimate links to the land in a rational way, no longer mediated by serfdom, lordship and an imbecile mystique of property. This is because the earth ceases to be an object of barter, and through free labor and free enjoyment once again becomes an authentic, personal property for man.

For Marx, communism was nothing other than the positive abolition of private property by means of association. Such positive communism 'as fully developed naturalism, equals humanism, and as fully developed humanism, equals naturalism; it is the genuine resolution of the conflict between man and nature, and between man and man, the true resolution of the conflict between existence and being, between freedom and necessity, between individual and species' (1975b: 348–349). This resolution exists only for associated or 'fully social' human beings. Marx argues further that society under communism, no longer alienated by the institution of private property is the 'perfected unity in essence of man with nature, the true resurrection of nature, the realized naturalism of man and the realized humanism of nature' (1975b: 349).

For Marx, advocacy for the abolition of private property pertained chiefly to agricultural land and over the means of production, i.e. factories and industry. He writes that 'the distinguishing feature of Communism is not the abolition of property generally, but the abolition of bourgeois property' (2008: 18). Such areas were to be owned collectively in association with others[1] and organised for the common good of the human community. Further, as mentioned in Chapter 2, one can also detect a minor thread in Marx that

---

1. I use the term 'organised' to distinguish a common property system with the 'open access' or unregulated property system that Garrett Hardin (1968) imagines in his influential essay 'The Tragedy of the Commons'. For a critique of Hardin, see Freyfogle (2003a: 157–178), Linebaugh (2009: 27) and Patel (2010: 91–110).

recognises the contradiction between private property and ecological sustainability. Marx (1993: 911) writes:

> From the standpoint of a higher socio-economic formation, the private property of particular individuals in the earth will appear just as absurd as the private property of one man in other men. Even the entire society, a nation, or all simultaneously existing societies taken together, are not owners of the earth. They are simply its possessors, its beneficiaries, and have to bequeath it in an improved state to succeeding generations, as *boni partes familias* [good heads of the household].

I am deeply sympathetic to this critique and its advocacy of common property. Similarly strong statements for common property have also been made by a variety of thinkers including the Nobel Prize-winning economist Eleanor Ostrom (1990), the historian Peter Linebaugh (2009), the political scientist Silvia Federici (2012) and the legal scholars Burns Weston and David Bollier (2013).

However, while I support the significant expansion of common property and polycentric governance mechanisms (Burdon 2013a), I also contend that the institution of private property is never going to be completely abolished. This is true even if the environment is recognised as having legal rights. Indeed, I contend that some advocates of Earth jurisprudence exaggerate the analogy between liberating slaves and liberating the environment from the institution of property. Human beings will always need to access nature and will thus require a legal and conceptual apparatus that explains that use and its relationship to the rest of the ecological community. In other words, some concept that fulfils the functions of private property (whether it is called that or not) will always be required.

Further, I contend that many of those who advocate for the total abolition of private property often neglect to articulate the benefits of the institution or theorise its role within a genuinely mixed property system (Cole 2002: 45–46). Moreover, many fail to consider the potential of legally restructuring private property for ecological goals. This has resulted in a premature and perhaps counter-productive advocacy for the abolition of private property. I consider each of these points in turn.

### 5.2.1 Private property and the ecology of place

Private property is built into the cultural fabric of Western culture. Joseph William Singer (2000: 1) notes: 'At the start of the twenty-first century, faith in private property as a mode of economic organization is as strong as it has ever been.' Under a capitalist mode of production, private property is the key legal institution that represents the commodification of the environment and facilitates its use and exploitation. As noted already, this has led some advocates of Earth jurisprudence to advocate for the abandonment of private property as an organising idea. However, before investigating how private property might be reconceptualised to reflect the great law, I wish to highlight the potential for private property to facilitate an intergenerational relationship with place.

Arguably, the most important writer on the relationship between property and place is the farmer and author Wendell Berry. Berry's short stories are all set in a fictionalised version of his hometown in Kentucky, in the United States. The most pertinent for present purpose is his story 'The Boundary' (2005: 75; Freytogle 1998: 79). Here Berry writes about the life of agrarian farmer, Mat Feltner. Feltner is portrayed as an honourable man who has enjoyed a long life in relationship with his demanding farm and lively community. At the beginning of the story, a weak Feltner gets the urge to inspect the barbed fence that surrounds his land. He worries that the fence might have fallen into disrepair and that the younger men might have been too busy with the upcoming harvest to make necessary repairs. As Feltner walks along the boundary to his land, he reflects on what the farm has meant to him over eight decades. He also thinks about those who came before him and the young people who will take over the farm after he is gone. At one point in the story, Feltner recalls accompanying his father and the work crew to install the wire fence. He also recalls leading his own son and a different work crew to make repairs. The two scenes merge and draw attention to how constant and similar life on the farm has been across generations. Checking the fence, Feltner soon realises that recent repairs had been made to the fence. The repairs were done with the same care and attention that Feltner or his father would have made them. Spurred on by these thoughts, Feltner continues to walk the boundary and comes to a place where he has trouble walking further. Rather than giving up, 'he chooses the difficult familiar way' (2005: 95). He is not ready to cross another boundary – the boundary into death.

As the day wears on, Feltner thinks about his loving wife Margaret and of the young men at work in the field. So familiar are their lives that the members of his community give rise to something greater than they are as isolated individuals. The land is part of them and they are part of it – there is a unity. Although tired, Feltner presses on:

> A shadowless love moves him now, not his, but a love that he belongs to, as he belongs to the place, and to the light over it. He is thinking of Margaret and of all that his plighting with her has led to. He is thinking of the members of the fields that he has belonged to all his life, and will belong to while he breathes, and afterward. He is thinking of the living ones of that membership – at work in the fields and that the dead were at work in before them. (2005: 96–96)

Reaching the crest, Feltner leans against an old walnut tree that 'stands alone outside the woods' (2005: 98). We are encouraged to reflect on just how like the old tree Feltner has become. They share a history and have both come to rest in the same spot. Just as the walnut tree has relinquished its seeds, so Feltner has given freely of himself, nourishing the land and giving rise to new life. Like the trees, Feltner has sunk deep roots and as the tree, so Feltner will die and become one again with the soil. At this point, Feltner is found and taken home by the young men who have finished work for the day.

Fundamentally, 'The Boundary' is a story about human association or relationship with place. The boundary fence provides the setting from which Berry explores lessons about property ethics and the good ways in which people and the land can come together. The fence marks not only the boundary of Feltner's farm, but also the boundary of his life. In association with this farm, the Feltner family have mixed generations of hard labour. They have grown together and become attentive to its many limits – its slopes, fragile soils and springs. Bounded to it, Feltner has forsaken all other lands and learned how to make it yield for the mutual benefit of the human and ecological community.

In 'The Boundary', Berry gives us a view of private property rarely seen in contemporary writing. For Feltner, boundaries can also offer positive virtues.[2] They mark out lines of responsibility. They allow for a special intergenerational bond between owner and soil. They nourish a sense of community and place across generations, fostering greater attention to those who will inherit the land and make a living from its productivity (Freytogle 1998: 79). A vital element of this continuity is the preserving of particular knowledge about a place that cannot be transported across location – as a dephysicalised conception of property would suggest. Indeed, over the decades Feltner learned to respect his farm and has also added to that vital fund of knowledge for future generations (Freytogle 1998: 79).

Feltner's informal concept of private property is obviously very different to the liberal 'ownership model' that I described in Chapter 2. Indeed, because the liberal theory of private property seeks to maximise individual choice, property owners and communities also have the freedom to adopt a more ecologically sensitive idea of private property. Once adopted, these informal or unofficial conceptions of private property represent a kind of 'vernacular law' (Weston & Bollier 2013: 104) and they highlight not only the flexibility of property but also its potential for producing positive outcomes for the Earth community. I now develop this argument further and consider how private property may be reformed to align with the great law.

### 5.2.2 The indeterminacy of private property

Private property is a dynamic social construct that is shaped by economic, legal, religious and philosophical factors. As C. Edwin Baker (1986: 744)

---

2. A fact that is sometimes exploited by advocates for the wholesale reduction of the environment to private property (Epstein 1985).

observes: 'Property rights are a cultural creation and a legal conclusion.' From this perspective, the concept of private property is indeterminate and lacks an objective and stable unitary structure that can be discovered through empirical analysis or logical deduction (Waldron 1988: 47–53).

The indeterminacy of property was illustrated with the historical narrative presented in Chapter 2. Seen from the perspective of four distinct points in history (antiquity, the scientific revolution, the Industrial Revolution and contemporary political philosophy), it was possible to observe how the concept of property has changed and adapted over time. This narrative finished with the contemporary and orthodox Hohfeld-Honoré conception of property. Yet even this sophisticated description is not fixed. While Honoré listed 11 standard incidents of ownership (1961: 161), he never claimed that his arrangement was the final word.

Even working within his framework, private property can take the shape of many different bundles of rights and duties and can even be fragmented into isolated incidents. As Tony Arnold (2002: 52) observes: 'The list is more an attempt at explanation than at codification of the incidents of property, and is clearly subject to substantial interpretation.' Furthermore, the incidents themselves are open to interpretation, making the articulation of an objective concept of private property all the more distant.

Drawing on the theory of law proposed in Earth jurisprudence, I will now attempt to develop the internal aspects of private property to align with the great law. Critical jurist, Roberto Unger (1986: 114), would describe this approach as giving private property 'internal development' or 'revolutionary form', and he has argued forcefully that this can bring about significant structural change – not just reformist tinkering – given the political will (Unger 1986: 114). Proceeding on that basis, I offer an ecological description of private property that conceives of the institution as a relationship between and among members of the Earth community through tangible or intangible items. This statement is incorporated into the following working definition:

> Private Property is a *human institution* that comprises a variety of *relationships* among members of the *Earth community, through* tangible or intangible items. For human beings, it is characterised by the allocation to individuals or groups of individuals of a degree of control over the use, alienation and exclusivity of scarce resources, as well as a measure of *obligation and responsibility* to all members of the Earth community in the exercise of the property right.[3]

Certainly, Thomas Berry (1999: 62) had something like this in mind, when in discussing what legal changes would be required to establish a viable human

---

3. This statement does not argue that non-human nature also carries obligations and responsibilities toward human beings or other parts of the Earth community. On this issue, see Rolston III (1993: 251).

presence on Earth he noted: 'The basic elements of personal security and personal property would be protected, although the sense of ownership would be a limited personal relation to property, which would demand use according to the well-being of the property and the well-being of the community, along with the well-being of the individual owner.'[4]

This perspective on private property has important consequences that are explored in this chapter. Due to space constraints, I have once again limited the discussion to real property or land law rather than intangible and personal property. I argue that private property ought to be limited by human social relationships, contain inherent and nonreciprocal obligations and responsibilities and bring some focus to bear on the item that is the subject matter of a property relationship.[5] While separated for the purpose of conceptual analysis, in reality each of these components is fundamentally related and integral to the ecocentric description of private property presented in this chapter.

## 5.3 Private property and human relationships

> Property rights are, by nature, social rights; they embody how we, as a society, have chosen to reward the claims of some people to finite and critical goods, and to deny the claims to the same goods by others. Try as we might to separate this right from choice, conflict, and vexing social questions, it cannot be done. (Underkuffler-Freund 1996: 1046)

Private property is a human institution and people will decide what the institution means and how it will be reflected in either positive or vernacular law. For this reason, an important consideration for private property is how it relates to human beings and communities. To be consistent with the concept of law proposed by Earth jurisprudence, I contend that private property must be characterised not in terms of individual rights, but as a social relationship. To paraphrase Jennifer Nedelsky (2013: 25), this perspective represents a shift from 'habits of individualistic thought' to 'habits of relational thought'.

The American legal realists provided the first sophisticated elucidation of the social or community aspect of property. Morris Cohen (1927: 16) for example, argued that 'it would be as absurd to argue that the distribution of property must never be modified by law as it would be to argue that the distribution of political power must never be changed.' He went on to argue that private property creates a legal relationship between the person holding

---

4. Berry (2006: 151) also recognises the importance of some mediated property relationships in his '10 Principles for Jurisprudence Revision': 'In a special manner, humans have not only a need for but also a right of access to the natural world to provide for the physical needs of humans and the wonder needed by human intelligence, the beauty needed by human imagination, and the intimacy needed by human emotions for personal fulfillment.'

5. This demarcation follows the analysis of good land use advocated by Freyfogle (2006: 144–157). For further analysis of agrarian land use, see Burdon (2010a: 708).

private property and others (1927: 16). In support, Felix Cohen (1954: 373) added an important modification to the dominant bundle of rights metaphor: 'Private property *is a relationship among human beings* such that the so-called owner can exclude others from certain activities or permit others to engage in those activities and in either case secure the assistance of the law in carrying out [that] decision.'

Building on this insight, scholars operating under the banner of critical legal studies have argued convincingly that the source and internal constitution of private property arises from social relationships (Singer & Beermann 1993). Indeed, private property is something that is defined and constructed by human beings. It is not handed down by divine grant, nor does it 'emerge fully formed like Athena from Zeus's head . . . it is closer to a piece of music that unfolds over time' (Singer 2000: 13). It gets its stability and certainty from an ongoing process of evaluation and adaptation to social, ethical and environmental tensions.

To support this analysis, social relations theorists present an alternative to the liberal conception of autonomy or freedom. 'What makes autonomy possible', argues Nedelsky (1993: 8; 2013), 'is not separation, but relationship.' From this perspective, the individualism that pertains to the liberal concept of private property is misconceived. People are not 'islands unto themselves' and best function to achieve their own goals in the context of 'social relations that support their own abilities to flourish' (Singer 2000: 131). Individuals achieve autonomy not in isolation from the community (both human and environmental) but by a mixture of dependence and independence (Nedelsky 1989: 7). Dependence is a necessary prerequisite for 'free' individuals (Freyfogle 2003a: 206–207). Ngaire Naffine (2013: 1) summarises this point and its consequence for law:

> Within relations we become what we are as persons; here, we must make sense of our lives, which in turn must be understood by scholars who wish to explain us. There is never a full separation between persons, and indeed, human beings draw their very identity from their relations. When they work well, relations are not only formative (but unavoidable) but also conducive to human autonomy and to the flourishing of the individual. It follows that the role of law is to regulate relations rather than to ward them off. Law's job is to ensure that they run smoothly and that they neither oppress nor harm us.

At their best, property rights represent enforceable rules that shape human relationships. If the community deems the rules to be fair and the rules contain an appropriate acknowledgement of the social aspect of property, then they can go a long way toward structuring a framework for allocation and distribution that serves the common good. The human interactions to be governed by law should not be seen primarily in terms of the clashing of individual rights – but in terms of the way 'patterns of relationship' can sustain a collective social life and the scope for individual autonomy' (Nedelsky 1993: 8). This is a fundamentally different perspective on personal freedom from the orthodox liberal conception of property. It simultaneously respects autonomy and also the need to develop oneself in relation to others (Underkuffler-Freund 1990: 129).

This description of private property does not abolish autonomy or boundaries, it simply reconceptualises them (Singer 2000: 4). Rather than understanding property rights as 'powers absolute within their spheres' (Kennedy 1980: 3), it interprets them as socially situated and contingent on their impact on others within the community. Put otherwise – a socially situated theory of private property gives rise mutual obligations between and among property owners. Singer (2000: 131) explains: 'Sometimes those obligations require nonowners to leave owners alone, but at times they require owners to exercise their property rights with due respect for the interests of others, including nonowners.' This statement recognises that property rights can come into conflict and when they do it is necessary that the rights be defined (at least partially) with reference to the relationships they instantiate.

In summary, shifting the focus of private property from individualism to relationship has the potential to promote the common good for human society. Lawmakers are more able to articulate laws for this purpose if they understand the kinds of relationship they want to foster or discourage. To this end, private property can play a role in facilitating communal living. This facilitative role consists partly of 'rules requiring individuals to respect the legitimate interests of others in controlling certain portions of the physical world' and rules 'designed to ensure that the property system as a whole functions well, with tolerable efficiency and justice' (Freyfogle 2003a: 232).

The social relations description of private property goes some way toward conforming with the principle of Earth community that is central to Earth jurisprudence. It recognises that property rights flow and evolve according to social factors. Further, by conceiving property in terms of 'relationship' it situates property holders and the choices they make within a vast network of relationships. However, while this social aspect is a necessary condition of the ecocentric conception of private property, it is not sufficient. To be consistent with the great law and the purpose of law as articulated within Earth jurisprudence, the concept of private property should also include broader ethical obligations toward the Earth community and the subject matter of a property relationship.

## 5.4 Private property and ethics

Alongside considerations pertaining to human social relationships are broader ethical considerations not obviously captured by social relations theory and its commitment to human relationships. There are a host of factors that might reasonably be considered under this heading. Some of the most important include duties toward future generations (Freyfogle 2006: 149–150), religious beliefs (Babie 2015; Engel 2011), recognition of indigenous ownership norms (Brown 1999) and individual virtue (Alexander 2011; Freyfogle 2006: 152; Thoreau 1995). There is also the fundamental issue of recognising human ignorance and the precautionary principle (Freyfogle 2006: 153–157).

Further to these considerations, I seek to contribute to the discourse concerning the recognition of nonreciprocal obligations and responsibilities as being integral to the concept of private property. I argue that such duties ought to be recognised for human beings and also the broader Earth community. In support of this argument I also consider an example of responsibility derived from indigenous Australian land use practices.

### 5.4.1 Obligation and responsibility

The description of private property presented in this chapter argues that for the institution to be reconciled with the great law it must recognise inherent and nonreciprocal obligations and responsibilities. Because of our interconnected and mutually dependant relationship to the rest of the environment, such considerations are central to the establishment of a mutually beneficial relationship with the Earth community and for the realisation of the comprehensive common good. Further, by defining private property in a way that includes responsibilities, the ecological description attempts to balance the existing 'rights' focus of liberal property theory and avoid the piecemeal and incremental approach of limiting the liberty of property holders through external legislation.

This description of private property draws partially on the work of Canadian theorist David Lametti (1998, 2003, 2010). More than any other contemporary theorist, Lametti has most fully developed a conceptual framework for recognising the duties and responsibilities as inherent to the concept of private property.

Lametti criticises the liberal theory of private property on the basis that it presents a picture of human beings as isolated, atomised and selfish. He also contends that private property cannot be morally justified with reference personal liberty and autonomy alone. While Lametti (1998: 669) recognises the value of freedom and its currency in Western culture, he contends that the liberal theory of private property does not adequately describe 'those aspects of the institution whose presence is not explainable or understandable in terms of rights.' More specifically, Lametti (1998: 670) contends that the concept of private property contains intrinsic 'duties and obligations' that are not adequately explained in terms of correlative rights and duties between individuals.

Lametti uses the term 'deon-telos' to capture these understated or neglected elements of property. The deon-telos is the 'deontology of private property' (1998: 670). The term is derived from the Greek – deon means duty or 'that which binds' and refers to specific obligations and responsibilities that derive from a variety of undefined sources. Further, the term '*telos*' means 'goal' or 'endpoint'. Consistent with the purposive description of human law outlined in Chapter 4, the term *deon-telos* captures the importance of social goals and values in property discourse. Moreover, it provides a basis from which to explore the larger ethical dimensions that are inherent to private property. Lametti (1998) outlines the intrinsic nature of the *deon-telos* in the following passage:

> Those aspects of private property captured by the rubric of the *deon-telos* are *an intrinsic* component of the concept of private property itself; any discussion of private property, whether in theory or practice is incomplete without them. Rights-based theories not only fail to capture this richness, they also lack the ability to discern a larger coherence among all these aspects of the institution. Without these elements, the explanatory force of any descriptive project is weakened. (1998: 671)

Lametti's critique of the liberal theory of private property and his advocacy for an integral ethical component accords with elements of the ecocentric description of private property advocated in this chapter. However, because Lametti was attempting to reconfigure the normative understanding of private property, his analysis has not sought to articulate the specific content of the *deon-telos* or other obligations and responsibilities that are integral to the concept of private property. Further, Lametti has not sought to argue if/how the concept of *deon-telos* pertains to duties or responsibilities to non-human animals or the broader Earth community. Such a step would go a long way toward moving away from what Aldo Leopold (1986: xviii) called the 'Abrahamic concept of land' and toward seeing the land as a 'community to which we belong'.

An important step in this direction can be noted with reference to the German constitutional law (Bosselmann 2011b; Dozer 1976; Raff 1998, 2003). Article 14(2) of the Constitution states: 'Property creates responsibilities. Its use shall at the same time serve the common good.' This Article assigns to the legislature the task of defining property in more detail, however, it prevents legislators from creating a concept of private property devoid of obligation (Raff 1998: 676). While this provision has been limited to duties toward human beings and the common human good,[6] it has also been interpreted to include environmental responsibility (Raff 2003: 172–179).

The most relevant principle in the interpretation of Article 14(2) is *Situationsgebundenheit* or 'environmental context'. Consistent with the social relations theory of private property, the German Federal Constitutional Court considers property rights to be limited by the social good. As a result, property rights are limited with reference to social and environmental context

---

6. See, further, *Economic Planning Case* (1954) 4 BVerfGE 7, [15]–[16] where section 14(2) of the Constitution was interpreted to highlight the importance of 'social connectedness and social bonding . . . without encroaching upon the intrinsic value of the person'.

(Raff 1998: 677). To determine whether a particular use of property has con-travened this standard, the Court will judge the sphere of protected property by considering what a reasonable and economically minded citizen would think when assessing the potential uses of the property in its social and envi-ronmental context in the absence of legal regulation (Raff 1998: 678).

One important application of Article 14(2) was the German High Court deci-sion in the *Cathedral of Beech Trees Case*.[7] In this case, the plaintiff had private property rights over a farm, on which were situated centuries-old beech trees (popularly known as the Cathedral of Beeches). The trees were provided legisla-tive protection in 1925 and the property owner applied several times for per-mission to cut down the trees. When this was denied, he sought compensation, arguing that their preservation amounted to an expropriation of his property.

In response, the German High Court found that the natural features of the land imposed a social obligation on the owner to preserve the trees for the com-munity. The imposition of this obligation did not amount to an expropriation and instead was consistent with what a reasonable and economically oriented owner of the land would recognise. The Court argued further that legislation or administrative action that imposes an obligation on a landowner is a concrete expression of social obligation, which encumbers a property right in view of its context. The Court reasoned: 'The limit lies at the point where the conserva-tion merits of the property would appear in the concrete situation to the owner, as a rational economically thinking person, when acquiring it as an economic asset with economic intentions or pursuing such intentions in relation to it.'

Subsequent decisions of the German courts have limited the application of Article 14(2) to obligations and responsibilities to other human beings. This was made plain in the *Water Gravel Mining Case*, in which the Federal Con-stitutional Court stated: 'Private land use is limited by the rights and interests of the general public, to have access to certain assets essential for human well-being such as water.'[8] This reasoning was supported in 1987 when the Federal Administrative Court ruled: 'The law cannot provide for the health of ecosystems per se, but only in so far as required to protect the rights of affected people.'[9] As the courts note, it would have been unlawful to restrict property rights on the basis ecological responsibilities under Article 14 of the Constitution.[10] These examples of anthropocentric reductionism fall far short

7   Cathedral of Beech Trees Case [1957] DVBT 856.
8.  BVerfGE 58, 300 at (342).
9.  BVerwG 4 C 56 at (58).
10. It is interesting to note that during late 1980s, the German government came under immense politi-cal pressure to amend Article 14(2) of the constitution to include ecological limitations to the concept of property. At this time, the draft wording being debated by the government read: 'Property implies duties. Its use should also serve the public well-being and the sustainability of natural conditions of life' (cited in Bosselmann 2011b: 38). During this debate, the Lower House resolved to install a 'Joint Commission for Constitutional Reform', which called for 'wide expert and public dialogue' about this change in its final report, which was presented in 1993. By this time, however, the political will required to implement such a radical change was lacking (Bosselmann 2011b: 38).

of the ecocentric description of private property advanced in this chapter. In order to extend the concept of property to include nonreciprocal obligations and responsibilities to the Earth community, I return to environmental ethics and the question – how can the environment be conceptualised as the subject of human ethics?

### 5.4.2 Ethics and earth community

> The reality of one planetary ecosystem and how to live within its boundaries can only be grasped if we learn to think globally, holistically and responsibly. (Bosselmann 2008a: ix)

In Earth jurisprudence, the motivation for expanding the concept of private property to include nonreciprocal obligations toward the comprehensive Earth community is based, first, in response to the great environmental harm currently being facilitated by the orthodox liberal conception of private property. The capacity of human beings to inflict environmental harm has increased in proportion to developments in technology and to the commodification of nature under the dominant neoliberal growth model of progress. While human beings have become a 'macrophase power' we only accept a 'microphase sense of responsibility and ethical judgment' (Berry 1999: 101). Against this, a persuasive argument can be made that the role of private property in facilitating the present environmental crisis provides a rational basis for humans to agree to expand restrictions on the exercise of freedom and to recognise duties toward the environment. Commenting on this extension, Berry (1991: 101) argues:

> [O]ur concern for the human community can only be fulfilled by a concern for the integrity of the natural world. The planet cannot support its human presence unless there is a reciprocal human support for the life systems of the planet. This more comprehensive perspective we might identify as macrophase ethics. This is something far beyond our ordinary ethical judgments involving individual actions, the actions of communities, or even of nations. We are presently concerned with ethical judgments on an entirely different order of magnitude. Indeed, the human community has never previously been forced to make ethical judgments on this scale because we never before had the capacity for deleterious actions with such consequences.

A similar argument for extending human ethics was made by the brilliant twentieth-century German philosopher Hans Jonas. Jonas's book, *The Imperative of Responsibility*, was one of the first to put on the international agenda the need for human beings to take responsibility for the future of the biosphere and the continuation of the authentic human moral life (1979: 7,

136–137). Jonas was a member of the Jewish Brigade of the British army in World War II and he explains how this experience etched deep into his consciousness an appreciation for the preciousness and vulnerability of earthly life and a mission to set out the ontological and ethical understanding that would bring humanity to respect and care for the Earth community. With respect to these impressions, Jonas (1980: xii) wrote: 'The apocalyptic state of things, the threatening collapse of a world, the climatic crisis of civilization, the proximity of death, the stark nakedness to which all the issues of life were stripped, all these were ground enough to take a new look at the very foundations for our being and to review the principles by which we guide our thinking on them.'

In response, Jonas posited the 'imperative of responsibility'. His primary objective was to design a new theory of moral responsibility, applicable to both the public and the private sphere. Like Berry, he recognised that new technologies have given humanity power to cause enormous harm to other humans, to future generations and to the balance between humans and nature. Given these circumstances, Jonas (1980: 130) argued that the 'ought' or 'obligation to do' or 'restrain from doing' arises as a form of self-control to consciously exercised power: 'In sum: that which binds (free) will and obligation together in the first place, power, is precisely that which today moves responsibility in[to] the centre of morality.'

In positing this ethical move, both Berry and Jonas run up against the limited criteria established in orthodox ethical discourse for identifying objects of responsibility. Arguably, the most important contributor to this discourse was Immanuel Kant. Kant's framework is expressly anthropocentric and limits the object of responsibility of duties to human beings. For example, Kant (1974: 124) reasons:

> The fact that man can have the idea 'I' raises him infinitely above all other beings living on earth. By this he is a *person* . . . that is, a being altogether different in rank and dignity from things such as irrational animals, which we can dispose of as we please. So far as animals are concerned, we have no direct duties. Animals are not self-conscious and are merely a means to an end. That end is man . . . our duties toward animals are merely indirect duties toward humanity.[11]

This statement is elaborated on in the *Groundwork of the Metaphysic(s) of Morals*. Here, Kant argues that only human beings may be the object of morality since we alone have the potential for moral reasoning (1998: 45).

---

11. Note that this passage is sometimes interpreted as suggesting that human beings have the highest value and are more valuable than all non-human entities. However, Kant does not take 'dignity' to imply such a value claim. Instead, 'dignity' refers to the status of humanity as subjects who are able of moral reasoning.

For Kant, moral status hinges on the value of reason. What grounds moral duty is a person's own unconditional commitment to following the moral law and it is the dictates of the moral law that generate moral obligations to others. Moreover, this rationality, which Kant identified with the capacity to act in accordance with moral principle, is taken both as qualifying human beings as moral agents and as objects of moral concern.

An implication of Kant's ethics is that the primary focus of morality is not the wellbeing of another but how an individual responds to their wellbeing. The fundamental focus is the individual and it is about the individual's moral development. A second implication is that moral agents can have no direct duties to non-moral agents and any duties we feel to animals or the environment are actually indirect duties to humanity. While Kant does claim that we should avoid callousness and indifference toward animals (1998: x) (on the basis that such actions are a form of self-harm), it is not the animals themselves that matter morally. For when we avoid such treatment (or even when we treat them well), the duty is not to our relation in the Earth community, but to humanity. Thus, for Kant, anybody who seeks to import moral obligations with regard to non-humans commits a moral fallacy (Ott 2008: 47).

Kant's ethical framework has been subject to robust critique by environmental and moral philosophers alike. Lawrence Johnson (1991: 63) observes that Kant 'is asking quite a lot of reason' to substantiate his moral theory. He argues further that moral reasoning is not exclusive to human beings and that it can be recognised in higher order animals. Johnson (1991: 63) notes: 'One can point to instances in animal behaviour of concern, kindness, loyalty and even more or less rudimentary sense of justice.'[12]

Hans Jonas is broader in his critique, arguing that Kant's analysis was only designed to facilitate interpersonal human interactions and is not sufficient to guide current human interactions with nature. Jonas (1984: 1) argues that all 'previous ethics . . . had these interconnected tacit premises in common: that the human condition, determined by the nature of man and the nature of things, was given once and for all; that the human good on that basis was readily determinable and that the range of human action and therefore responsibility was narrowly circumscribed.' For Jonas, this did not mean that Kantian interpersonal ethics were wrong, but rather that it was not 'designed to cope with the current and prospective scope of human agency' (Levy 2002: 84).

Arguably, the most developed international document for articulating the current scope of human agency is the International Earth Charter.[13] With

---

12. Kant might still deny moral value to these animals on the basis that they do not act from principle per se. To be consistent, Kant would also need to judge a human being who saved the life of another from a position of instinct or compassion to be morally neutral. Christine Korsgaard (2005) provides a fascinating defence of a Kantian conception of duties to other animals.

13. The IUCN Draft International Covenant on Environment and Development recognises a 'duty of all to respect and care for the environment and promote sustainable development'.

specific respect to the concept of property under discussion in this chapter, I draw your attention to the following Earth Charter principles:

*Principle 2.* Care for the community of life with understanding, compassion, and love.

a. Accept that with the right to own, manage, and use natural resources comes the duty to prevent environmental harm and to protect the rights of people.

b. Affirm that with increased freedom, knowledge, and power comes increased responsibility to promote the common good.

*Principle 4.* Secure Earth's bounty and beauty for present and future generations.

a. Recognise that the freedom of action of each generation is qualified by the needs of future generations.

*Principle 6.* Prevent harm as the best method of environmental protection and, when knowledge is limited, apply a precautionary approach. [ . . . ]

b. Place the burden of proof on those who argue that a proposed activity will not cause significant harm, and make the responsible parties liable for environmental harm.

These principles articulated clear limitations to important preexisting legal property rights in a manner that potentially gives legal meaning to the concept of 'common but differentiated' responsibility. Article 6 also needs to be highlighted because it reshapes the precautionary principle by shifting the burden of proof from the opponents of property exploitation and development to the proponents (Engel 2011: 83).

Ron Engel, one of the principle drafters of the Earth Charter reflects on the immediate influence that thinkers such as Leopold and Jonas had on the basic normative framework of the charter (Engel 2011: 83). More specifically, Engel notes that Leopold's contribution is evidenced by the fact that the entire second section of the Earth Charter is devoted to the principle of 'ecological integrity', which I outlined in Chapter 4 of this book. Similarly, Jonas's influence is most evident in the preamble to the Earth Charter, which reads:

[W]e must decide to live with a sense of universal responsibility, identifying ourselves with the whole Earth community as well as our local communities. We are at once citizens of different nations and of one world in which the local and global are linked. Everyone shares responsibility for the present and future well-being of the human family and the larger living world. The spirit of human solidarity and kinship with all life is strengthened when we live with reverence for the mystery of being, gratitude for the gift of life, and humility regarding the human place in nature.[14]

14. To read the whole text visit: http://www.earthcharterinaction.org/invent/images/uploads/echarter_english.pd.

The Charter also affirms universal human rights, but they are embraced within a relational understanding of human responsibility to the whole community of life. As Engel (2011: 83) contends, the Earth Charter is 'virtually unique among prominent international declarations' in adopting this perspective.

Alongside 'soft law' documents such as the Earth Charter, environmental philosophers have made many unique attempts to transcend the Kantian framework and recognise nature as an object of human responsibility (Agar 2001; Johnson 1991; Jonas 1984; Rolston III 1988; Taylor 1986; Westra 1998). In my interpretation, Earth jurisprudence adopts a similar normative position to the Earth Charter in its recognition of the moral value of each member of the Earth community. From the perspective of this more compressive community, it is no longer defensible that obligations and responsibilities are owed to human beings alone. This insight requires human beings to consider not only their own interests, but potentially the wellbeing and integrity of all entities affected by their decisions. In support of this more comprehensive ethical perspective, Albert Einstein (cited in Bosselmann 2008a: 319) writes:

> A human being is a part of a whole, called by us 'universe', a part limited in time and space. He experiences himself, his thoughts and feelings as something separated from the rest . . . a kind of optical delusion of his consciousness. This delusion is a kind of prison for us, restricting us to our personal desires and to affection for a few persons nearest to us. Our task must be to free ourselves from this prison by widening our circle of compassion to embrace all living creates and the whole of nature in its beauty.

In contrast to Kantian ethics, the ethical approach advanced in Earth jurisprudence is holistic and inclusive. Indeed, rather than starting with a class of beings that are assumed to be moral subjects and working outward, Earth jurisprudence presumes membership to the moral community. This shifts the burden of persuasion onto detractors who are then required to advance arguments as to why an entity should be excluded. Konrad Ott (2008: 45) describes this approach as the 'route from the outside'.

Importantly, this reasoning does not deny the moral status of human beings or claim that all forms of non-human nature have moral equivalence with humanity. To be clear, I think that it would be absurd to claim that bacteria had moral equivalence to a human being or to a chimpanzee. However, I also think it equally absurd to claim that the moral claims of human beings trump all others. In all ethical systems, there needs to be some mechanism for resolving conflicting between competing moral claims and in 'hard cases'.[15] Such determinations

---

15. To assist with decision making in hard cases, Lowe and Gleeson (1998) consider three qualifications to their argument for extending human ethics to include nature. They argue that life has moral precedence over non-life; that individualised life takes moral precedence over life forms that exist in communities; and that humans take precedence over all other life forms.

can only be made in the concrete particular and not in the abstract. However, as Berry (1999: 105) suggests, the 'present urgency' is to begin thinking within the context of the whole planet, the 'integral Earth community with all its human and other-than-human components'. From this perspective, human ethics concern the principles and values that we give expression to at the rational level that govern this more comprehensive community. The ecological is not subordinate to human beings and the ecological imperative is not derivative of human ethics. Rather, Berry (1999: 105) argues that 'human ethics are derivative from the ecological imperative.' The basic ethical norm is the wellbeing of the Earth community and the attainment of human wellbeing within that context.

The comprehensive perspective advocated in Earth jurisprudence has the capacity to change radically the institution of private property. While property rights would still be limited by the competing rights of other human beings, they would also be limited by the integral responsibilities we have to the Earth community. Thus, property rights would be shaped, restricted and given formal content by reference to the common good of the comprehensive community. If this position were adopted in the vernacular law of individuals, communities and eventually formalised by the state, it could change the role of private property, from being a fundamental cause of the present environmental crisis, to being an agent for its mitigation.

To assist Western law to assimilate the description of private property just described I think that it is useful to consider an example of a 'property system' where nonreciprocal obligations and responsibilities have been recognised in practice. Perhaps the best example can be seen in the many indigenous cultures in Australia[16] who perfected sustainable land management practices for over 40,000 years (Gammage 2013).[17] This example is particularly powerful because it represents a concept of property that governed human social relationships over a vast landscape that is now being exploited by a system of property law that reflects the liberal concept of private property. While indigenous traditions are currently being violently suppressed in Australia (and other Commonwealth countries), I contend that their wisdom is a necessary component of any genuine transition toward an ecocentric era. To be effective, the dominant culture needs to approach such conversations with humility and with the understanding that the liberation of the Earth community is commensurate with the liberation of indigenous people around the world.

### 5.4.3 Responsibility in practice

Today, laws enacted with reference to the liberal theory of private property govern human interactions with the Australian landscape. This was not always

16. Harris (1996) describes indigenous systems of land management as 'communitarian property'.
17. In making this assertion, I am cognisant of Tim Flannery's (1994) excellent survey of the extinction of mega-fauna on the Australian continent prior to European invasion.

the case. Human interaction with these same plains, rivers, mountains and deserts was once entirely governed by the cultural norms of approximately 500 distinct nations. In order to understand how contemporary society can shift toward the establishment of a mutually beneficial relationship with the Earth, Berry (1999: 176–177) argues that we should reflect on the practices of indigenous traditions: 'As the years pass it becomes ever more clear that dialogue with native peoples . . . throughout the world is urgently needed to provide the human community with models of a more integral human presence on Earth.'

In support, Nicole Graham (2011: 197–198) contends that indigenous laws and models of people–place relations 'constitute an obvious and sensible source of reflection on modern property relations because in addition to containing concepts of responsibility, Indigenous land laws are demonstrably successful regulatory systems over a long period of time'. There are many reasons for this success, some of which relate to geography itself, while others relate to the worldview or paradigm that supported indigenous law.

While I acknowledge that no single indigenous perspective can be taken as representative for a community or nation, I find it instructive how consistently sentiments like that expressed by Paddy Roe, lawman and guardian of the Lurujarri nation in Western Australia, are articulated by indigenous Australians. For Roe, the land and his self are inseparable and ownership 'must be understood in terms of relationship and responsibility'. He argues further that the western way of understanding the environment is 'killing his country', which also involves 'killing the people' (Sinatra & Murphy 1999: 11).

Tanganekald-Meintangk[18] elder Irene Watson expresses a similar worldview to Roe. Watson (2002: 257) also contends that her own conception of property is 'irreconcilable to the Western legal property law system, as it is to fit a sphere on top of a pyramid'. To give full expression to this perspective, I quote Watson at length:

> The earth is our mother: this is a relationship that is based on caring and sharing. From birth we learn the sacredness and the connectedness of all things to the creation. Every aspect of the natural world is honoured and respected. And from an early age Nungas learn to tread lightly on the Earth. All life forms are related. The law speaks to principles. One is respect. It is a respect for all of creation, not just humanity but the total ecological environment: trees, birds, animals the entire wholeness and oneness of creation. (2002: 38)[19]

18. The Tanganekald-Meintangk peoples are custodians of the place now known as the Coorong and the lower southeast of South Australia.
19. The term 'Nunga' refers to an aboriginal person in the southern areas of South Australia.

Watson (2002: 46) argues further that indigenous relationship to the land contains both obligations and rights. The relationship to land is both as a traditional owner and a custodian. Both exist at the same time. Further, obligations are dynamic and place specific to the particular of land:

> Ownership is not exclusive. And it does not define the owned object as a commodity: instead it defines it as the concern of a limited group of people who stand in a particular relationship to the owner and whose various responsibilities depend on that relationship. There are both managers and bosses, for example. And each has a different responsibility or right. The obligations I speak of here are to the law-song of place handed on to the song holder from the ancestors. For example, for the ancestor Tjirbruki, the obligation was not to kill the female emu in the hunt, for the preservation of the species. (Watson 2002: 46–47)

Central to Watson's comments is that indigenous knowledge of place and ideas of ownership are learned and experienced within specific places over long periods of time. The knowledge of place that is central to indigenous law 'comes through the living of it' (Watson 2002: 255). I will return to this point later in the chapter, but for now it is essential to highlight the importance of local, place-based knowledge for any reformation of the Western concept of private property (Jackson 1994; Sale 1991).

While many indigenous communities around Australia continue informally to practice an ethic of responsibility in land management, I would be derelict not to explicitly state that their worldview has not been accommodated by Australian property or native title law. For example, in the 1999 Federal Court decision, *The Members of the Yorta Yorta Aboriginal Community v State of Victoria and Others*, it was ruled that the relation between the Yorta Yorta[20] people and their land was extinguished at colonisation. On this point, Justice Olney made a revealing pronouncement that it was impossible to 're-establish' a connection with the land once it was interrupted.

Further to this decision, the Federal Court ruling in *Western Australia v Ward* sought to adapt Indigenous descriptions of ownership into the Hohfeldian bundle of rights framework articulated in Chapter 2.[21] The majority (Beaumont and von Doussa JJ) conceived indigenous ownership as a 'bundle of rights'[22] that could be partially extinguished by removing some of the rights that make up the bundle. The Court held:

---

20. The Yorta Yorta people traditionally lived around the junction of the Goulburn and Murray Rivers in present-day northeast Victoria. *Members of the Yorta Yorta Aboriginal Community v State of Victoria and Others (2002) 214 CLR 422.*
21. See pages 37–38.
22. This issue framing was rejected by the trial judge in *Western Australia v Ward* (1998) 159 ALR 483. Citing law from Canada, his Honour held at [508]: 'Native title at common law is a communal "right to land" arising from the significant connection of an Indigenous society with land under its customs

In our opinion the rights and interests of Indigenous people which together make up native title are aptly described as a 'bundle of rights'. It is possible for some only of those rights to be extinguished by the creation of inconsistent rights by laws or executive acts. Where this happens 'partial extinguishment' occurs. In a particular case a bundle of rights that was so extensive as to be in the nature of a proprietary interest, by partial extinguishment may be so reduced that the rights which remain no longer have that character. Further, it is possible that a succession of different grants may have a cumulative effect, such that native title rights and interests that survived one grant that brought about partial extinguishment, may later be extinguished by another grant.

The translation of indigenous conceptions of land to the bundle of rights framework has forced traditional owners such as Watson (2002: 260) to reject the formal native title system, arguing that it is a 'further erosion and subversion of Nunga identities'. Watson (2002: 260) contends further that 'native title does not help us care for country' and continues to observe the law of her people outside formal legal mechanisms.[23]

This discussion is of clear relevance for those who adopt an ecocentric worldview and regard private property as including inherent obligations and responsibility. Ultimately, the formal legal recognition of both ecocentric and indigenous descriptions of private property are related and there is the potential for great benefit from a dialogue and shared learning from both perspectives. Until both are recognised, we would do well to follow the advice of indigenous elder Dennis Walker (cited in Watson 2000: 34), speaking at a ceremony to celebrate the Aboriginal Tent Embassy in 1995:

> The real land and law business has not been done. And what I would like to point out to you is that in terms of our land and our law it needs to be understood, as my mother said, we are custodians of this land. And when people say 'oh we lost this land or we lost that land', we didn't lose it anywhere. The land is still here and we still have got the responsibility of being custodians of that land. The problem is that we haven't been

and culture. It is not a mere "bundle of rights"': see *Delgamuukw v British Columbia* [1997] 153 DLR (4th) 193 per Lamer CJ at [240]–[241]. Interestingly, this interpretation was also rejected in the High Court decision *R v Toohey, Ex parte Meneling Station Pty Ltd* [1982] HCA 69. Here, Brennan J argued: 'Aboriginal ownership is primarily a spiritual affair rather than a bundle of rights.' While not overturned, the construction of native title as a 'bundle of rights' was further criticised in the High Court decision *Western Australia and o'rs v Ward and o'rs* [2002] HCA 28. Gleeson CJ, Gaudron, Gummow and Hayne JJ noted at [14]: 'The difficulty of expressing a relationship between a community or group of Aboriginal people and the land in terms of rights and interests is evident. Yet that is required by the Native Title Act. The spiritual or religious is translated into the legal. This requires the fragmentation of an integrated view of the ordering of affairs into rights and interests which are considered apart from the duties and obligations which go with them.'

23. This decision resonates with what Weston and Bollier (2013: 104) term 'vernacular law'.

given the power in the non-Aboriginal legal system to fulfil that custodial right. Until our Elders in Council decide on these matters through their customary laws and until that consent, which Captain Cook was supposed to get, is properly given, then we still live under bad laws.

In the next section, I consider how private property can shift to pay greater attention to the 'thing' that is the subject matter of a property relationship. While the orthodox narrative of private property celebrates human conquest and separation from the environment, I argue that the 'thing', which is the subject matter of a property relationship, should also play a role in influencing and limiting property choices. This analysis is supported by an eclectic range of intellectual sources including literature, property theory, case law and agrarian land use practices.

## 5.5 Property and things

An ecological interpretation of private property will consider human social relationships and ethical considerations at length. However, I contend that for a description of private property to be consistent with the great law it should also refer to the item, which is the subject matter of a property relationship.

As described in Chapter 2, the orthodox Hohfeldian interpretation of private property entrenches a person–person relationship with respect to things (Penner 1996: 713–714). Here, rights are held against other people, who owe a corresponding duty to respect the right. As Jeremy Waldron (1988: 27) explains: 'legal relations cannot exist between people and [objects], because [objects] cannot have rights or duties of be bound by or recognise rules.' The ecological conception of private property advanced in this chapter seeks to extend this dominant framework by describing private property as a relationship facilitated *through* or *by* an item of property (tangible or intangible). This shift maintains that private property is fundamentally a human institution, while giving explicit recognition to the fact that the thing itself is an important part of a property relationship. As Lametti (2003: 329) contends: 'private property is a relationship both *to* and *through* objects of social wealth.'

In support of this description of private property, the profound shortcomings of a purely person–person description must first be explored. To initiate this discussion, I return to literature and offer an imaginary journey across the Adelaide plains to see what ownership means in practice. We only need a few stops to appreciate how private property is more than a person–person relationship and the consequences it has for the broader Earth community.

The Adelaide plains stretch west from the Adelaide Hills to the Southern Ocean. As a traveller journeys into this open land and across a series of ancient creek and river systems the land gives rise to a mixture of suburbs and broad acreage. We begin in the western watershed of the Mount Lofty

Rangers and move northwest along Brown Hill Creek. The creek receives its modern name from the dominating hill behind Mitcham called Brown Hill that was grazed early in the history of Adelaide's European settlement. The Kaurna peoples named this creek Wirraparinga, meaning 'creek or scrub place' and oral history surrounding its constant flow of water are commonplace. However, in less than two centuries of settlement, Brown Hill Creek has been reduced to a trickle. As we venture northwest along the creek bed, the reason for this dramatic reduction in water level becomes immediately obvious.

Stretching alongside the entrance to the creek are rows and rows of houses, whose backyards enter onto the creek. Each house makes use of the creek in its own distinct way. Some houses have extended their gardens into the creek, growing both ornamental and vegetable plants along the side of the embankment. Others have planted apple trees and invasive varieties of prickly pear that are pollinated by the European bee. There are also a multitude of makeshift irrigation pipes drawing water illegally to sustain English rose gardens, lawns or tropical plantations.

Nestled within suburbia, the landscape changes dramatically as the traveller comes to a clearing and parkland. Here one finds an array of native birdlife including the Adelaide rosella, bandit rosella, common blackbird and starling. Pools of water cluster amidst ancient stone and provide a home for fish and amphibian young to develop and await the winter rain and increased water flow.

At the end of the park, the soil consistency of the creek shifts gradually from dense clay to a sandy loam. This is short lived as the soft creek bed is covered by kilometres of cement that extends up along the embankment. This stretch of creek bed is all but devoid of habitation and culminates in a 200-metre passage in complete darkness under a shopping plaza. Walking through this passage one hears the muted sound of traffic from above and the occasional crunch of the bones of fish whose seasonal journey along the creek has been cut short by the impermeable cement.

When one returns to the open, further access along this waterway is blocked by development. However, from a crouching position, the traveller can glimpse a small gap and continuation of the river through more concrete, fencing and housing.

From this brief narrative, several points stand out as particularly important. To begin, it is clear that it is not only human beings, but also the land itself and non-human animals that are affected by the choices we make when exercising property rights. This is true whether we are considering the impact of human settlement on a waterway; land clearing on privately owned land or the construction of human-made objects such as a car, books or even a paperclip. While perhaps an obvious point, it is not one that is expressly acknowledged in either the orthodox or social relations descriptions of private property.

From this narrative it can also be argued that the environment and non-human animals play a role in shaping the interactions people have with the land. The neglected importance of the nonhuman world in shaping human choices is a subject actively theorised by Aldo Leopold (1986: 241):

> Many historical events, hitherto explained solely in terms of human enterprise, were actually biotic interactions between people and the land. The characteristics of the land determined the facts quite as potently as the characteristics of the men who lived on it.

The dominant liberal theory of private property does not (arguably, it cannot) acknowledge this point and instead focuses on human dominion and myriad ways in which human beings control objects of property. However, on further reflection it is apparent that our interaction with the land is far from one sided. In the narrative that I provided earlier, it must be acknowledged that the 'decision' to settle and construct housing around Brown Hill Creek was determined largely by factors such as water availability, fertile soil, protection from the surrounding hills, food and ocean access. Further, the choices property owners have made in regard to their blocks have also been influenced heavily by ecological factors. Soil type, rainfall, and wind speed, for example, play a crucial role in determining what varieties of plant life an ecosystem will sustain. The 'choice' to plant an apple orchard or prickly pear cactus in the creek bed was only realised because the ecosystem could sustain those plants.

If we step further outside the images of ownership advanced by contemporary liberal theories of private property, one can find other examples of how nature has shaped human beings. This is perhaps most acute when considering the variety of choices human beings make in their own backyards. Author Michael Pollan (2002: xiii–xiv) writes:

> Gardeners like me tend to think [our] choices are our sovereign prerogative: in the space of this garden, I tell myself, I alone determine which species will thrive and which will disappear. I'm in charge here, in other words, and behind me stand other humans still more in charge: the long chain of botanists, plant breeders, and these days, genetic engineers who 'selected', 'developed' or 'bred' the particular potato that I decided to plant. Even our grammar makes the terms of this relationship perfectly clear: *I choose the plants, I pull the weeds, I harvest the crops.* We divide the world into subjects and objects, and here in the garden, as in nature generally, we humans are the subjects.
>
> But [one] afternoon in the garden I found myself wondering: What if that grammar is all wrong? What if it's really nothing more than self-serving conceit? The bumblebee would probably also regard himself as a subject in the garden and the bloom he's plundering for its drop of nectar as an object. But we know that this is just a failure of his imagination.

> The truth of the matter is that the flower has cleverly manipulated the bee into hauling its pollen from blossom to blossom.

In this passage, Pollan touches on a key ecological concept called co-evolution (Scheffer 2001; Wilson 1992). Co-evolution is a kind of community evolution involving 'reciprocal selective interaction' between two significant species with a close ecological relationship (Odum 1971: 273). This can be witnessed in my earlier narrative, where the apple tree has struck a co-evolutionary bargain with the European bee. Here the two parties work together to advance their individual interests and wind up trading favours – transportation for the apple genes and food for the bee. Far from conscious, this transaction blurs the traditional distinction between subject and object (Pollan 2002: xiv).

Is the situation very different for the property owner planted a row of apple trees in the creek bed? Certainly, it is at least arguable that the gardener and the apple tree are partners in a co-evolutionary relationship. The size, variety and taste of apples have been selected over countless generations by human beings. Like bees, human beings have criteria for selection, which includes symmetry, sweetness and nutritional value (Pollan 2002: xiv). The fact that humans have evolved to become intermittently aware of our desire makes no substantial difference to coevolution (Odum 1971: 273).

Reflecting on the concept of co-evolution, it can be argued that what the orthodox liberal theory of private property regards simply as a one-way exercise of control, is actually a complex reciprocal and mutually beneficial relationship. Of course, this is not true for all items of private property, i.e. many items of personal property, but where it is true, our legal concepts ought to be broad enough to recognise this fact. This is important both for the breadth and accuracy of our thinking on private property and also because it highlights the importance of the 'thing' itself in the choices property holders can make.

The importance of explicitly recognising the 'thing' as part of the concept of private property has been advocated by a significant number of property theorists. I will consider the contribution of A.M. Honoré and James E. Penner to this discourse. Following this, I will consider examples of 'things in practice' with reference to an important decision of the United States Supreme Court and also agrarian farm practices.

### 5.5.1 Things in theory

Within the contemporary analytic tradition, Honoré (1961: 161) first articulated the argument for analysing private property with reference to the 'thing'. Honoré discusses ownership in close proximity to objects and gradually extends his enumeration across a variety of items. Importantly, as he moves away from corporeal items, he argues that the nature of property rights change in response to the item of property. He writes:

Our investigation has revealed what we began by suspecting, that the notions of ownership and of the thing owned are interdependent. We are left not with an inclination to adopt a terminology which confines ownership to material objects, but with an understanding of a certain shift of meaning as ownership is applied to different classes of things owned. (1961: 183)

While Honoré does not pursue this point further, it highlights an important point for further discussion – that the nature of ownership varies according to the subject matter of a property relationship. While this injects a degree of emphasis on the object, Honoré is vague on the extent to which objects are important conceptually to the property bundle, which he largely supports.

A significant contributor to this debate is James E. Penner (1996, 1997). Penner's analysis of property begins by critiquing the person–person conception of private property on the basis that it does not represent how ordinary people understand and engage with private property. To make this point, Penner considers the example of selling a house. While this process alters the legal relationship between contracting parties, it has no impact on the community at large who still have the same rights/responsibilities vis-à-vis the property. In this situation, Penner (1997: 25–26) claims that it is more accurate to characterise property norms as 'norms *in rem*' – literally meaning power about or against 'the thing':

> To understand rights *in rem* we must not only discard Hohfeld's dogma that rights are always relations between two persons, but also the idea that a right *in rem* is a simple relation between one person and a set of indefinitely many others.
>
> [I]f we pay attention to the fact that rights and duties *in rem* do not refer to persons, not in the sense that property is not owned by persons, but in the sense that nothing to do with any particular individual's personality is involved in the normative guidance they offer, we may get somewhere.

Penner's argument is that the distinction between *in rem*/*in personam* applies to all categories of norm and that the distinction is the basis for our interaction with objects. A norm *in rem* requires a relationship to a thing and is framed with reference to the object. Penner (1997: 29) argues:

> A duty *in rem* is a duty not to interfere with the property of others, or some state to which all others are equally entitled. Thus, a person is a holder of a right *in rem* when he benefits from that general duty. The holder of a right *in rem* benefits from the existence of an exclusionary reason, but one which does not apply to him alone. Note that in some sense the correlativity here is not symmetrical. The duty-owner's duty applies to more cases than that of the individual right holder.

Penner's insight is that norms can apply in a special, impersonal way *through* objects and have consequences for other persons. Correlativity between people is thus mediated by things, which can carry special types of rights and duties. The distinction between Penner and orthodox Hohfeldian property theorists is one of symmetry and asymmetry. The Hohfeldian picture of bilateral legal relations can be characterised as simple symmetry or one-to-one relationship. Here, each right holder has a corresponding duty holder. However, Penner (1997: 34) argues that in reality, there is no such symmetry in property relations. Property holders understand their right as being good against the whole world – not just an individual.

By the same token, duty holders owe a duty not to interfere with all items of private property that are not their own. Their duty not to interfere with another's property is focused on the object itself and in this sense the human owner is irrelevant. As a consequence Penner (1997: 35) argues that the supposed bilateral nature of property relationships is undermined by the existence of asymmetry – the singular duty holder and non-identified right holders of owned objects. While Hohfeld's framework might have value for some private law relationships, it becomes distorted when applied to private property. Arguably, the identification of this asymmetry might stand as Penner's most important contribution to the 'property as things' discourse (Lametti 2003: 343).

The notion of asymmetry can be used to support the ecological description of private property advanced in this chapter. The structure of Penner's analysis, also illustrates the shortcomings of Hohfeld's person–person bilateral characterisation of private property. As noted, most items of private property are derived from nature and their creation and/or use impact the environment in some way. Nature can also play a role in shaping property choices. The inclusion of such considerations into our understanding and analysis of private property can only be supported by an asymmetrical framework, which recognises the role and importance of things. Thus, I describe private property as a relationship *between* persons and a relationship *with* things. It is circular and contrary to the anthropocentric separation drawn by orthodox theories between nature/things and human beings.

One consequence of recognising the 'thing' itself as being integral to our description of private property is that it brings the object into focus and helps shape the particular rights and duties that attach to private property. As Lametti (2003: 328) argues: 'Contrary to the rights-based paradigm, the redefinition allows specific objects of property to carry with them duties of stewardship or obligations to be used in a certain manner.' Lametti (2003: 344) argues further that inherent duties may attach to the 'ownership of certain resources' and that '*in rem* norms might arise from the unique characteristics of certain objects of social wealth.' For example: '[T]he ownership of a specifically situated plot of land or building might entail specific, non-correlative, and asymmetrical duties to non-owners: stewardship of an environmentally sensitive area or heritage building' (2003: 344). In this instance, the asymmetry is object specific. This subtlety cannot be accommodated internally by the orthodox liberal concept of private property. Curiously, neither Penner nor Lametti examines the possible implications of this step in great detail. If they did, they would find many instances where *in rem* duties have attached themselves to the ownership of specific things.

The most celebrated example of *in rem* duties attaching to objects of ownership is the 1972 decision of the Wisconsin Supreme Court, *Just v Mariette County*.[24] In that case, the plaintiff purchased 36.4 acres of land along the fore shore of Lake Noquebaby in Marionette County. In 1967 the county enacted an ordinance designed to protect the shore land by banning people from dumping garbage and waste into wetlands without a permit. Later in the same year and contrary to the ordinance the plaintiff dumped a large quantity of sand into the wetland without a permit. Marionette County objected and the plaintiff filed suit, requesting that the court declare the ordinance unconstitutional as a takings of their property in violation of the fifth amendment of the United States Constitution.

The Wisconsin Supreme Court summed up the dispute in the following terms: 'A conflict between the public interest in stopping the despoliation of natural resources, which our citizens until recently have taken for granted as inevitable and an owner's asserted right to use his property as he wishes.' The Court noted further that the intention of the ordinance was not 'to secure a benefit for the public' by forcing or compelling the plaintiff to 'cease activity on their property'. Instead the intention was to prevent harm to the natural character of the plaintiff's property. To decide what impact the ordinance had on the plaintiff, the Court had to determine the exact nature of their property right. If the plaintiff did not have the right to dump sand in the wetland, then the ordinance could not possibly amount to a taking.

In deliberating on this issue, the court posed the following question: 'Is the ownership of a parcel of land so absolute that man can change its nature to suit any of its purposes?' The Court responded in the negative, holding:

> An owner of land has no absolute and unlimited right to change the essential natural character of his land so as to use it for a purpose for which it was unsuited in its natural state and which injures the rights of others. The exercise of the police power in zoning must be reasonable and we think it is not an unreasonable exercise of that power to prevent harm to public rights by limiting the use of private property to its natural uses.

24. *Just u Marietee County, 56 Wisconsin 2d 7 (1972).*

Contrary to liberal theory of private property, the Court held that plaintiffs possessed the right to use their land 'for natural and Indigenous uses' and stressed that such use had to be 'consistent with the nature of the land.' That is – the specific nature of the wetland in question played a key role in determining the uses that landowners could engage in. Put otherwise, the private property rights of the owner were restricted to use that consistent with the continued health of the wetland and the baseline of a landowner's entitlement was nature itself (Freyfogle 2003a: 96). Expressed in the terminology of Earth jurisprudence, the Court held that the environment acted as a bedrock standard or measure for human land use practices.

While heralded by environmentalists (Rome 2001: 234) the decision in *Just* was overruled by the United States Supreme Court in *Lucas v South Carolina Coastal Watch*.[25] In this case, Justice Scalia held it was unlawful for the states to regulate land use by requiring landowners to maintain their property in its natural state as part of a functioning ecosystem (Sax 1992–1993: 1438). Freyfogle (1988: 108) explains this reluctance with reference to the overt conservatism of the Supreme Court. Further to this, Freyfogle comments on the Court's concern with letting the environment guide human decision making. Freyfogle (1988: 108) states: 'To embrace nature itself as the source of rules, binding on lawmakers and without human interpretation, tinkers with much more than the law of private property: it alters the entire idea of sovereignty and public power.' To be consistent with democratic values, Freyfogle argues that the judgement needs revision. In a statement that is remarkably consistent with the idea of great law proposed in Earth jurisprudence, Freyfogle (1988: 108) contends: 'Nature's integrity can remain a bedrock value and limit, but humans must control the lawmaking process, interpreting the land scientifically and ethically and translating their conclusions and choices into new landownership norms.'

While the person–person conception of property remains dominant in orthodox property discourse, the notion of recognising the importance of 'things' and recognising the land itself as limiting use rights has been informally adopted by a growing number of individuals, communities and organisations around the world. In the next section, I provide an example of this with reference to the practice of agrarian farming. I contend that agrarian land use practices contain valuable insight for those engaged in developing an ecocentric description of property that recognises the importance of the 'thing' that mediates a property relationship.

### 5.5.2 Things in practice

As detailed already, agrarian farming is a practice that encourages a deep connection with place and conceives ownerships norms in such a way as to

---

25. *Lucas v South Carolina Coastal Watch 05 US Supreme Court 1003 (1992).*

preserve the health of the human and non-human community. Commenting on this description Wendell Berry notes: 'Land health is the one value . . . the one absolute good' that upholds the entire web of life (1972: 186). In his description of private property, Berry draws on the English botanist, Sir Albert Howard. Howard (1947: 11) urged people to adopt a holistic perspective and understand the 'problem of land health in soil, plant, animal and man as one great subject'. Consistent with the concept of Earth community, Berry (1993: 14) defines 'community' in broad terms:

> If we speak of a *healthy* community, we cannot be speaking of a community that is merely human. We are talking about a neighbourhood of humans in a place, plus the place itself: its soil, its water, its air, and all the families and tries of the nonhuman creatures that belong to it. If the place is well preserved, if its entire membership, natural and human, is present in it, and if the human economy is in practical harmony with the nature of the place, then the community is healthy.

Berry also draws on important elements of natural rights reasoning when dealing with the limits of private property. 'I am an uneasy believer in the right of private property', Berry writes, 'because I know that this right can be understood as the right to destroy, which is to say the natural or the given world' (1995: 50). He continues, stating that: 'I do not believe that such a right exists, even though its presumed existence has covered the destruction of a lot of land' (1995: 50). Accordingly, for Berry the entire institution of private property is infused with ethical considerations toward the land. Berry (1984: 30) argues further that private property functions best when owners act in relationship with each other and with the land itself:

> Property belongs to a family of words, if we can free them from the denigration that shallow politics and social fashion have imposed on them, are the words and ideas, that govern our connections with the world and with one another: property, proper, appropriate, propriety. The word property . . . if we use it in its full sense (that is, with a proper respect for the pattern of meaning that surrounds it) always implies the intimate involvement of a proprietary mind – not the mind of ownership, as the term is necessarily defined by the industrial economy, but a mind possessed of the knowledge, affection, and skill appropriate to the keeping and use of its property.

Berry's writing has been influential on other agrarian farmers such as Wes Jackson and the Land Institute. Since 1976, Jackson and his colleagues have run a Natural Systems Agriculture Program (Jackson 2010, 2011). The programme challenges conventional ideas of ownership by conducting agriculture in a way that utilises and respects the naturally occurring ecological processes of the specific piece of land they are using and disturbing the pre-existing ecosystem as little as possible. Jackson (2002: 44) notes that 'we took the never-plowed native prairie to be our teacher.' Prairies are excellent teachers for Jackson's work because they sustain a great diversity of species, which are nearly all perennial. Further, plant roots on a prairie do not rot away like annual roots. Instead, they hold soil though all seasons and as a consequence can be studied all year round. Moreover, perennial plants actually build soil and give back to the ecological system. The ecosystem thus maintains its own health, fuelled by the energy from the sun and recycled nutrients. All of this is achieved at no cost or detriment to human beings or to the Earth community. Jackson (2002: 44) explains:

> [W]herever there is a prairie, four functional groups are featured: warm-season grasses, cool-season grasses, legumes, and composites. Other species are present, but these groups are featured. Different species fill different roles. Some thrive in dry years, others in wet ones. Some provide fertility by fixing atmospheric nitrogen. Some tolerate shade, others require direct sunlight. Some repel insect predators. Some do better on poor, rocky soils while others need rich, deep soil. Diversity provides the system with built-in-resilience to changes and cycles in climate, water, insects and pests, grazers and other natural disturbances.

The challenge set by Jackson and his team is to combine species diversity and perennialism. To match the needs of the prairie, they use four functional groups in their polyculture and seek to ensure that the groups produce harvestable grain for direct human consumption. They then imitate the prairie and produce harvest through the services it naturally performs. The results of this work have been extraordinary and Jackson (2002: 44) contends: 'Properly designed, the system itself should virtually eliminate the ecological degradation characteristic of conventional agriculture and minimise the need for human intervention.'

This vision of land use promotes a process of constant reassessment and adjustment to match the ecological needs of place. As the landowner becomes intimate with the land, his rights and obligations bend and dynamic from season to season. Rather than dictating to the land, ownership practices unfold over time in conversation with a 'coequal subject rather than a mere object' (Freyfogle 1998: 135). Guided by nature, private property could express a 'community's growing understanding of nature' and their 'willingness to respect nature's limits' (Freyfogle 1998: 135). It could also provide a tool for dealing with recalcitrant landowners, inclined to continue to exploit the land for individual preference satisfaction. Further to these factors, an ecological interpretation of private property could promote a more aesthetically pleasing landscape and fulfil the common human desire to live in harmony with nature – as one member of the Earth community. Certainly, 'none of us lives to the fullest, who does not study the natural order, and more than that, none is wise who does not ultimately make peace with it' (Rolston III 1998: 44).

## 5.6 Conclusion

Over the centuries, dominant Western culture and lawmakers have never seriously considered giving up the institution of private property or reducing its importance. However, there has been rigorous debate about what private property means. I contend that this is where a theory of Earth jurisprudence can exercise the most influence, particularly its description of private property as a relationship between and among members of the Earth community, through tangible or intangible items. In this context, private property is more than an individual right and includes relationship with community, the land and ethical considerations. Consistent with the legal philosophy of Earth jurisprudence, a theory of private property that overlooks any of these considerations is defective and deserves to be labelled as such.

In conducting this analysis, I acknowledge that any transition toward an ecocentric conception of private property would require extensive structural reform to the institution of property. I also acknowledge that the reforms outlined in this chapter will be attacked on the grounds of 'inefficiency' or perhaps 'utopianism', which is commonly levelled at proposals for 'interventionist' or 'regulatory' structural reform of the property system (Epstein 1985: 970). However, I contend that this objection loses much of its vigour when considered in light of the role private property plays in facilitating environmental harm. There are persuasive arguments for human beings to rationally agree to limit their own efficiency and environmental impact. In this sense, what is utopian is not Earth jurisprudence or an ecocentric theory of private property. What is truly utopian is the misguided belief that human law and legal concepts do not need to change and we can continue to exploit the environment for human benefit. From this perspective, the charges of inefficiency or utopianism ought to be embraced, not as an indictment but as a defence to existing ecological need.

Importantly, the key to evolving the concept of private property lies within the concept itself. As noted, private property is a concept that has many conceptions and interpretations, such that the past and present forms of private property by no means exhaust the range of institutional possibilities. The indeterminate nature of private property opens up theoretical space for systems of property that are radically different from contemporary interpretations.

Further, for all its shortcomings, the liberal theory of private property allows individuals and the collective to choose their own concept of private property within set constraints. This was illustrated most poignantly with reference to Indigenous ideas of ownership and agrarian land use practices. Thus, while the current rights-based theory promotes individual preference satisfaction, we can choose not to follow these ownership norms and interact with the land responsibly, ethically and with consideration of place. Making this choice is an example of vernacular law and is the most immediate way that individual and communities can reform the concept of private property so that it is consistent with the great law. As Paul Babie contends, exercising choice is fundamental to reshaping the institution of private property (2010a : 527). If conducted on a broad scale and given the political will, ecocentric examples of property ownership can help transform the institution of private property. If we can reconceptualise our relationship with the land from individual rights to the concept of Earth community, then there is every chance that we can interact with the environment in a sustainable way for many years to come.

# Epilogue: the great work

## Concluding remarks

> History is governed by those overarching movements that give shape and meaning to life by relating the human venture to the larger destinies of the universe. Creating such a movement might be called the Great Work of a people. (Berry 1999: 1)

In his final book before his death (in 2009), Thomas Berry identified a 'great work' that lies before humankind. 'The Great Work now' he writes 'is to carry out the transition from a period of human devastation of the Earth to a period when humans would be present to the planet in a mutually beneficial manner' (1999: 3). Berry was under no illusion of the immensity of this task, neither was he unaware of its urgency. Indeed, reflecting on the present environmental crisis, he argues that perhaps the most 'valuable heritage' we can provide for future generations is some indication of how this work can be fulfilled in an effective manner (1999: 7). This is not a task we have chosen for ourselves. However, Berry (1999: 7) maintains that '[T]he nobility of our lives . . . depends upon the manner in which we come to understand and fulfil our assigned role.' This book represents a modest contribution to the great work and is part of a vast tapestry of ideas and actions that are striving toward a sustainable human presence with the Earth community.

As we approach the immense task that is before us, we would do well to follow Berry's lead and confront what C. Wright Mills (1956: 346) called the 'higher immorality' that dominates our society and law. That is, those unjustifiable hierarchical values and structures that are ultimately responsible for the exploitation of the planet and human suffering. Chief among these is anthropocentrism and the tyranny of money power. These instances of higher immorality are so institutionalised in society that they hardly appear as immoral at all. Nevertheless, all other moral standards and bases of community are forced to give way before them. Thus, if land – the essential human connection to the earth – is turned into mere property to be bought, sold or exploited, it is due to this reduction of everything into human and economic values. In contemporary capitalist societies, these values have become the real community and the measure of all worth.

No sustained progress can be achieved for the protection of the Earth community unless we confront this higher immorality head on. Hence today, we are seeing a rise throughout the world of an ecological critique of law and governance. As articulated in this book, this critique rests on two propositions:

1    that law reflects unjustifiable anthropocentric values and is a vehicle which those in power use to exploit both the human and ecological community; and
2    that a concept of private property that disconnects people from a sense of being native to some place and all ecological roots is incompatible with ecological stability.

Eventually, it seems clear that both these propositions will need to shift if we are to realise a mutually enhancing human–Earth relationship that reflects the paradigm of Earth community. While important work is being carried out in this regard, the project of transitioning toward the Ecozoic era is still in its infancy. Because of the importance Western culture places on law and the institution of private property, a paradigm shift toward ecocentrism will require a fundamental rethinking of both institutions and the purposes they intend to serve. More fundamentally, it will require struggle and for all parts of civil society to fight for social and environmental justice. In outlining a theory of social change, as well as an ecocentric concept of law, this book has aimed to provide some groundwork needed to advance this most important task.

# Bibliography

## Books

Agar, Nicholas, *Life's Intrinsic Value* (Columbia University Press, 2001)

Alexander, Frank, 'Property and Christian theology' in John Witte Jr and Frank Alexander (eds), *Christianity and Law: An Introduction* (Cambridge University Press, 2008)

Alexander, Gregory, *Commodity and Propriety: Competing Visions of Property in American Legal Thought* (University of Chicago Press, 1999)

Alexander, Samuel, *Voluntary Simplicity: The Poetic Alternative to Consumer Culture* (Stead and Daughters, 2009).

Alexander, Samuel, 'Property beyond Growth: Toward a Politics of Voluntary Simplicity' in David Grinlinton and Prue Taylor, *Property Rights and Sustainability: The Evolution of Property Rights to Meet Ecological Challenges* (Martinus Nijhoff, 2011)

Alexy, Robert, *The Argument for Injustice: A Reply to Legal Positivism* (Oxford University Press, 2002)

Allot, Phillip, *Eunomia: New Order for a New World* (Oxford University Press, 1990)

Anderson, Anthony and Clinton Jenkins, *Applying Nature's Design: Corridors as a Strategy for Biodiversity Conservation* (Columbia University Press, 2006)

Angermeier, Paul L., and James R. Karr, 'Protecting Biotic Resources: Biological Integrity versus Biological Diversity as Policy Directives' (1994) *BioScience* 44(10): 690–697

Aquinas, Thomas, *Summa Theologica* (Christian Classics, 1981) [first published 1274]

Aquinas, Thomas, *Summa Contra Gentiles* (University of Notre Dame Press, 1991) [first published 1264]

Aquinas, Thomas, *Treatise on Law: Summa Theologica, Questions 90–97* (Gateway Editions, 1996)

Arendt, Hannah, *The Human Condition* (University of Chicago Press, 1958)

Aristotle, 'History of Animals' in Barnes, Jonathan (ed.), The Complete Works of Aristotle, Vol. 1 (Princeton University Press, 1984)

Armstrong, David, *What is a Law of Nature?* (Cambridge University Press, 1983)

Attfield, Robin, *Environmental Philosophy: Principles and Prospects* (Ashgate Publishing, 1994)

Augustine, St, *City of God* (Penguin Classics, 2003)

Babie, Paul, 'Climate Change and the Concept of Private Property' in Rosemary Lyster (ed.), *In the Wilds of Climate Law* (Australian Academic Press, 2010)

Babie, Paul, 'Private Property and Human Consequence' in Peter Burdon (ed.), *An Invitation to Wild Law* (Wakefield Press, 2011)

Babie, Paul, *Private Property, Climate Change and The Children of Abraham* (University of British Columbia Press, 2015)

Bacon, Francis, *The Essays* (Penguin Classics, 1986)

Bacon, Francis, *Francis Bacon: The Major Works* (Oxford University Press, 1985)

Bacon, Francis, *The New Atlantis* (Cambridge University Press, 1990) [first published 1626]

Barnes, Jonathan (ed.), *The Complete Works of Aristotle* (Princeton University Press, 1984)

Bates, Gerry, *Environmental Law in Australia*, 6th edn (Butterworths, 2002)

Bateson, Gregory, *Mind and Nature: A Necessary Unity* (Hampton Press, 2002)

Baxi, Upendra, The Future of Human Rights (Oxford University Press, 2006)

Becker, Lawrence C., *Property Rights: Philosophical Foundations* (Routledge & Kegan Paul, 1977)

Bedau, Hugo (ed.), *Civil Disobedience in Focus* (Routledge, 1991)

Begon, Michael, *Ecology: Individuals, Populations and Communities* (Sinauer Associates, 1996)

Bennett, Jane, *Vibrant Matter: A Political Ecology of Things* (Duke University Press Books, 2010)

Bentham, Jeremy, *A Theory of Legislation* (Elibron Classics, 1931) [first published 1789]

Bentham, Jeremy, *A Bentham Reader* (Pegasus, 1969)

Bentham, Jeremy, *Commentary on the Commentaries* (Oxford University Press, 1978) [first published 1823]

Bentham, Jeremy, 'Deontology' in Ammon Goldworth (ed), *The Collected Works of Jeremy Bentham* (Oxford University Press, 1985)

Benyus, Janine M., *Biomimicry: Innovation Inspired by Nature* (Harper Perennial, 2007)

Berger, Peter and Thomas Luckmann, *The Social Construction of Reality: A Treatise in the Sociology of Knowledge* (Anchor, 1966)

Bergin, Thomas and Max Fisch, *The New Science of Giambattista Vico* (Cornell University Press, 1970)

Berlin, Isaiah, *Liberty: Incorporating Four Essays on Liberty* (Oxford University Press, 2002)

Berman, Harold J., *Law and Revolution: The Formation of the Western Legal Tradition* (Harvard University Press, 1983)

Berman, Harold J., *Law and Revolution, II: The Impact of the Protestant Reformations on the Western Legal Tradition* (Harvard University Press, 2006)

Berman, Morris, *The Re-enchantment of the World* (Cornell University Press, 1981)

Berry, Thomas, *The Historical Theory of Giambattista Vico* (PhD thesis, American Catholic University, 1949)

Berry, Thomas, 'The New Story' in *Teilhard Studies* (Anima Books, 1977)

Berry, Thomas, 'Perspectives on Creativity: Openness to a Free Future' in Francis A. Eigo (ed.), *Whither Creativity, Freedom, Suffering? Humanity, Cosmos, God* (Villanova University Theology Institute Publishers, 1981)

Berry, Thomas, *The Dream of the Earth* (Sierra Club Books, 1988)

Berry, Thomas, *Human Presence in the Earth Community: Tape Five* (1989) Audiotape

Berry, Thomas, *Befriending the Earth: A Theology of Reconciliation Between Humans and the Earth* (Twenty-Third Publications, 1991)

Berry, Thomas, *Thomas Berry and the New Cosmology* (Twenty-Third Publications, 1991)

Berry, Thomas, *The Great Work: Our Way into the Future* (Bell Tower, 1999)

Berry, Thomas, 'The Story and the Dream: The Next Step in the Evolutionary Epic' in J.B. Miller (ed.), *The Epic of Evolution: Science and Religion in Dialogue* (Prentice Hall, 2003)

Berry, Thomas, 'Legal Conditions for Earth Survival' in Mary-Evelyn Tucker (ed.), *Evening Thoughts: Reflections on Earth as Sacred Community* (Sierra Club Books, 2006)

Berry, Thomas, 'The Spirituality of the Earth' in Charles Birch et al (eds), *Liberating Life: Contemporary Approaches in Ecological Theology* (Wipf & Stock, 1990)

Berry, Thomas, *The Sacred Universe: Earth, Spirituality and Religion in the Twenty-First Century* (Columbia University Press, 2009)

Berry, Wendell, *A Continuous Harmony: Essays Cultural and Agricultural* (Harcourt Brace Jovanovich, 1972)

Berry, Wendell, 'Whose Head is the Farmer Using? Whose Head is Using the Farmer?' in Wes Jackson, Wendell Berry and Bruce Coleman (eds), *Meeting the Expectations of the Land* (North Point Press, 1984)

Berry, Wendell, *Sex, Economy, Freedom and Community* (Pantheon Books, 1993)

Berry, Wendell, *Another Turn of the Crank* (Counterpoint, 1995)

Berry, Wendell, *The Unsettling of America: Culture and Agriculture* (Sierra Club Books, 1996)

Berry, Wendell, *The Art of the Commonplace: The Agrarian Essays of Wendell Berry* (Counterpoint, 2003)

Berry, Wendell, *That Distant Land: The Collected Stories* (Counterpoint, 2005)

Bertalanffy, Ludwig von, *General Systems Theory* (George Braziller, 1968)

Best, Steven, 'The Commodification of Reality and the Reality of Commodification' in Douglas Kellner (ed.), *Baudrillard: A Critical Reader* (Oxford University Press, 1994)

Best, Steven, *Igniting a Revolution: Voices in Defense of the Earth* (AK Press, 2006)

Birch, Charles, *Biology and the Riddle of Life* (University of New South Wales Press, 1999)

Bix, Brian H., *A Dictionary of Legal Theory* (Oxford University Press, 2004)

Bix, Brian H., 'The Natural Law Tradition' in Joel Fienberg and Jules Coleman (eds), *Philosophy of Law* (Wadsworth Publishing, 2004)

Bix, Brian H., *Jurisprudence: Theory and Context* (Carolina Academic Press, 2009)

Blackshield, Tony and George Williams, *Australian Constitutional Law and Theory*, 3rd edn (Federation Press, 2002)

Blackstone, Sir William, *The Commentaries on the Laws of England* (Oxford University Press, 1966) [first published 1796]

Blomley, Nicholas, *Law, Space and the Geographies of Power* (Guilford Press, 1994)

Blomley, Nicholas, D. Delaney and R. Ford, *The Legal Geographies Reader: Law, Power and Space* (Wiley-Blackwell, 2001)

Bohm, David, 'Postmodern Science and a Postmodern World' in Carolyn Merchant (ed.), *Ecology* (Humanity Books, 1994)

Bonyhady, T. and T. Griffiths, *Words for Country: Landscape and Language* (University of New South Wales Press, 2002)

Bookchin, Murray, *The Ecology of Freedom: The Emergence and Dissolution of Hierarchy* (Cheshire Books, 1982)

Bookchin, Murray, *The Rise of Urbanization and the Decline of Citizenship* (Sierra Club Books, 1987)

Bookchin, Murray, *Remaking Society: Pathways to a Green Future* (South End Press, 1990)

Bookchin, Murray, *Toward an Ecological Society* (Black Rose Books, 1996)

Bookchin, Murray and Dave Forman, *Defending the Earth: A Dialogue Between Murray Bookchin and Dave Foreman* (South End Press, 1999)

Bosselmann, Klaus, *When Two Worlds Collide: Society and Ecology* (RSVP, 1995)

Bosselmann, Klaus, *The Principle of Sustainability: Transforming Law and Governance* (Ashgate, 2008)

Bosselmann, Klaus, 'The Way Forward: Governance and Ecological Integrity', in Laura Westra, Klaus Bosselmann and Richard Westra *Reconciling Human Existence with Ecological Integrity* (Earthscan, 2008)

Bosselmann, Klaus, 'Earth Democracy: Institutionalizing Sustainability and Ecological Integrity' in J. Ronald Engel, Laura Westra and Klaus Bosselmann (eds), *Democracy, Ecological Integrity and International Law* (Cambridge Scholars Press, 2010)

Bosselmann, Klaus, 'From Reductionist Environmental Law to Sustainability Law' in Peter Burdon (ed.), *Wild Law: An Invitation* (Wakefield Press, 2011a)

Bosselmann, Klaus, 'Property Rights and Sustainability: Can They Be Reconciled?' in David Grinlinton and Prue Taylor (eds), *Property Rights and Sustainability: The Evolution of Property Rights to Meet Ecological Challenges* (Martinus Nijhoff, 2011b)

Bosselmann, Klaus and David Grinlinton (eds), *Environmental Law for a Sustainable Society* (NZCEL Monograph Series, 2002)

Boughey, Arthur, *Man and the Environment: Introduction to Human Ecology and Evolution* (Macmillan, 1975)

Boyd, Brian, *On the Origin of Stories: Evolution, Cognition, and Fiction* (Belknap Press of Harvard University Press, 2010)

Bressler, J.B., *Human Ecology* (Addison-Wesley, 1966)

Brooks, Richard O., Ross Jones and Ross A. Virginia, *Law and Ecology: The Rise of the Ecosystem Regime* (Ashgate, 2002)

Brown, Andrew, *J.D. Bernal: The Sage of Science* (Oxford University Press, 2007)

Brown, Brian Edward, *Religion, Law and the Land: Native Americans and the Judicial Interpretation of Sacred Land* (Greenwood Press, 1999)

Brown, Lester R., *Plan 4:0 Mobilizing to Save Civilization* (World Watch Institute, 2009)

Buckland, William, *Roman Law of Slavery: The Condition of The Slave In Private Law From Augustus To Justinian* (Kessinger Publishing, 2010) [first published 1908]

Bullard, Robert D., *Dumping in Dixie: Race, Class, and Environmental Quality* (Westview Press, 2000).

Burdon, Peter, 'The Ecozoic Paradigm' in Peter Burdon (ed.), *An Invitation to Wild Law* (Wakefield Press, 2011)

Burdon, Peter, 'The Great Law' in Peter Burdon (ed.), *An Invitation to Wild Law* (Wakefield Press, 2011)

Burdon, Peter, 'The Project of Earth Democracy' in *Confronting Collapse: What Agencies, Institutions and Strategies are Needed for a Better World? How to Achieve Environmental Justice?* (Routledge, 2013)

Burdon, Peter, 'Environmental Human Rights: A Constructive Critique' in Anna Grear and Louis Kotz (eds), *Research Handbook on Human Rights and the Environment* (Edward Elgar, 2014)

Burns Thomas, 'Hierarchical Evolution in Ecological Networks' in Masahiko Higashi and Thomas Burns, *Theoretical Studies of Ecosystems: The Network Perspective* (Cambridge University Press, 1991)

Butt, Peter, *Land Law* (Law Book Company, 2001)

Campbell, Joseph, *The Inner Reaches of Outer Space: Metaphor as Myth and as Religion* (New World Library, 2002)

Capra, Fritjof, *The Turning Point: Science, Society, and the Rising Culture* (Bantam, 1983)

Capra, Fritjof, 'Systems Theory and the New Paradigm' in Carolyn Merchant (ed.), *Ecology* (Humanity Books, 1994)

Capra, Fritjof, *The Web of Life: A New Scientific Understanding of Living Systems* (Anchor Books, 1996)

Capra, Fritjof, *The Tao of Physics: An Exploration of the Parallels between Modern Physics and Eastern Mysticism* (Shambhala, 2010)

Carson, Rachel, *Silent Spring* (Mariner Books, 1962)

Carter, Paul, *The Lie of the Land* (Faber & Faber, 1996)

Carlyle, A.J., *Property, its Rights and Duties* (Macmillan, 1922)

Cashford, Jules, 'Dedication to Thomas Berry' in Peter Burdon (ed.), *An Invitation to Wild Law* (Wakefield Press, 2011)

Chardin, Teilhard de, *The Phenomenon of Man* (Collins Sons & Co Ltd, 1959)

Chardin, Pierre Teilhard de, *The Divine Milieu* (Harper & Row, 1960)

Chardin, Pierre Teilhard de, *Science and Christ* (Harper & Row, 1968)

Chardin, Pierre Teilhard de, *The Future of Man* (Harper & Row, 1977)

Chardin, Pierre Teilhard de, *The Phenomenon of Man* (Harper Perennial, 2008)

Christ, Carol, 'Why Women Need the Goddess' in Carol Christ and Judith Plaskow (eds), *Womanspirit Rising: A Feminist Reader in Religion* (Harper and Row, 1979)

Churchill, Ward, *Pacifism as Pathology* (AK Press, 2007)

Cicero, *The Nature of the Gods* (Oxford University Press, 2008)

Cicero, *The Republic and the Laws* (Oxford University Press, 2008)

Clark, Ronald W., *Einstein: The Life and Times* (Harper Perennial, 2007)

Clay, Jason, *World Agriculture and the Environment* (Island Press, 2004)

Code, Lorraine, Ecological Thinking: The Politics of Epistemic Location (Oxford University Press, 2006)

Cohen, G.A., *Karl Marx's Theory of History: A Defence* (Oxford University Press, 1978)

Cole, Daniel, *Pollution and Property: Comparing Ownership Institutions for Environmental Protection* (Cambridge University Press, 2002)

Comte, Auguste, *Introduction to Positive Philosophy* (Hackett Publishing Company, 1988)

Cooper, John M (ed.), *Plato: Complete Works* (Hackett Publishing Company, 1997)

Cotterell, Roger, *Law, Culture and Society: Legal Ideas in the Mirror of Social Theory* (Ashgate Publishing, 2006)

Coyle, Sean and Karen Morrow, *The Philosophical Foundations of Environmental Law: Property, Rights and Nature* (Hart Publishing, 2004)

Craig, Edward (ed.), *The Shorter Routledge Encyclopedia of Philosophy* (Routledge, 2005)

Cronon, William (ed.), *Uncommon Ground: Rethinking the Human Place in Nature* (WW Norton and Company, 1996)

Crooks, Kevin and M Sanjayan (eds), *Connectivity Conservation* (Cambridge University Press, 2006)

Cullinan, Cormac, *Wild Law: A Manifesto for Earth Justice* (Green Books, 2003)

Cullinan, Cormac, *Wild Law: A Manifesto for Earth Justice* (Chelsea Green Publishing, 2011a)

Cullinan, Cormac, 'A History of Wild Law' in Peter Burdon (ed.), *An Invitation to Wild Law* (Wakefield Press, 2011b)

Cullis, Tara and David Suzuki, *The Declaration of Interdependence: A Pledge to Planet Earth* (Greystone Books, 2010)

Curd, Martin, 'The Laws of Nature' in Martin Curd and J.A Cover, *Philosophy of Science: The Central Issues* (WW Norton and Company, 1998)

Dalton, Anne Marie, *A Theology for the Earth: The Contributions of Thomas Berry and Bernard Lonergan* (University of Ottawa Press, 1999)

Darwin, Charles, *The Origin of Species: 150th Anniversary Edition* (Signet Classics, 2003)

Davies, Margaret, *Property, Meanings, Histories, Theories* (Routledge, 2007)

Davies, Margaret, *Asking the Law Question* (Thomson Reuters, 2008)

Derrida, Jacques, 'Before the Law' in David Attridge (ed.), *Acts of Literature* (Routledge, 1992)

Descartes, René in John Cottingham (ed.), *The Philosophical Writings of Descartes* (Cambridge University Press, 1985)

Descartes, René, *Discourse on the Method for Conducting One's Reason Well and for Seeking Truth in the Sciences* (Hackett Publishing Company, 1998)

Descartes, René, *Meditations, Objections, and Replies* (Hackett Publishing Company, 2006)

DesJardin, Joseph, *Environmental Ethics: Concepts, Policy, and Theory* (McGraw- Hill, 1998)

Dessler, Andrew and Edward Parson, *The Science and Politics of Global Climate Change: A Guide to the Debate* (Cambridge University Press, 2010)

Devall, Bill and George Sessions (eds), *Deep Ecology: Living as if Nature Mattered* (Gibbs Smith, 1985)

Diamond, Jared, *Guns, Germs, and Steel: The Fates of Human Societies* (WW Norton and Company, 2005)

Dokuchaev, Vasilievich, *Cartography of Russian Soils* (St Petersburg, 1879)

Downton, Paul, *Ecopolis: Architecture and Cities for a Changing Climate* (Springer, Press, 2009)

Dozer, Rudolf, *Property and Environment: The Social Obligation Inherent to Ownership – A Study of German Constitutional Setting* (International Union for Conservation of Nature and Natural Resources, 1976)

Dubos, René, 'A Theology of the Earth' in Ian Barbour (ed.), *Western Man and Environmental Ethics* (Longman Higher Education, 1973)

Dunn, Stephen, Thomas Clarke and Anne Lonergan, *Befriending the Earth: A Theology of Reconciliation Between Humans and the Earth: Thomas Berry and Thomas Clark* (Twenty-Third Publications, 1991)

Dworkin, Ronald, *Taking Rights Seriously* (Harvard University Press, 1978)

Eagleton, Terry, *Why Marx was Right* (Yale University Press, 2012)

Eckersley, Robyn, *Environmentalism and Political Theory: Toward an Ecocentric Approach* (State University of New York Press, 1992)

Eckersley, Robyn, *The Green State: Rethinking Democracy and Sovereignty* (MIT Press, 2004)

Ehrenfeld, David, *The Arrogance of Humanism* (Oxford University Press, 1978)

Ehrlich, Paul, *The Population Bomb* (MacMillan, 1972)

Eiseley, Loren, *The Immense Journey* (Vintage, 1946)

Eiseley, Loren, *The Firmament of Time* (Bison Books, 1960)

Embree, Lester, *Environmental Philosophy and Environmental Activism* (Rowman & Littlefield Publishers, 1995)

Engel, J. 'Contesting Democracy' in J. Ronald Engel, Laura Westra and Klaus Bosselmann (eds), *Democracy, Ecological Integrity and International Law* (Cambridge Scholars Press, 2010)

Engel, Ron, *Sacred Sands: The Struggle for Community in the Indiana Dunes* (Wesleyan Press, 1986).

Engel, J. Ronald, 'Property: Faustian Pact or New Covenant with Earth?' in David Grinlington and Prue Taylor (eds), *Property Rights and Sustainability: The Evolution of Property Rights to Meet Ecological Challenges* (Martinus Nijhoff, 2011)

Engel, J. Ronald, 'The Summons to a New Axial Age: The Promise, Limits and Future of the Earth Charter' in Laura Westra and Mirian Vilela (eds), *The Earth Charter, Ecological Integrity and Social Movements* (Routledge, 2014)

Engel, J. Ronald and Brendan Mackey, 'The Earth Charter, Covenants, and Earth Jurisprudence' in Peter Burdon (ed.), *An Invitation to Wild Law* (Wakefield Press, 2011)

Epstein, Richard, *Takings: Private Property and the Power of Eminent Domain* (Harvard University Press, 1985)

Esjörn-Hargens, Sean, 'Ecological Interiority: Thomas Berry's Integral Ecology Legacy' in Ervin Laszlo and Allan Combs (eds), *Thomas Berry, Dreamer of the Earth: The Spiritual Ecology of the Father of Environmentalism* (Inner Traditions, 2011)

Esjörn-Hargens, Sean and Michael E. Zimmerman, *Integral Ecology: Uniting Multiple Perspectives on the Natural World* (Integral Books, 2009)

Etzioni, Amitai, *The Essential Communitarian Reader* (Rowman & Littlefield Publishers, 1998)

Evernden, Neil, *The Social Creation of Nature* (Johns Hopkins University Press, 1992)

Evernden, Neil, *The Natural Alien: Human Kind and the Environment* (University of Toronto Press, 1999)

Fairweather, N., 'The Future of Environmental Direct Action: A Case for Tolerating Disobedience' in N. Fairweather, Sue Elworthy, Matt Stroh and Piers Stephens (eds), *Environmental Futures* (Palgrave Macmillan, 1999)

Farrington, Benjamin, *Francis Bacon: Philosopher of Industrial Science* (Schumann, 1949)

Fiere, Ronald, 'The Sceptical Perspective: Science Without Laws of Nature' in Friedel Weinert (ed.), *Laws of Nature: Essays on the Philosophical, Scientific and Historical Dimensions* (Walter de Gruyter, 1995)

Finnis, John, *Natural Law and Natural Rights* (Oxford University Press, 1980)

Finnis, John, 'Law, Problems in Philosophy' in Ted Honderich (ed.), *Oxford Companion to Philosophy* (Oxford University Press, 1995)

Finnis, John, 'The Truth in Legal Positivism' in Robert P. George (ed.), *The Autonomy of Law: Essays in Legal Positivism* (Oxford University Press, 1996)

Finnis, John, *Aquinas: Moral, Political, and Legal Theory* (Oxford University Press, 1998)

Finocchiaro, Maurice A. (ed.), *The Essential* Galileo (Hackett Publishing Company, 2008)

Fish, Stanley, *Doing What Comes Naturally: Change, Rhetoric, and the Practice of Theory in Literary and Legal Studies, Post-contemporary Interventions* (Duke University Press Books, 1990)

Fitzpatrick, Peter, *The Mythology of Modern Law* (Routledge, 1992)

Flader, Susan, and J. Baird Callicott, *The River of the Mother of God and Other Essays by Aldo Leopold* (University of Wisconsin Press, 1991)

Flannery, Tim, *The Future Eaters* (Grove Press, 1994)

Folse, Henry, *The Philosophy of Niels Bohr: The Framework of Complementarily* (North Holland, 1985)

Forbes, Stephen, *The Lake as a Microcosm* (Bobbs-Merrill, 1925)

Foster, John Bellamy, *Marx's Ecology: Materialism and Nature* (Monthly Review Press, 2000)

Foster, John Bellamy, *Ecology Against Capitalism* (Monthly Review Press, 2002)

Foster, John Bellamy, *The Ecological Revolution: Making Peace with the Planet* (Monthly Review Press, 2009)

Foster, John Bellamy, *The Ecological Rift: Capitalism's War on the Earth* (Monthly Review Press, 2010)

Fourier, Charles, Gareth Jones and Ian Patterson, *Fourier: The Theory of the Four Movements* (Cambridge University Press, 1996)

Fox, Matthew, 'Some Thoughts on Thomas Berry's Contributions to the Western Spiritual Tradition' in Ervin Laszlo and Allan Combs (eds), *Thomas Berry, Dreamer of the Earth: The Spiritual Ecology of the Father of Environmentalism* (Inner Traditions, 2011)

Freeman, M.D.A., *Current Legal Problems* (Oxford University Press, 1982)

Freeman, M.D.A., *Lloyd's Introduction to Jurisprudence* (Thomson Reuters, 2008)

Freud, Sigmund, *Civilization and Its Discontents* (WW Norton and Company, 1989)

Freyfogle, Eric T., *Justice and Earth: Images of Our Planetary Survival* (Free Press, 1993)

Freyfogle, Eric T., *Bounded People, Boundless Lands: Envisioning A New Land Ethic* (Island Press, 1998)

Freyfogle, Eric T., *The New Agrarianism: Land, Culture, and the Community of Life* (Island Press, 2001)

Freyfogle, Eric T., *The Land We Share: Private Property and the Common Good* (Shearwater Books, 2003)

Freyfogle, Eric T., 'Private Property in Land: An Agrarian View' in Norman Wirzba (ed.), *The Essential Agrarian Reader: The Future of Culture, Community and the Land* (Counterpoint, 2003)

Freyfogle, Eric T., *Why Conservation is Failing and How it Can Regain Ground* (Yale University Press, 2006)

Freyfogle, Eric T., *Agrarianism and the Good Society: Land, Culture, Conflict, and Hope* (University Press of Kentucky, 2007)

Freyfogle, Eric T., *On Private Property: Finding Common Ground on the Ownership of Land* (Beacon Press, 2007)

Freyfogle, Eric T., *On Private Property: Finding Common Ground on the Ownership of Land* (Beacon Press, 2009)

Freyfogle, Eric T. and Dale D. Goble, *Wildlife Law Cases and Materials: Cases and Materials* (Foundation Press, 2009)

Freyfogle, Eric T., and Dale D. Goble, *Wildlife Law: A Primer* (Island Press, 2009)

Francione, Gary, *Animals Property and the Law* (Temple University Press, 2005)

Fuller, Lon, *The Law in Quest of Itself* (Beacon Press, 1940)

Fuller, Lon, *The Morality of Law* (Yale University Press, 1964)

Fuller, Lon, *The Principles of Social Order* (Duke University Press, 1981)

Gardner, Garry, *Inspiring Progress: Religion's Contribution to Sustainable Development* (Worldwatch Institute, 2006)

Gammage, Bill, *The Biggest Estate on Earth: How Aborigines Made Australia* (Allen & Unwin, 2013)

Garber, Daniel, 'René Descartes' in Edward Craig (ed.), *The Shorter Routledge Encyclopedia of Philosophy* (Routledge, 2005)

Gelderloos, Peter, *How Nonviolence Protects the State* (Southend Press, 2007)

Getzler, Joshua, 'Roman Ideas of Landownership' in Susan Bright and John Dewar (eds), *Land Law: Themes and Perspectives* (Oxford University Press, 1998)

Godden, Lee and Jacqueline Peel, *Environmental Law: Scientific, Policy and Regulatory Dimensions* (Oxford University Press, 2010)

Goldstein, Robert, *Ecology and Environmental Ethics: Green Wood in the Bundle of Sticks* (Ashgate Publishing, 2004)

Goldworth, A. (ed.), *The Collected Works of Jeremy Bentham* (Oxford University Press, 1983)

Golan, Tal, *Laws of Men and Laws of Nature: The History of Scientific Expert Testimony in England and America* (Harvard University Press, 2007)

Gordon, Robert, 'Paradoxical Property' in John Brewer and Susan Staves (eds), *Early Modern Conceptions of Property* (Routledge, 1995)

Gottlieb, Roger S. (ed.), *The Ecological Community* (Routledge, 1996)

Gottlieb, Roger S., *This Sacred Earth: Religion, Nature, Environment* (Routledge, 1996)

Gottlieb, Roger S., *The Oxford Handbook of Religion and Ecology* (Oxford University Press, 2010)

Graham, Nicole, *Lawscape: Paradigm and Place in Australian Property Law* (PhD thesis, University of Sydney, 2003)

Graham, Nicole, 'Restoring the "Real" to Real Property Law' in Wilfred Press (ed.), *Blackstone and His Commentaries: Biography, Law, History* (Hart Publishing, 2009)

Graham, Nicole, *Lawscape: Property, Environment, Law* (Routledge, 2011)

Gray, Janice, 'Watered Down Legal Constructs, Tradable Entitlement and the Regulation of Water' in Devleena Ghosh, Heather Goodall and Stephanie Hemelryk Donald (eds), *Water, Sovereignty and Borders in Asia and Oceania* (Routledge, 2008)

Green, T.H., *Lectures on the Principles of Political Obligation* (Cambridge University Press, 1907)

Grundmann, Reiner, *Marxism and Ecology* (Oxford University Press, 1991)

Guttman, Amy and Dennis Thompson, *Democracy and Disagreement* (Harvard University Press, 1996)

Hall, Kermit, Paul Finkelman and James Ely, *American Legal History: Cases and Materials* (Oxford University Press, 2004)

Hall, Kermit and Peter Karsten, *The Magic Mirror: Law in American History* (Oxford University Press, 2009)

Hanna, Susan, Carl Folke, Karl-Goran Maler and Kenneth Arrow, *Rights to Nature* (Island Press, 1996)

Harris, J.W., *Property and Justice* (Oxford University Press, 1996)

Harris, J.W., *Legal Philosophies* (Oxford University Press, 2004)

Hart, H.L.A., *The Concept of Law* (Oxford University Press, 1961)

Hart, H.L.A., *Essays in Jurisprudence and Philosophy* (Oxford University Press, 1983)

Harvey, David, *Justice, Nature and the Geography of Difference* (Blackwell Publishers, 1996)

Harvey, David, *A Brief History of Neoliberalism* (Oxford University Press, 2007)

Harvey, David, *A Companion to Marx's Capital* (Verso, 2010)

Harvey, David, *The Enigma of Capital* (Oxford University Press, 2011)

Harvey, David, *Rebel Cities: From the Right to the City to the Urban Revolution* (Verso, 2012)

Hauerwas, Stanley and L. Gregory Jones, *Why Narrative? Readings in Narrative Theology* (Wipf & Stock Publishers, 1997)

Havel, Norman, *Ecology and Bible – Green & Grey* (ATF Press, 2008)

Hawken, Paul, *The Ecology of Commerce* (Harper Paperbacks, 1994)

Hawken, Paul, *Blessed Unrest: How the Largest Movement in the World Came into Being and Why No One Saw it Coming* (Viking Press, 2007)

Hawken, Paul, *Natural Capitalism: Creating the Next Industrial Revolution* (Back Bay Books, 2008)

Hay, Peter, *Main Currents in Western Environmental Thought* (Indiana University Press, 2002)

Haywood, Bill, Dave Foreman and Edward Abbey, *Ecodefense: A Field Guide to Monkeywrenching* (Abzug Press, 1993)

Hegel, G.W.F., *Early Theological Writings* (University of Pennsylvania Press, 1971)

Hegel, G.W.F., *Lectures on the Philosophy of History* (Cambridge University Press, 1981) [first published 1840]

Heidegger, Martin, *The Question Concerning Technology, and Other Essays* (Harper Torchbooks, 1982)

Heisenberg, Werner, *Philosophy and Physics* (Harper & Row, 1967)

Heisenberg, Werner, *Physics and Philosophy: The Revolution in Modern Science* (Harper Perennial, 2007)

Heisenberg, Werner and Arnold Pomerans, *The Physicists Conception of Nature* (Greenwood Press, 1970)

Hettinger, Ned, 'Environmental Disobedience' in Dale Jamieson (ed.), *A Companion to Environmental Philosophy* (Wiley-Blackwell, 2003)

Hittinger, Russell, *A Critique of the New Natural Law Theory* (University of Notre Dame Press, 1989)

Hobbes, Thomas, *Leviathan* (Oxford University Press, 2009) [first published 1651]

Hohfeld, Wesley Newcomb, *Fundamental Legal Conceptions as Applied in Judicial Reasoning* (Lawbook Exchange, 2010)

Holloway, John, *Change the World Without Taking Power: The Meaning of Revolution Today* (Pluto Press, 2002)

Holmes Jr, Oliver Wendell, *The Speeches of Oliver Wendell Holmes* (Cambridge University Press, 1891)

Honoré, Tony, 'Ownership' in Anthony Guest, *Oxford Essays in Jurisprudence* (Oxford University Press, 1961)

Hooker, C.A., 'Laws, Natural' in Edward Craig (ed.), *The Shorter Routledge Encyclopedia of Philosophy* (Routledge, 2005)

Horwitz, Morton, *The Transformation of American Law, 1780–1860* (Harvard University Press, 1977)

Howard, Albert, *The Soil and Health: A Study of Organic Agriculture* (Devin-Adair, 1947)

Hughes, R.I.G., *Philosophical Perspectives on Newtonian Science* (MIT Press, 1990)

Hume, David, *A Treatise of Human Nature* (Oxford University Press, 2002) [first published 1740]

Humfress, Caroline, 'Law and Legal Practice in the Age of Justinian' in Michael Maas (ed.), *The Cambridge Companion to the Age of Justinian* (Cambridge University Press, 2005)

Humphreys, W. Lee, 'Pitfalls and Promises of the Biblical Texts as a Basis for a Theology of Nature' in Glenn C. Stone (ed), *A New Ethic for a New Earth* (Andover, 1971)

Hurd, Heidi, *Moral Combat* (Cambridge University Press, 2008)

Hutchinson, Terry, *Researching and Writing in Law* (Lawbook Co., 2010)

Isaacson, Walter, *Einstein: His Life and Universe* (Simon & Schuster, 2008)

Jackson, Wes, *New Roots for Agriculture* (University of Nebraska Press, 1980)

Jackson, Wes, 'Farming in Nature's Image: Natural Systems of Agriculture' in Andrew Kimbrell (ed.), *Fatal Harvest: The Tragedy of Industrial Agriculture* (Island Press, 2002)

Jackson, Wes, *Nature as Measure: The Selected Essays of Wes Jackson* (Counterpoint, 2011)

Jackson, Wes, *Consulting the Genius of the Place: An Ecological Approach to a New Agriculture* (Counterpoint, 2010)

Jackson, Wes, Becoming Native to This Place (Counterpoint, 1994)

Jacob, Margaret, *The Scientific Revolution: A Brief History with Documents* (Bedford/St. Martin's, 2009)

Jamieson, Dale, *Ethics and the Environment: An Introduction* (Cambridge University Press, 2008)

Jensen, Derrick, *Listening to the Land: Conversations about Nature, Culture and Eros* (Chelsea Green, 2004)

Jensen, Derrick, *Endgame Vol. 2: Resistance* (Seven Stories Press, 2006)

Jensen, Derrick, *Thought to Exist in the Wild: Awakening From the Nightmare of Zoos* (No Voice Unheard, 2007)

Jonas, Hans, *The Phenomenon of Life* (Delta, 1966)

Jonas, Hans, *Philosophical Essays: From Ancient Creed to Technological Man* (University of Chicago Press, 1980)

Jonas, Hans, *The Imperative of Responsibility: In Search of an Ethics for the Technological Age* (University of Chicago Press, 1979)

Johnson, Lawrence E., *A Morally Deep World: An Essay on Moral Significance and Environmental Ethics* (Cambridge University Press, 1991)

Kairys, David, *The Politics of Law: A Progressive Critique* (Basic Books, 1998)

Kant, Immanuel, *Lectures on Ethics* (Harper & Row, 1963)

Kant, Immanuel, *Anthropology from a Pragmatic Point of View* (Martinus Nijhoff, 1974) [first published 1798]

Kant, Immanuel, *Groundwork of the Metaphysic(s) of Morals* (Cambridge University Press, 1998) [first published 1785]

Katz, Eric and Andrew Light (eds), *Environmental Pragmatism* (Routledge, 1996)

Karr, James 'Health, Integrity and Biological Assessment: The Importance of Whole Things' in David Pimentel, Laura Westra and Reed Noss, *Ecological Integrity: Integrating Environment, Conservation and Health* (Island Press, 2000)

Karr, James, R., and Ellen W. Chu, Restoring Life in Running Waters (Island Press, 1999)

Karr, James R, 'Ecological Integrity and Ecological Health Are Not the Same' in Peter C

Keith, Lierre, *The Vegetarian Myth: Food, Justice and Sustainability* (PM Press, 2009)

Kelman, Mark, *A Guide to Critical Legal Studies* (Harvard University Press, 1990)

Kelsen, Hans, *General Theory of Law and State* (Harvard University Press, 1949)

Klein, Naomi, *The Shock Doctrine: The Rise of Disaster Capitalism* (Picador, 2008)

Knudtson, Peter and David Suzuki, *Wisdom of the Elders: Native and Scientific Ways of Knowing about Nature* (Douglas and McIntyre, 2006)

Koestler, Arthur, *The Ghost in the Machine* (Macmillan, 1967)

Korsgaard, Christine, 'Fellow Creatures: Kantian Ethics and Our Duties to Animals' in Grethe B. Peterson (ed.), *Tanner Lectures on Human Values* (University of Utah Press, 2005)

Korten, David C., *The Great Turning: From Empire to Earth Community* (Berrett-Koehler Publishers, 2007)

Kovel, Joel, *The Enemy of Nature: The End of Capitalism or the End of the World?* (Zed Books, 2007)

Krech, Shepard, *The Ecological Indian: Myth and History* (WW Norton and Company, 1999)

Kuhn, Thomas, *The Structure of Scientific Revolutions* (University of Chicago Press, 1996)

Kunnie Julian E. and Nomalungelo Goduka, *Indigenous Peoples' Wisdom and Power: Affirming Our Knowledge Through Narratives* (Ashgate Publishing, 2006)

Lametti, David, *The Deon-Telos of Private Property* (PhD thesis, Oxford University, 1999)

Lametti, David, 'The Morality of James Harris's Theory of Property' in T. Endicott, J. Getzler and E. Peel (eds), *The Properties of Law: Essays in Honour of James Harris* (Oxford University Press, 2006)

Lametti, David, 'The Objects of Virtue' in G. Alexander and E. Peñalver (eds), *Property and Community* (Oxford University Press, 2010)

Lapo, Andrey, *Traces of Bygone Biospheres* (Synergetic Press, 1979)

Laster, Kathy, *Law as Culture* (Federation Press, 2001)

Laszlo, Ervin and Allan Combs, *Thomas Berry, Dreamer of the Earth: The Spiritual Ecology of the Father of Environmentalism* (Inner Traditions, 2011)

Latour, Bruno, *We Have Never Been Modern* (Harvard University Press, 1993)

Latour, Bruno, *Pandora's Hope: Essays on the Reality of Science Studies* (Harvard University Press, 1999)

Latour, Bruno, *Politics of Nature: How to Bring the Sciences into Democracy* (Harvard University Press, 2004)

Leiss, William, *The Domination of Nature* (McGill-Queen's University Press, 1994)

Lemert, Edwin, *The Juvenile Court System: Social Action and Legal Change* (Transaction Publishers, 2009)

Lennox, James G., *Aristotle's Philosophy of Biology: Studies in the Origins of Life Science* (Cambridge University Press, 2000)

Boff, Leonardo, *Cry of the Earth, Cry of the Poor* (Orbis Books, 1997)

Leopold, Aldo, *A Sand County Almanac: Essays on Conservation from Round River* (Ballantine Books, 1986)

Leopold, Aldo, *The River of the Mother of God: and Other Essays by Aldo Leopold* (University of Wisconsin Press, 1992)

Leopold, Aldo, *For the Health of the Land: Previously Unpublished Essays and Other Writings* (Island Press, 2001)

Levy, David, *Hans Jonas: The Integrity of Thinking* (University of Missouri Press, 2002)

Lindenmayer, David and Joern Fischer, *Habitat Fragmentation and Landscape Change: An Ecological and Conservation Synthesis* (Island Press, 2006)

Linebaugh, Peter, *The Magna Carta Manifesto: Liberties and Commons for All* (University of California Press, 2009)

Linzey, Thomas, *Be the Change: How To Get What You Want in Your Community* (Gibbs Smith, 2010)

Livingston, John, *Arctic Oil* (Canadian Broadcasting Corporation, 1981)

Livingston, John, *Rogue Primate: An Exploration of Human Domestication* (Roberts Rinehart Publishers, 1994)

Llewellyn, Karl, *Jurisprudence: Realism in Theory and Practice* (Transaction Publishers, 1962)

Lloyd, Dennis, *Idea of Law* (Penguin UK, 1991) [first published 1964]

Locke, John, *Two Treatise of Government* (Cambridge University Press, 1970) [first published 1689]

Long, A.A., *Hellenistic Philosophy: Stoics, Epicureans, Sceptics* (University of California Press, 1986)

Lopez, Barry (ed.), *The Future of Nature: Writing on Human Ecology from Orion Magazine* (Milkweed Editions, 2007)

Louv, Richard, *Last Child in the Woods: Saving Our Children From Nature-Deficit Disorder* (Algonquin Books, 2008)

Lovejoy, Arthur O., *The Great Chain of Being* (Harper Torchbooks, 1960)

Lovelock, James, *Gaia: A New Look at Life on Earth* (Oxford University Press, 1979)

Lovelock, James, 'Gaia' in Carolyn Merchant (ed.), *Ecology* (Humanity Books, 1994)

Low, Nicholas and Gleeson, Brendan, *Justice, Society and Nature* (Routledge, 1998)

Luxemburg, Rosa, The Accumulation of Capital (Routledge, 2003)

Lovelock, James, *Gaia: The Practical Science of Planetary Medicine* (Gaia Books, 2000)

Lyell, Charles and James Secord, *Principles of Geology* (Penguin Classics, 1998)

Lyon, Pamela, 'Extracting Norms From Nature: A Biogenic Approach to Ethics' in Peter Burdon (ed.), *An Invitation to Wild Law* (Wakefield Press, 2011)

Lyons, Oren, 'The Leadership Imperative: An Interview with Oren Lyons' in Barry Lopez, *The Future of Nature: Writing on a Human Ecology From Orion Magazine* (Milkweed Editions, 2007).

McCann, Michael, *Law and Social Movements* (Ashgate, 2006a)

McClellan, James and Harold Dorn, *Science and Technology in World History: An Introduction* (Johns Hopkins University Press, 2006)

MacCormick, Neil, 'Natural Law and the Separation of Law and Morals' in Robert P. George (ed.), *Natural Law Theory: Contemporary Essays* (Oxford University Press, 1992)

McCusker, Brian, *The Quest for Quarks* (Cambridge University Press, 1983)

McDonough, William and Michael Braungart, *Cradle to Cradle: Remaking the Way We Make Things* (North Point Press, 2002)

McInery, Ralph, *St Thomas Aquinas* (University of Notre Dame Press, 1977)

Macpherson, C.B., *The Political Theory of Possessive Individualism: Hobbes to Locke* (Oxford University Press, 1962)

Macpherson, C.B., 'Capitalism and the Changing Concept of Property' in Eugene Kamenka and R.S. Neal (eds), *Feudalism, Capitalism and Beyond* (Hodder & Stoughton Educational, 1975)

Macpherson, C.B. (ed.), *Property: Mainstream and Critical Positions* (University of Toronto Press, 1978)

McRae, Heather, Garth Nettheim, Laura Beacroft and Luke McNamara (eds), *Indigenous Legal Issues: Commentary and Materials* (Lawbook Co., 2003)

Macy, Joanna and Molly Young Brown, *Coming Back to Life: Practices to Reconnect Out Lives, Our* World (New Society Publishers, 1998)

Maloney, Michelle, 'Ecological Limits, Planetary Boundaries and Earth Jurisprudence' in Michelle Maloney and Peter Burdon (eds) *Wild Law: In Practice* (Routledge, 2014)

Manning, David, *Liberalism* (Dent, 1976)

Margulis, Lyn and Dorion Sagan, *What is Life?* (University of California Press, 1995)

Margulis, Lyn and Dorion Sagan, *Dazzle Gradually: Reflections on the Nature of Nature* (Chelsea Green Publishing, 2007)

Marietta, Don, *People and the Planet: Holism and Humanism in Environmental Ethics* (Temple University Press, 1994)

Marshall, Peter, *Nature's Web: Rethinking Our Place on Earth* (Paragon, 1994)

Marx, Karl, *The Poverty of Philosophy* (Progress Publishers, 1975a) [first published 1847]

Marx, Karl, 'Economic and Philosophic Manuscripts' in *Early Writings* (Vintage, 1975b)

Marx, Karl, 'For the Ruthless Criticism of Everything Existing' in Robert C. Tucker (ed.), The Marx-Engels Reader (WW Norton and Company, 1978)

Marx, Karl, *Capital: Vol. One: A Critique of Political Economy* (Penguin Books, 1992) [first published 1867]

Marx, Karl, *Capital: Vol. Three* (Penguin Classics, 1993) [first published 1894]

Marx, Karl, 'Proletarians and Communists' and Jeremy Bentham, 'Security and Equality of Property' in C.B. Macpherson (ed.), *Property: Mainstream and Critical Positions* (University of Toronto Press, 1999)

Marx, Karl, *The Communist Manifesto* (Oxford University Press, 2008)

Matthews, Freya, *The Ecological Self* (Routledge, 1994)

Matthews, Freya, *Ecology and Democracy* (Routledge, 1996)

Maturana, Humberto, *Biology of Cognition* (D. Reidel Publishing Co., 1970)

Maturana Humberto, and Francisco Varela, *Autopoiesis and Cognition: The Realization of the Living* (D. Reidel Publishing Co., 1980)

McInerny, Ralph, 'Forward' to Aquinas, Thomas, *Treatise on Law: Summa Theologica, Questions 90–97* (Gateway Editions, 1996)

McInerny, Ralph, 'Forward' to Aquinas, Thomas, *Thomas Aquinas: Selected Writings* (Penguin Classics, 1999)

Meadows, Donella H., *Thinking in Systems: A Primer* (Chelsea Green, 2008)

Merchant, Carolyn, *The Death of Nature: Women, Ecology and the Scientific Revolution* (Harper & Row, 1980)

Merleau-Ponty, Maurice, *Phenomenology of Perception* (Routledge, 2002) [first published 1945]

Metzner, Ralph, *Green Psychology* (Park Street Press, 1999)

Meyerson, Denise, *Jurisprudence* (Oxford University Press, 2011)

Milsom, S.F.C., *Historical Foundations of the Common* (Lexis Law Publishing, 1981)

Milton, John, 'Francis Bacon' in Edward Craig (ed.), *The Shorter Routledge Encyclopedia of Philosophy* (Routledge, 2005)

Mill, John Stuart, *On Liberty* (Penguin Books, 1974)

Mill, John Stuart, *On Liberty and Other Writings* (Cambridge University Press, 1989)

Miller, Donald (ed.), *Liberty* (Oxford University Press, 1991)

Mills, C.W., *The Power Elite* (Oxford University Press, 1956)

Molles, Manuel, *Ecology: Concepts and Applications* (McGraw-Hill, 2009)

Moore, George Edward, *Principia Ethics* (Dover Publications, 2004) [first published 1903]

Morton, Timothy, *Ecology without Nature: Rethinking Environmental Aesthetics* (Harvard University Press, 2009)

Morton, Timothy, *The Ecological Thought* (Harvard University Press, 2012)

Morton, Timothy, *Hyperobjects: Philosophy and Ecology after the End of the World* (University of Minnesota Press, 2013)

Moyers, Bill, *Genesis: A Living Conversation* (Anchor, 1997)

Mumford, Lewis, *The Transformations of Man* (Harper Torchbooks, 1956)

Mumford, Lewis, *Technics and Human Development* (Harcourt, 1967)

Munzer, Stephen, *A Theory of Property* (Cambridge University Press, 1990)

Munzer, Stephen, 'Property as Social Relations' in Stephen Munzer (ed.), *New Essays in the Legal and Political Theory of Property* (Cambridge University Press, 2001)

Murphy, Mark C., *Natural Law in Jurisprudence and Politics* (Cambridge University Press, 2006)

Murphy, Mark C., *Philosophies of Law* (Wiley-Blackwell, 2007)

Næss, Arne, Jens Chrisophersen and Kjell Kvalo, *Democracy, Ideology and Objectivity* (Oxford University Press, 1956)

Næss, Arne, *Freedom, Emotion and Self-Subsistence: The Structure of a Central Part of Spinoza's Ethics* (Universitetsforl, 1975)

Næss, Arne, *Ecology, Community and Lifestyle: Outline of an Ecosophy* (Cambridge University Press, 1993)

Næss, Arne, *The Ecology of Wisdom: Writings by Arne Næss* (Counterpoint, 2010)

Nagel, Thomas, *Mortal Questions* (Cambridge University Press, 1992)

Nash, Roderick, *The Rights of Nature: A History of Environmental Ethics* (University of Wisconsin Press, 1989)

Nash, Roderick, *Wilderness and the American Mind* (Yale University Press, 2001)

Neeson, Jennifer, *Commoners: Common Right, Enclosure and Social Change in England, 1700–1820* (Cambridge University Press, 1996)

Nedelsky, Jennifer, *Law's Relations: A Relational Theory of Self, Autonomy, and Law* (Oxford University Press, 2013)

Nicholas, Barry, *An Introduction to Roman Law* (Oxford University Press, 1962)

Norton, Bryan, *Toward Unity Among Environmentalists* (Oxford University Press, 1991)

Novak, David, 'Natural Law in a Theological Context' in John Goyette, Mark S. Latkovic and Richard S. Myers, *St Thomas Aquinas and the Natural Law Tradition: Contemporary Perspectives* (Catholic University of America Press, 2004)

Nozick, Robert, *Anarchy, State and Utopia* (Basic Books, 1974)

Odahl, Charles M., *Constantine and the Christian Empire* (Routledge, 2006)

Odum, Eugene, *Fundamentals of Ecology* (WB Saunders Company, 1971)

Odum, Eugene, *Ecology: A Bridge Between Science and Society* (Sinauer Associates, 1997)

Onions, C.T., *The Oxford Dictionary of English Etymology* (Oxford University Press, 1996)

Orr, David, 'Love It or Lose It: The Coming Biophilia Revolution' in Edward O. Wilson (ed.), *The Biophilia Hypothesis* (Island Press, 1993)

Ostrom, Elinor, *Governing the Commons: The Evolution of Institutions for Collective Action* (Cambridge University Press, 1990)

Ott, Konrad, 'A Modest Proposal about How to Proceed in Order to Solve the Problem of Inherent Moral Value in Nature' in Laura Westra, Klaus Bosselmann and Richard Westra (eds), *Reconciling Human Existence with Ecological Integrity* (Earthscan, 2008)

Pashukanis, Evgeny, *Law and Marxism: A General Theory* (Pluto Press, 1989)

Patel, Raj, *The Value of Nothing: How to Reshape Market Society and Redefine Democracy* (Picador, 2010)

Patten, Bernard, 'Network Ecology' in M. Higashi and T.B. Burns, *Theoretical Studies of Ecosystem: The Network Perspective* (Cambridge University Press, 1991)

Pearce, Fred, *With Speed and Violence: Why Scientists Fear Tipping Points in Climate Change* (Beacon Press, 2007)

Pelzynski, Z.A. and J.N. Gray (eds), *Conceptions of Liberty in Political Philosophy* (Athlone Press, 1984)

Penner, James, *The Idea of Property in Law* (Oxford University Press, 1997)

Pipes, Richard, *Property and Freedom* (Alfred Knopf, 1999)

Plato, 'Theatetus' in Cooper, John M (ed.), Plato: Complete Works (Hackett Publishing Company, 1997)

Plato, 'Timaeus' in Cooper, John M (ed.), Plato: Complete Works (Hackett Publishing Company, 1997)

Plato, 'Parmenides' in Cooper, John M (ed.), Plato: Complete Works (Hackett Publishing Company, 1997)

Plumwood, Val, *Feminism and the Mastery of Nature* (Routledge, 1993)

Pollan, Michael, *The Botany of Desire: A Plant's-Eye View of the World* (Random House Trade Paperbacks, 2002)

Pollan, Michael, *The Omnivore's Dilemma* (Penguin, 2006)

Posner, Richard, *Takings: Private Property and the Power of Eminent Domain* (Harvard University Press, 1985)

Posner, Richard, *Economic Analysis of Law* (Aspen, 1986)

Postema, Gerald, *Bentham and the Common Law Tradition* (Clarendon Press, 1986)

Pottage, Alain and Martha Mundy (eds), *Law, Anthropology and the Constitution of the Social: Making Persons and Things* (Cambridge University Press, 2004)

Prentice, Jessica, *Full Moon Feast: Food and the Hunger for Connection* (Chelsea Green, 2006)

Price, Andy, *Recovering Bookchin: Social Ecology and the Crises of Our Time* (New Compass Press, 2012)

Proudhon, P.J., *What is Property: An Inquiry into the Principle of Right and of Government* (Dover, 1970) [first published 1840]

Quinn, Daniel, *Ishmael: An Adventure of the Mind and Spirit* (Bantam, 1992)

Quinn, Daniel, Ishmael: *An Adventure of the Mind and Spirit* (Bantam, 1995)

Radin, Margaret Jane, *Reinterpreting Property* (University of Chicago Press, 1993)

Raff, Murray, *Private Property and Environmental Responsibility* (Kluwer Law International, 2003)

Raff, Murray, 'Toward an Ecologically Sustainable Property Concept' in Elizabeth Cooke (ed.), *Modern Studies in Property Law* (Hart Publishing, 2005)

Rasmussen, Larry L., *Earth Community, Earth Ethics* (Orbis Books, 1997)

Rawls, John, *A Theory of Justice* (Oxford University Press, 1999)

Raz, Joseph, *The Authority of Law* (Oxford University Press, 1986)

Reid, Peter, *Belonging: Australians, Place and Aboriginal Ownership* (Cambridge University Press, 2000)

Reismann, Michael W., *Law in Brief Encounters* (Yale University Press, 1999)

Reisner, Marc, *Cadillac Desert: The American West and Its Disappearing Water* (Penguin Books, 2003)

Register, Richard, *EcoCities: Rebuilding Cities in Balance with Nature* (Berkley Hills Books, 2006)

Renteln, Alison Dundes, *Folk Law: Essays in the Theory and Practice of Lex Non Scripta* (University of Wisconsin Press, 1995)

Revetz, Jerome, *Scientific Knowledge and its Social Problems* (Transaction Publishers, 1971)

Rickaby, Joseph, *Of God and His Creatures: An Annotated Translation of the Summa Contra Gentiles of Saint Thomas Aquinas* (Kessinger Publishing, 2006)

Rindos, David, *Origins of Agriculture: An Evolutionary Perspective* (Academic Press, 1984)

Robbins, Paul, *Political Ecology: A Critical Introduction* (Wiley-Blackwell, 2004)

Rodgers, Alan, *Owners and Neighbours in Roman Law* (Oxford University Press, 1972)

Rolston III, Holmes, *Philosophy Gone Wild: Environmental Ethics* (Prometheus Books, 1986)

Rolston III, Holmes, *Environmental Ethics: Duties to and Values in the Natural World* (Temple, 1988)

Rome, Adam, *The Bulldozer in the Countryside: Suburban Sprawl and the Rise of American Environmentalism* (Cambridge University Press, 2001)

Rose, Carol, *Property and Persuasion: Essays on the History, Theory and Rhetoric of Ownership* (Westview Press, 1994)

Rosen, Lawrence, *Law as Culture: An Invitation* (Princeton University Press, 2006)

Russell, Bertrand, *A History of Western Philosophy* (Simon & Schuster, 1967)

Russell, Bertrand, *The Autobiography of Bertrand Russell* (Routledge, 1969)

Ryan, Alan, *Property and Political Theory* (Basil Blackwell, 1984)

Sagan, Dorion, *Biospheres: Metamorphosis of Planet Earth* (McGraw-Hill, 1990)

Sale, Kirkpatrick, *Dwellers in the Land: The Bioregional Vision* (University of Georgia Press, 1991)

Said, Edward, *Representations of the Intellectual: The 1993 Reith Lectures* (Vintage, 1996)

Sandel, Michael J., *Liberalism and its Critics* (New York University Press, 1984)

Sandel, Michael J., *What Money Can't Buy: The Moral Limits of Markets* (Farrar, Straus & Giroux, 2012)

Sax, Joseph, 'Environmental Law Forty Years Later: Looking Back and Looking Ahead' in M. Jeffery (ed.), *IUCN Academy of Environmental Law Research Studies: Biodiversity, Conservation, Law and Livelihoods* (Cambridge University Press, 2008)

Scarman, Leslie, *English Law: The New Dimension* (Stevens Publishing, 1975)

Schaab, Gloria, 'Beyond Dominion and Stewardship' in Peter Burdon (ed.), *An Invitation to Wild Law* (Wakefield Press, 2011)

Scheffer, Victor, *Spire of Form: Glimpses of Evolution* (Harcourt, 2001)

Schlatter, Richard, *Private Property: The History of an Idea* (Allen & Unwin, 1951)

Schneider, Stephen and Boston, Penelope, *Scientists on Gaia* (MIT Press, 1991)

Schneider, Stephen, *Scientists Debate Gaia: The Next Century* (MIT Press, 2004)

Schrödinger, Erwin, *Nature and the Greeks and Science and Humanism* (Cambridge University Press, 1996)

Schröter, Michael, *Mensch, Erde, Recht: Grundfragen ökologischer Rechtstheorie* (Nomos Publishers, 1999)

Sedley, David, 'Stoicism' in Edward Craig (ed.), *The Shorter Routledge Encyclopedia of Philosophy* (Routledge, 2005)

Seneca, *Letters from a Stoic* (Penguin Books, 1969)

Sessions, George (ed.), *Deep Ecology for the 21st Century: Readings on the Philosophy of the New Environmentalism* (Shambhala, 1995)

Sessions, George and Bill Devall (eds), *Deep Ecology: Living as if Nature Mattered* (Gibbs Smith, 2001)

Shabecoff, Philip, *A Fierce Green Fire: The American Environmental Movement* (Island Press, 2003)

Shapin, Steven, *The Scientific Revolution* (University of Chicago Press, 1998)

Shapiro, J., 'Authority', in Jules Coleman, Scott Shapiro and Kenneth Einar Himma (eds), *The Oxford Handbook of Jurisprudence and Philosophy of Law* (Oxford University Press, 2002)

Shiva, Vandana, *Earth Democracy: Justice, Sustainability, and Peace* (Seven Stories Press, 2005)

Siddali, Silvana, *From Property To Person: Slavery and The Confiscation Acts, 1861–1862* (Louisiana State University Press, 2005)

Federici, Silvia, *Revolution at Point Zero: Housework, Reproduction, and Feminist Struggle* (PM Press, 2012)

Sinatra, J. and P. Murphy, *Listen to People Listen to the Land* (Melbourne University Publishing, 1999)

Singer, Peter, *Democracy and Disobedience* (Oxford University Press, 1973)

Singer, Peter, *Animal Liberation* (Jonathon Cape, 1975)

Singer, Peter *The Expanding Circle: Ethics and Sociobiology* (Oxford University Press, 1981)

Singer, Joseph William, *The Edges of the Field: Lessons on the Obligations of Ownership* (Beacon Press 2000)

Singer, Joseph William, *Entitlement: The Paradoxes of Property* (Yale University Press, 2000)

Singer, Joseph William, 'Property and Social Relations: From Title to Entitlement' in Charles Geisler and Gail Daneker (eds), *Property and Values: Alternatives to Public and Private Ownership* (Island Press, 2000)

Singer, Joseph William, *Introduction to Property* (Aspen Publishers, 2005)

Skyrms, Brian, *Evolution of the Social Contract* (Cambridge University Press, 1996)

Smith, J.C. and David Weisstub, *The Western Idea of Law* (Butterworths, 1983)

Smith, M.B.E., 'The Duty to Obey the Law' in D. Patterson (ed.), *A Companion to Philosophy of Law and Legal Theory* (Wiley-Blackwell, 1996)

Snyder, Gary, *Turtle Island* (New Directions Publishing Corporation, 1969)

Sontheimer, Sally, *Women and the Environment: A Reader Crisis and Development in the Third World* (Monthly Review Press, 1991).

Sorokin, Pitirim, *Social and Cultural Dynamics* (Extending Horizons Books, 1970)

Sorrell, Roger, *St. Francis of Assisi and Nature: Tradition and Innovation in Western Christian Attitudes toward the Environment* (Oxford University Press, 2009)

Spinoza, Baruch, 'The Ethics' in Michael L. Morgan (ed.), *Spinoza: Complete Works* (Hackett Publishing Company, 2002)

Starhawk, *The Fifth Sacred Thing* (Bantam, 1994)

Stein, Peter, *Character and Influence of the Roman Civil Law* (Bloomsbury Academic, 2003)

Steinberg, Theodore, *Slide Mountain: Or, The Folly of Owning Nature* (University of California Press, 1996)

Steinberg, Theodore, *Nature Incorporated: Industrialization and the Waters of New England* (Cambridge University Press, 2004)

Steinberg, Theodore, *Down to Earth: Nature's Role in American History* (Oxford University Press, 2008)

Steiner, Dean Frederick, *Human Ecology: Following Nature's Lead* (Oxford University Press, 2002)

Tarnas, Richard, *The Passion of the Western Mind: Understanding the Ideas that Have Shaped Our World View* (Ballantine, 1993)

Stone, Christopher D., *Should Trees Have Standing: Law Morality and the Environment* (Oxford University Press, 2010)

Suess, Edward, *The Face of the Earth* (Oxford University Press, 1924)

Suzuki, Daisetz T., 'The Role of Nature in Zen Buddhism' in Olga Frobe Kapteyn (ed.), *Mensch und Erde* (Rhein-Verlag, 1954)

Suzuki, David, *The Sacred Balance: Rediscovering Our Place in Nature* (Allen & Unwin, 1997)

Suzuki, David, *The Legacy: An Elder's Vision for our Sustainable Future* (Allen & Unwin, 2010)

Sveiby, Karl-Erik and Tex Skuthorpe, *Treading Lightly: The Hidden Wisdom of the World's Oldest People* (Allen & Unwin Academic, 2006)

Swimme, Brian, *The Universe is a Green Dragon: A Cosmic Creation Story* (Bear & Company, 1984)

Swimme, Brian, *The Hidden Heart of the Cosmos: Humanity and the New Story* (Orbis Books, 1998)

Swimme, Brian and Matthew Fox, *Manifesto! For A Global Civilization* (Bear & Company, 1982)

Brian Swimme, Berry and Thomas, *The Universe Story: From the Primordial Flaring Forth to the Ecozoic Era, A Celebration of the Unfolding of the Cosmos* (Harper San Francisco, 1992)

Swimme, Brian, and Mary-Evelyn Tucker, *Journey of the Universe* (Yale University Press, 2011)

Tarrow, Sidney, *Struggling to Reform: Social Movements and Policy Change During Cycles of Protest* (Cornell University Press, 1983)

Taylor, Bron (ed.), *Ecological Resistance Movements: The Global Emergence of Radical and Popular Environmentalism* (State University of New York Press, 1995)

Taylor, Paul, *Respect for Nature: A Theory of Environmental Ethics* (Princeton University Press, 1986)

Taylor, Prue, 'The Imperative of Responsibility in a Legal Context: Reconciling Responsibilities and Rights' in J. Ronald Engel, Laura Westra, Klaus Bosselmann (eds), *Democracy, Ecological Integrity and International Law* (Cambridge Scholars Publishing, 2010)

Thoreau, Henry David, *Walden or Life in the Woods* (Dover Publications, 1995) [first published 1854]

Thoreau, Henry David, *The Higher Law: Thoreau on Civil Disobedience and Reform* (Princeton University Press, 2004)

Tilly, Charles, 'Social Movements and National Politics' in Charles Bright and Susan Harding (eds), *Statemaking and Social Movements: Essays in History and Theory* (University of Michigan Press, 1984)

Tomlinson, John, *Cultural Imperialism: A Critical Introduction* (ACLS Humanities E-Book, 2008)

Tucker, Mary-Evelyn, *Worldly Wonder: Religions Enter Their Ecological Phase* (Open Court, 2003)

Tucker, Mary-Evelyn, 'Editor's Afterword: An Intellectual Biography of Thomas Berry' in Mary-Evelyn Tucker (ed.), *Evening Thoughts: Reflecting on Earth as Sacred Community* (Sierra Club Books, 2006)

Tucker, Robert C. (ed.), *The Marx-Engels Reader* (Norton, 1978)

Tyson, Lois, *Critical Theory Today: A User-Friendly Guide* (Routledge, 2006)

Uexküll, Jakob, 'A Stroll Through the Worlds of Animals and Men: A Picture Book of Invisible Worlds, in Claire H. Schiller (ed.), *Instinctive Behavior: The Development of a Modern Concept* (International Universities Press, 1957)

UKELA and Gaia Foundation, *Wild Law: Is There Any Evidence of Earth Jurisprudence in Existing Law and Practice* (UKELA, 2009)

Underkuffler, Laura S., *The Idea of Property: Its Meaning and Power* (Oxford University Press, 2003)

Unger, Roberto, *The Critical Legal Studies Movement* (Harvard University Press, 1986)

Unger, Roberto, *False Necessity: Anti-Necessitarian Social Theory in the Service of Radical Democracy* (Verso, 2001)

Vernadsky, Ivanovick, *The Biosphere: Complete Annotated Edition* (Springer, 1992) [first published 1926]

Vico, Giambattista, *The New Science* (Cornell University Press, 1976) [first published 1725]

Waldau, Paul and Kimberley Patton (eds), *A Communion of Subjects: Animals in Religion, Science and Ethics* (Columbia University Press, 2006)

Waldron, Jeremy, *The Right to Private Property* (Oxford University Press, 1987)

Waldron, Jeremy, *Nonsense upon Stilts: Bentham, Burke and Marx on the Rights of Man* (Methuen, 1988)

Waldron, Jeremy, 'Liberalism' in Edward Craig (ed.), *The Shorter Routledge Encyclopaedia of Philosophy* (Routledge, 2005)

Wallerstein, Immanuel, *The Modern World-System IV: Centrist Liberalism Triumphant, 1789 – 1914* (University of California Press, 2011a)

Wallerstein, Immanuel, *Historical Capitalism with Capitalist Civilization* (Verso, 2011b)

Watson, Irene, *Raw Law: The Coming of the Muldarbi and the Path to its Demise* (DPhil thesis, University of Adelaide, 1999)

Weber, Max, 'The Ideal Type' in K. Thompson and J. Tunstall (eds), *Sociological Perspectives* (Penguin, 1971)

Weightman, Gavin, *The Industrial Revolutionaries: The Making of the Modern World 1776–1914* (Grove Press, 2010)

Weinreb, Lloyd, *Natural Law and Justice* (Harvard University Press, 1987)

Weir, Jessica, *Murray River Country: An Ecological Dialogue with Traditional Owners* (Aboriginal Studies Press, 2009)

Weiss, Paul, *Hierarchically Organized Systems in Theory and Practice* (Hafner Publishing Company, 1971)

Weiss, Paul, *The Science of Life: The Living System – A System for Living* (Futura Publishing Company, 1973)

Wellmann, Christopher and A. John Simmons, *Is There A Duty to Obey the Law?* (Cambridge University Press, 2005)

Weston, Burns H., 'The Role of Law in Promoting Peace and Violence: A Matter of Definition, Social Values and Individual Responsibility' in W. Michael Reisman and Burns H. Weston (eds) *Toward World Order and Human Dignity* (Free Press, 1976)

Weston, Burns H and Bollier, David, *Green Governance: Ecological Survival, Human Rights and the Law of the Commons* (Cambridge University Press, 2013)

Westen, Anthony (ed.), *An Invitation to Environmental Philosophy* (Oxford University Press, 1999)

Westra, Laura, *Living in Integrity: A Global Ethic to Restore a Fragmented Earth* (Rowman & Littlefield Publishers, 1998)

Westra, Laura, 'Institutionalized Violence and Human Rights' in David Pimentel, Laura Westra, and Reed F. Noss (eds), *Ecological Integrity: Integrating Environment, Conservation and Health* (Island Press, 2000)

Whitehead, Alfred North, *Modes of Thought* (Macmillan, 1938)

Whitehead, Alfred North, *Process and Reality* (Free Press, 1979)

Wilber, Ken, *Sex, Ecology, Spirituality: The Spirit of Evolution* (Shambhala, 1995)

Wilson, Edward O., *The Diversity of Life* (WW Norton and Company, 1992)

Wilson, Edward O., *Biophilia* (Harvard University Press, 1994)

Wilson, Edward O., *Biodiversity* (National Academy of Sciences, 1996)

Wittgenstein, Ludwig, *Philosophical Investigations* (Wiley-Blackwell, 2009) [first published 1953]

Wolff, Robert Paul, *Robert Nozick: Property, Justice, and the Minimal State* (Stanford University Press, 1991)

Wolff, Robert Paul, *In Defense of Anarchism* (University of California Press, 1998)

World Commission on Environmental Development, *Our Common Future* (Oxford University Press, 1987)

Worster, Donald, *Nature's Economy: A History of Ecological Ideas* (Cambridge University Press, 1994)

Wuerthner, George, 'The Destruction of Wildlife Habitat by Agriculture' in Andrew Kimbrell (ed.), *Fatal Harvest: The Tragedy of Industrial Agriculture* (Island Press, 2002)

Zimmerman, Michael E. (ed.), *Environmental Philosophy: From Animal Rights to Radical Ecology* (Prentice Hall, 2001)

Zinn, Howard, *Disobedience and Democracy: Nine Fallacies on Law and Order* (South End Press, 2002)

Zinn, Howard, *A People's History of the United States: 1492 to Present* (Harper Perennial Modern Classics, 2005)

Žižek, Slavoj, *In Defense of Lost Causes* (Verso, 2009)

Zondervan, *NIV Study Bible* (Zondervan, 2008)

## Journal articles

Ahlers, Glen Peter, 'Earth Jurisprudence: A Pathfinder' (2009) 11 *Barry Law Review* 121

Arneil, Barbara, 'Trade, Plantations and Property: John Locke and the Economic Defence of Colonialism' (1994) 55(4) *Journal of the History of Ideas* 591

Arnold, Tony, 'The Reconstitution of Property: Property as a Web of Interests' (2002) 26 *Harvard Environmental Law Review* 281

Babie, Paul, 'Private Property, the Environment and Christianity' (2002) 15 *Pacifica: Australasian Theological Studies* 307

Babie, Paul, 'Two Voices of the Morality of Private Property' (2007) 23 *Journal of Law and Religion* 101

Babie, Paul, 'Idea, Sovereignty, Eco-colonialism and the Future: Four Reflections on Private Property and Climate Change' (2010) 19 *Griffith Law Review* 527

Babie, Paul, 'Private Property: the Solution or the Source of the Problem?' (2010) 2(2) *Amsterdam Law Forum*; http://ojs.ubvu.vu.nl/alf/article/view/124

Baker, C. Edwin, *Property and its Relation to Constitutionally Protected Liberty* (1986) 134 *University of Pennsylvania Law Review* 741

Becker, Lawrence C., 'The Moral Basis of Property Rights' (1980) 22 *Nomos* 187

Bedau, H.A., 'On Civil Disobedience' (1961) 58 *Journal of Philosophy* 653

Bell, Mike, 'Thomas Berry and an Earth Jurisprudence' (2003) 19(1) *The Trumpeter* 69

Bender, L., 'A Lawyer's Primer on Feminist Theory and Tort' (1988) 38 *Journal Legal Education* 3

Bernstein, J.M., 'Love and Law: Hegel's Critique of Morality' (2003) 70(2) *Social Research* 393

Berry, Thomas, 'The New Story' (1978) 1 *Teilhard Studies* 1

Berry, Thomas, 'Technology and the Nation State in the Ecological Age' (1981) *Riverdale Papers VIII* 27

Berry, Thomas, 'The Viable Human' (1987) 9(2) *Revision* 1

Berry, Thomas, 'The Gaia Theory: Its Religious Implications' (1994) 22 *ARC: Journal of the Faculty of Religious Studies, McGill University* 7

Beyleveld, D. and F. Brownsword, 'The Practical Difference Between Natural Law Theory and Legal Positivism' (1985) 5(1) *Oxford Journal of Legal Studies* 1

Birch, Thomas, 'Moral Considerability and Universal Consideration' (1993) 15(4) *Environmental Ethics* 313

Birks, Peter, 'The Roman Law Concept of Dominium and the Idea of Absolute Ownership' (1985) *Acta Juridica* 1

Bix, Brian H., 'On the Dividing Line Between Natural Law Theory and Legal Positivism' (1999 –2000) 75 *Notre Dame Law Review* 1613

Blomley, Nicholas, 'Landscapes of Property' (1998) 32(3) *Law and Society Review* 567

Bodian, Stephan, 'Simple in Means, Rich in Ends: A Conversation with Arne Næss' (1982) *The Ten Directions* 11

Bohen, F., 'The Rule in Rylands v Fletcher' (1911) 59 *University of Pennsylvania Law Review* 298

Bosselmann, Fred P. and A.D. Tarlock, 'The Influence of Ecological Science on American Law: An Introduction' (1993–1994) 69 *Chicago Kent Law Review* 847

Boyle, J., 'Natural Law, Ownership and the World's Natural Resources' (1989) 23 *Journal of Value Inquiry* 191

Burdon, Peter, 'The Rights of Nature: Reconsidered' (2010) 49 *Australian Humanities Review* 69

Burdon, Peter, 'What is Good Land Use? From Rights to Relationship' (2010) 34(2) *Melbourne University Law Review* 708

Burdon, Peter, 'Wild Law: The Philosophy of Earth Jurisprudence' (2010) 35(2) *Alternative Law Journal* 62

Burdon, Peter, 'The Jurisprudence of Thomas Berry' (2011) 11 *Worldviews: Global Religions, Culture, and Ecology* 151

Burdon, Peter, 'Rights of Nature: The Theory' (2011) 1 *IUCN Environmental Law Journal*

Burdon, Peter, 'A Theory of Earth Jurisprudence' (2012) *Australian Journal of Legal Philosophy* 28

Burdon, Peter, 'The Future of a River: Earth Jurisprudence and the Murray Darling Basin' (2012) 37(2) *Alternative Law Journal* 82

Burns, Robert, 'Blackstone's Theory of the "Absolute" Rights of Property' (1985) 54 *University of Cincinnati Law Review* 67

Butler, Lynda, 'The Pathology of Property Norms: Living Within Nature's Boundaries' (2000) 73 *Southern California Law Review* 927

Bynum, William F., 'The Great Chain of Being after Forty Years: An Appraisal' (1975) 13 *History of Science* 1

Byrne, Peter, 'Green Property' (1990) 7 *Constitutional Commentary* 239

Capra, Fritjof, 'Paradigms and Paradigm Shift' (1985) 9(1) *Revision* 11

Chakrabarty, Dipesh, 'The Climate of History: Four Theses' (2009) 35 *Critical Inquiry* 197

Circo, Carl, 'Does Sustainability Require a New Theory of Property Rights?' (2009) 58(1) *University of Kansas Law Review* 91

Coase, Ronald, 'The Problem of Social Cost' (1960) 3 *Journal Law and Economics* 1

Coglianese, Cary, 'Social Movements, Law and Society: The Institutionalization of the Environment Movement' (2001) 150 *University of Pennsylvania Law Review* 85

Cohen, Carl, 'Militant Morality: Civil Disobedience and Bioethics' (1989) 19(6) *Hastings Center Report* 23

Cohen, Felix S., 'Dialogue on Private Property' (1954) 9 *Rutgers Law Review* 357

Cohen, Morris, 'Property and Sovereignty' (1927) 13 *Cornell Law Quarterly* 8:

Crutzen, Paul and E.F. Stoermer, 'The Anthropocene' (2000) 41 *Global Change Newsletter* 17

Cullinan, Cormac, 'Do Humans Have Standing to Deny Trees Rights?' (2009) 11 *Barry Law Review* 11

Dworkin, Ronald, 'On Not Prosecuting Civil Disobedience' (1968) 10(11) *New York Review of Books* 14

Eaton, Heather, 'Introduction to the Special Edition on Thomas Berry's The Great Work' (2001) 5(1) *Worldviews: Global Religions, Culture, and Ecology* 1

Ehrlich, Paul and Peter Raven, 'Butterflies and Plants: A Study of Coevolution' (1964) 18 *Evolution* 586

Ellickson, Robert C., 'Alternatives to Zoning: Covenants, Nuisance Rules and Fines as Land Use Controls (1973) 40 *University of Chicago Law Review* 681

Ellickson, Robert C., 'Property in Land' (1993) 102 *Yale Law Journal* 1364

Epstein, Richard, 'Property as a Fundamental Civil Right' (1998) 29 California Western Law Review 187

Why Restrain Alienation?' (1985) 85 *Columbia Law Review* 970

Fleming, Donald, 'Roots of the New Conservation Movement' (1972) 6 *Perspectives in American History* 18

Frazier, Terry, 'The Green Alternative to Classical Liberal Property Theory' (1995) 20 *Vermont Law Review* 299

Frazier, Terry, 'Protecting Ecological Integrity within the Balancing Function of Property Law' (1998) 28(1) *Environmental Law* 53

Freyfogle, Eric .T, 'Ownership and Ecology' (1993) 43(4) *Case Western Law Review* 1269

Freyfogle, Eric T., 'Property Rights, The Markets and Environmental Change in Twentieth-Century America' (2001) 1 *Illinois Public Law and Legal Theory Research Papers Series* 1

Freyfogle, Eric T., 'Property Rights, the Market, and Environmental Change in 20th century America' (2002) 31 *Environmental Law Reporter* 10254

Freyfogle, Eric T., 'The Tragedy of Fragmentation' (2002) 32 *Environmental Law Reporter* 11321

Freyfogle, Eric T., 'Property and Liberty' (2007) *Illinois Public Law and Legal Theory Research Papers Series* Available at SSRN: http://ssrn.com/abstract=1024574

Fuller, Lon, 'Human Purpose and Natural Law' 53 (1956) *Journal of Philosophy* 697

Fuller, Lon, 'Positivism and Fidelity to Law' (1958) 71 *Harvard Law Review* 630

Getzler, Joshua, 'Theories of Property and Economic Development' (1996) 26(4) *Journal of Interdisciplinary History* 639

Godden, Lee, 'Preserving Natural Heritage: Nature as Other' (1998) 22 *Melbourne University Law Review* 719

Gould, Stephan Jay, 'Kropotkin was no Crackpot' (1997) 106 *Natural History* 12

Gray, Kevin, 'Property in Thin Air' (1991) 50 *Cambridge Law Journal* 252

Grisez, Germain, 'The First Principle of Practical Reason: A Commentary on the *Summa Theologica*, 1–2, Question 94, Article 2' (1965) 10 *Natural Law Forum* 174

Guth, Joseph, 'Law for the Ecological Age' (2009) 9 *Vermont Journal of Environmental Law* 431

Hart, H.L.A., 'Positivism and the Separation of Law and Morals' (1958) 71 *Harvard Law Review* 593

Heller, Michael, 'The Tragedy of the Anticommons: Property in the Transition from Marx to Markets'? (1998) 111 *Harvard Law Review* 621

Hohfeld, Wesley Newcomb, 'Some Fundamental Legal Conceptions as Applied in Judicial Reasoning' (1913) 23 *Yale Law Journal* 16

Hohfeld, Wesley Newcomb, 'Some Fundamental Legal Conceptions as Applied in Judicial Reasoning' (1917) 26 *Yale Law Journal* 710

Hunter, David, 'An Ecological Perspective on Property' (1988) 12 *Harvard Environmental Law Review* 311

Hutton, Patrick H., 'Vico's Significance for the New Cultural History' (1985) 3 *New Vico Studies* 74

Janzen, Daniel, 'The Future of Tropical Ecology' (1986) 17 *Annual Review of Ecology and Systematic* 305

Karr, James, 'Protecting Ecological Integrity: An Urgent Societal Goal' (1993) 18(1) *Yale Journal of International Law* 297

Katz, Larrisa, 'Exclusion and Exclusivity in Property Law' (2008) 58(3) *University of Toronto Law Review* 275

Kennedy, Duncan, 'Toward a Historical Understanding of Legal Consciousness: The Case of Classical Legal Thought in America 1850–1940' (1980) *Research in Law and Sociology* 3

Kennedy, Duncan, 'The Stages of Decline of the Public/Private Distinction' (1982) 130(6) *University of Pennsylvania Law Review* 1349

Kimbrell, Andrew, 'Breaking the Law of Life' May/June (1997) 182 *Resurgence Magazine* 9

Kimbrell, Andrew, 'Halting the Global Meltdown: Can Environmental Law Play a Role?' (2008) 20 *Environmental Law and Management* 64

Kirchner, James, 'The Gaia Hypothesis: Fact, Theory, and Wishful Thinking' (2002) 52(4) *Climatic Change* 391

Krauthammer, Charles, 'The Spotted Owl' (1991) 6 *Time Magazine* 17

Lametti, David, 'Property and (Perhaps) Justice' (1998) 43 *McGill Law Journal* 665

Lametti, David 'The Concept of Property: Relations through Objects of Social Wealth' (2003) 53 *University of Toronto Law Journal* 325

Lenton, Timothy, 'Gaia and Natural Selection' (1998) 394 *Nature* 439

Leopold, Aldo, 'Some Fundamentals of Conservation in the Southwest' (1979) 1 *Environmental Ethics* 131

Lovelock, James and Lynn Margulis, 'Biological Modulation of the Earth's Atmosphere' (1974) 21 *Icarus* 471

Lyon, Pamela, 'Autopoiesis and Knowing: Reflections on Manturana's Biogenic Explanation of Cognition' (2004) 11(4) *Cybernetics and Human Knowing* 21

McCann, Michael, 'Law and Social Movements: Contemporary Perspectives' (2006b) 2 *Annual Review of Law and Social Science* 17

MacKinnon, Catherine, 'Feminism, Marxism, Method and the State: Toward Feminist Jurisprudence' (1983) 8 *Signs* 636

Mahoney, Paul, 'The Common Law and Economic Growth: Hayek Might Be Right' (2001) 30 *Journal of Legal Studies* 503

Merrill, Thomas W, 'Property and the Right to Exclude' (1998) 77 *Nebraska Law Journal* 746

Meyer, John, 'The Concept of Private Property and the Limits of the Environmental Imagination' (2009) 37(1) *Political Theory* 99

Næss, Arne, 'The Shallow and the Deep, Long-Range Ecology Movement: A Summary' (1973) 16 *Inquiry* 95

Næss, Arne, 'The Deep Ecology Movement: Some Philosophical Aspects' (1986) 8 *Philosophical Inquiry* 10

Naffine, Ngaire, 'The Liberal Legal Individual Accused: The Relational Case' (2013) *Canadian Journal of Law and Society* 1

Nedelsky, Jennifer, 'Reconceiving Autonomy: Sources, Thoughts and Possibilities' (1989) 1 *Yale Journal of Law and Feminism* 7

Nedelsky, Jennifer, 'Reconceiving Rights as Relationship' (1993) 1 *Review of Constitutional Studies* 1

Odum, William, 'Environmental Degradation and the Tyranny of Small Decisions' (1982) 32 *Bioscience* 728

Otteson, James, 'Kantian Individualism and Political Libertarianism' (2009) *Independent Review* 389

Penner, James E., 'The 'Bundle of Rights' Picture of Property' (1996) 43 *UCLA Law Review* 711

Penner, James E., 'The Idea of Property in Law' (1998) 43 *McGill Law Journal* 663

Plumwood, Val, 'Androcentrism and Anthrocentrism: Parallels and Politics' (1996) *Ethics and the Environment* 1

Posner, Richard, 'Utilitarianism, Economics, and Legal Theory' (1979) 8(1) *Journal Legal Studies* 103

Posner, Richard, 'Wealth Maximization Revisited' (1985) 2 *Notre Dame Journal Law, Ethics and Public Policy* 85

Pottage, Alain, 'The Measure of Land' (1994) 57(3) *Modern Law Review* 361

Pottage, Alain, 'Instituting Property' (1998) 18 *Oxford Journal of Legal Studies* 331

Pound, Roscoe, 'Symbiosis and Mutualism' (1893) 27 *American Naturalist* 509

Pound, Roscoe, 'The Need for a Sociological Jurisprudence' (1907) 19 *Green Bag* 607

Radbruch, G., 'Statutory Lawlessness and Supra-Statutory Law' (2006) 26 *Oxford Journal of Legal Studies* 7

Radin, Margaret Jane, 'Property and Personhood' (1982) 34 *Stanford Law Review* 957

Radin, Margaret Jane, 'The Consequences of Conceptualism' (1986) 41 *University of Miami Law Review* 239

Raff, Murray, 'Environmental Obligations and the Western Liberal Property Concept' (1998) 22 *Melbourne University Law Review* 657

Raz, Joseph, 'The Morality of Obedience' (1985) 83 *Michigan Law Review* 732

Reich, Charles, 'The New Property' (1964) 73 *Yale Law Journal* 733

Rockström, J et al, 'Planetary Boundaries: Exploring the Safe Operating Space for Humanity,' *Ecology and Society* 14(2) 32

Rolston III, Holmes, 'Rights and Responsibilities on the Home Planet' (1993) 18 *Yale Journal of International Law* 251

Rose, Deborah Bird, 'Exploring an Aboriginal Land Ethic' (1988) 2 *Meanjin* 379

Rosenblueth, A., 'Behaviour, Purpose and Teology' (1943) 10(1) *Philosophy of Science* 18

Rubin, Edward, 'Passing Through the Door: Social Movement Literature and Legal Scholarship' (2001) 150 *University of Pennsylvania Law Review* 1

Sax, Joseph, 'Takings, Property and Public Rights' (1971) 81 *Yale Law Journal* 149

Sax, Joseph, 'Property Rights and the Economy of Nature: Understanding Lucas v. South Carolina Coastal Council' (1992–1993) 45 *Stanford Law Review* 1433

Sax, Joseph, 'Property Rights and the Economy of Nature' (1993) 45 *Stanford Law Review* 201

Sessions, George, 'Spinoza and Jeffers on Man in Nature' 20 (1977) *Inquiry* 481

Sen, Amartya, 'Consequential Evaluation and Practical Reason' (2000) 97 *Journal of Philosophy* 477

Singer, Joseph William, 'How Property Norms Construct the Externalities of Ownership' (2008) *Harvard Law School Public Law Working Papers* No. 08–06

Singer, Joseph William and Jack Beermann, 'The Social Origins of Property' (1993) 6 *Canadian Journal of Law and Jurisprudence* 217

Singh, Raghuveer, 'Herakleitos and the Law of Nature' 24 (1963) *Journal of the History of Ideas* 457

Smith, M.B.E., 'Do We have a Prima Facie Obligation to Obey the Law?' (1973) 82 *Yale Law Journal* 950

Sokol, Mary, 'Bentham and Blackstone on Incorporeal Hereditaments' (1994) 15 *Journal of Legal History* 287

Stapp, Henry, 'S-Matrix Interpretation in Quantum Theory' (1971) 3 *Physical Review D* 15

Strum, Douglas, 'Identity and Alterity: Summons to a New Axial Age' (2000) 1 *Journal of Liberal Religion: An Online Theological Journal* 2.

Swimme, Brian, 'Berry's Cosmology' (1987) 2–3 *Cross Currents* 218

Tolan, Patrick, 'Ecocentric Perspectives on Global Warming: Toward an Earth Jurisprudence' (2008) 1(4) *Global Studies Journal* 39

Underkuffler-Freund, Laura, 'On Property: An Essay' (1990) 100 *Yale Law Journal* 127

Underkuffler-Freund, Laura, 'Property: A Special Right' (1996) 1 *Notre Dame Law Review* 1033

Vandevelde, Kenneth, 'The New Property of the Nineteenth Century: The Development of the Modern Concept of Property' (1980) 29 *Buffalo Law Review* 325

Warren, Lynda, 'Wild Law—the Theory' (2006) 18 *Environmental Law and Management* 11

Watson, Irene, 'Power of the Muldarbi and the Road to its Demise' (1998) 11 *Australian Feminist Law Journal* 28

Watson, Irene, 'Kaldowinyeri-Munaintaya-In the Beginning' (2000) 4 *Flinders Journal of Law Reform* 3

Watson, Irene, 'Buried Alive' (2002) 13(3) *Law and Critique* 253

White Jnr, Lynn, 'The Historical Roots of Our Ecologic Crisis' (1967) 155 *Science* 1203

Winston, Kenneth, 'The Ideal Element in a Definition of Law' (1986) 5 *Law and Philosophy* 89

Zamboni, Mauro, 'Social in Social Law: An Analysis of a Concept in Disguise' (2008) 9 *Journal of Law and Society* 63

## Other sources (media and internet)

Berry, Thomas, *The Ecozoic Era* (1991) http://www.smallisbeautiful.org/publications/berry_91.html

Berry, Thomas, *Biography* (2011) http://www.thomasberry.org/Biography/

Burdon, Peter, *Environmental Protection and the Limits of Rights Talk* (2012) http://rightnow.org.au/topics/environment/environmental-protection-and-the-limits-of-rights-talk/

Burdon, Peter, 'Environmental Legal Aid Cuts an "Act of Barbarism"' *ABC Environment* (2013) http://www.abc.net.au/environment/articles/2013/12/18/ 3914079.htm

Earth Charter (2000) http://www.earthcharterinaction.org/content/pages/Read-the-Charter.html

*The 11th Hour: Turn Mankind's Darkest Hour Into Its Finest* (directed by Leonardo DiCaprio, Warner Brothers Pictures, 2007)

Fox, Matthew, *Matthew Fox Tribute to Thomas Berry* (2002) http://www.earth-community.org/images/FoxTribute.pdf

Hardin, Garrett, *The Tragedy of the Commons* (1968) http://www.garretthardinsociety.org/articles/art_tragedy_of_the_commons.htm

International Union for the Conservation of Nature, *Draft International Covenant on Environment and Development* (1995) http://www.i-c-e-l.org/english/ EPLP31EN_rev2.pdf

Latour, Bruno, *Waiting for Gaia. Composing the Common World Through Arts and Politics*, Lecture at the French Institute, London, November (2011) http://www.bruno-latour.fr/node/446

Latour, Bruno, *Facing Gaia: A New Enquiry into Natural Religion*, Gifford Lectures (2013) http://www.bruno-latour.fr/node/486

Leonard, Matthew, *Al Gore Calling for Direct Action Against Coal* (2007) http://understory.ran.org/2007/08/16/al-gore-calling-for-direct-action-against-coal/

Linzey, Thomas, *Of Corporations, Law, and Democracy: Claiming the Rights of Communities and Nature* (2005) http://www.smallisbeautiful.org/publications/linzey_06.html

Linzey, Thomas, *Global Civil Rights: The Author of Spokane's Community Bill of Rights on Fighting for Nature* (2011) http://www.inlander.com/spokane/global-civil-rights/Content?oid=2135290

Mackenzie, John, Margaret Ayre, Peter Oliver, Poh Ling Tan, Sue Jackson and Wendy Proctor, *Collaborative Water Planning: Context and Practice. Literature Review* (2010) http://lwa.gov.au/files/products/track/pn21213/pn21213.pdf

Margulis, Lynn, *Gaia is a Tough Bitch* (2007) http://www.edge.org/documents/Third Culture/n-Ch.7.html

Marx, Karl, *Debates on the Law on Thefts of Wood* (1996) http://www.marxists.org/archive/marx/works/1842/10/25.htm [first published 1842]

Millennium Ecosystem Assessment, *Ecosystems and Human Well-Being: Biodiversity* (2005) http://www.MAweb.org/en/index.aspx

Nichols, Michelle, *Gore Urges Civil Disobedience to Stop Coal Plants* (2008) http://uk.reuters.com/article/idUKTRE48N7AA20080924

Morton, Timothy, *Rethinking Ecology* (2011) http://www.againstthegrain.org/program/490/id/442328/tues-11-01-11-rethinking-ecology

Rose, Deborah Bird, *Indigenous Kinship with the Natural World* (2003) http://www.environment.nsw.gov.au/resources/cultureheritage/IndigenousKinship.pdf

Rose, Deborah Bird, *Sharing Kinship with Nature: How Reconciliation is Transforming the NSW National Parks and Wildlife Service* (2003) http://www.environment.nsw.gov.au/resources/cultureheritage/SharingKinship.pdf

Shuttleworth, Kate, 'Agreement Entitles Whanganui River to Legal Identity', *New Zealand Herald*, 30 August (2012) http://www.nzherald.co.nz/nz/news/article.cfm?c_id=1andobjectid=10830586

Union of Concerned Scientists, *World Scientists Warning to Humanity* (1992) http://www.ucsusa.org/about/1992-world-scientists.html

United Kingdom Environmental Law Association, *Wild Law: Is There Any Evidence of Earth Jurisprudence in Existing Law and Practice?* (2009) http://www.ukela.org/content/page/1090/Wild%20Law%20Research%20Report%20published%20March%202009.pdf

Vidal, John, *Bolivia Enshrines Natural World's Rights with Equal Status for Mother Earth* (2011) http://www.guardian.co.uk/environment/2011/apr/10/bolivia-enshrines-natural-worlds-rights

Weston, Burns and Bach, Tracy, *Recalibrating the Law of Humans with the Laws of Nature: Climate Change, Human Rights and International Justice* (2009) http://www.vermontlaw.edu/Documents/CLI%20Policy%20Paper/CLI_Policy_Paper.pdf

Westra, Laura, *Ecological Integrity* (2005) http://www.globalecointegrity.net/pdf/Westra%20on%20Ecological%20Integrity.pdf

Wilber, Ken, *An Integral Age at the Leading Edge* (2011) http://wilber.shambhala.com/html/books/kosmos/excerptA/notes-1.cfm

World Watch Institute, *State of the World* (2010) http://www.worldwatch.org/taxonomy/term/38

World Wild Life Fund, *Living Planet Report* (2008) http://assets.panda.org/downloads/living_planet_report_2008.pdf


## Case law

### Australia

*Members of the Yorta Yorta Aboriginal Community v State of Victoria and Others* (2002) 214 CLR 422

*R v Toohey, Ex parte Meneling Station Pty Ltd* [1982] HCA 69

*Yorta Aboriginal Community v State of Victoria and Others* (1998) 1606 FCA 130

*Western Australia v Ward* (1998) 159 ALR 483

*Western Australia v Ward* [2000] FCA 191

*Western Australia and o'rs v Ward and o'rs* [2002] HCA 28

### England

*Omychund v Baker* (1744) 26 English Reports 15

### Germany

*Cathedral of Beech Trees Case* [1957] DVBl 856

*Economic Planning Case* (1954) 4 BVerfGE 7

*Gravel Extraction Case* (1984) 14 *Agrarrecht* 281

### North America

*Bryant v Lefever*, 4 Common Please Division 172 (1879)

*Delgamuukw v British Columbia* [1997] 153 DLR (4th) 193

*Just v Mariette County*, 56 Wisconsin 2d 7 (1972)

*Losee v Buchanan* 51 New York Supreme Court 476 (1873)

*Lucas v South Carolina Coastal Watch* 05 US Supreme Court 1003 (1992)

*Palmer v Mulligan* 3 Cai. R. 307 (1805)

*Platt v Johnson and Root* 15 New York Supreme Court 213 (1818)


## Legislation

### Australia

Environmental Protection and Biodiversity Act 1999 (Cth)

Roxby Downs Indenture Ratification Act 1981 (SA)

# Index

Murphy, Mark C. 97
mutual enhancement 81
mythology 69

Naess, Arne 83, 93n18
Naffine, Ngaire 109
Nagel, Thomas 48
Native Title Act 122n22
naturalism 103
natural law 13, 21, 34, 36, 80–4, 91,
    96n24, 98
natural philosophers 17n4
natural resource management 92
natural rights 131
Natural Systems Agriculture Program 131
natural use 32
naturalistic fallacy 89–90, 94
nature 66, 67, 70, 75n26; and Earth
    community 8; and Earth jurisprudence
    86; and law xiii; and property choices
    128; Bacon on 29; Descartes on
    30; integrity of 130; mechanistic
    description of 30n18; Morton on
    60–3; rights of 93
necessitarian accounts 86–7
Nedelsky, Jennifer 108, 109
neoliberalism 6,11, 16, 41–6, 44
neo-Thomism 83, 84
networks 54, 55, 76, 77
network theory 54
New Atlantis, The 28
'new story' 66, 68–73, 77, 78
Newton, Sir Isaac 30n18; law of motion
    87
New Zealand 75
Nichomachean Ethics xiii
Nimrod 25n13
nöosphere 58
nuisance laws 32
Nungas 120, 122

object-oriented ontology 60n14
obligation 111–14
Olney, Justice 121
operational closure 56n6
Origin of Species 10, 63, 72
Ostrom, Eleanor 104
otherworldliness 18, 19
Ott, Konrad 118
overpopulation 3
ownership 102, 119–21, 127
ownership model 43, 44, 45, 106

Pachamama 75n26
Palmer v Mulligan 33, 34
paradigm crisis 7, 49
paradigms xiv, 1, 6–10, 49–65; ecocentric
    102
paradigm shift 1, 6–10, 49–65, 70
Parmenides 18n7
patriarchy 3
Patten, Bernard 55
Penner, James E. 126, 127, 128
perennialism 132
Phenomenon of Man 9
place-based knowledge 121
planning law 92
Plato 11, 17, 18, 19
plentitude 18, 19, 26
plenum formarum 18
Pneuma 20
political philosophy 11
Pollan, Michael 125
pollutants 32
population 2; control 62
positive law 33, 80, 92; Bentham on 35–7
positivism 5–6, 13, 34, 78, 81, 82, 84, 91,
    95, 97
Posner, Richard 6, 44
power: and culture 4–5; and law 4–5; and
    the legal system 13; of money 135
'powers of soul' 20
Practical Science of Planetary Medicine 62
prairies 131, 132
precautionary principle 111
'present urgency' 119
principle of indeterminacy 52
private property, see property
privatisation 6
procedural democracy 94n20
production 66, 67
Project for Earth Democracy 93, 94
Prometheus 28
property 101–34; and anthropocentrism
    1, 6, 15–47; and attitudes 17; and
    Christianity 23; and Earth jurisprudence
    13–14, 78; and ecological stability 136;
    and ethics 110–19, 131, 133; and great
    law 133; and liberalism 16, 41–6; and
    neoliberalism 16, 41–6; and obligation
    114; and place-based knowledge 121; and
    relationships 108–10; and rights xiii, 6,
    14–16, 107–12, 119–20; and Roman
    Stoicism 11; and sustainability 104;
    and the anthropocene 2; and the Earth

*Timaeus* 19
tino ('there is no alternative') ideology xiv
totality 61
Tragedy of the Commons 103n1
transnational corporations 93n19
trespass laws 32
Tucker, Mary Evelyn 66, 71n21, 73
*Two Treatises of Government* 35

Unger, Roberto 107
United Nations Millennium Assessment 1
use values 39
utopianism 133

Vandevelde, Kenneth 37
Varela, Francisco 56, 59
vernacular law 13, 80, 95, 96, 99, 106,
    122n23
Vernadsky, Ivanovick 57, 58
Viable Human, The 81
Vico, Giambattista 69, 70
virtue 111

Waldron, Jeremy 43, 123
Walker, Dennis 122

Warren, Lynda 82
water bottling 75
*Water Gravel Mining Case* 113
water resources 2
waterwheels 32
Watson, Irene 16, 120–1
webs of relationships 55
*Western Australia v Ward* 121, 122n22
Weston, Burns 104
Westra, Laura 88
wetlands 1
Whanganui River 75
Whitehead, Alfred North 94
Wilber, Ken 55n5
*Wild Law* 86
wild law 95
wildlife law 43
women: and environmental crisis 4; rights
    67
World Scientists' Warning to
    Humanity 2

Yorta Yorta 121

Zeno of Citium 20